POPULAR RELIGION IN SOUTHEAST ASIA

Books by Robert L. Winzeler

Ethnic Relations in Kelantan: Malays and non-Malays in an East Coast Malay State. Singapore: Oxford University Press, 1985

The Seen and the Unseen: Shamanism, Mediumship and Spirit Possession in Borneo. Borneo Research Council Monograph Number 2. 1993 (Editor and contributor)

Latah in Southeast Asia: The History and Ethnography of a Culture-Bound Syndrome. Cambridge: Cambridge University Press, 1995

Indigenous Peoples and the State: Politics, Land and Ethnicity in the Malay Peninsula and Borneo. Monograph No. 46. Yale University Southeast Asian Studies, Yale Center for International and Area Studies, 1997 (Editor and contributor)

Indigenous Architecture of Borneo. Borneo Research Council, Proceedings Series Number Five, 1998 (Editor and contributor)

The Architecture of Life and Death in Borneo. Honolulu: The University of Hawaii Press, 2004

Religion: What We Know, Think and Question. New York: AltaMira Press, 2008

The Peoples of Southeast Asia Today: Ethnography, Ethnology and Change in a Complex Region. New York: AltaMira Press, 2011

Anthropology and Religion: What We Know, Think and Question, 2nd Edition. New York: AltaMira Press, 2012

POPULAR RELIGION IN SOUTHEAST ASIA

Robert L. Winzeler

ROWMAN & LITTLEFIELD
Lanham • Boulder • New York • London

Published by Rowman & Littlefield
A wholly owned subsidiary of
The Rowman & Littlefield Publishing Group, Inc.
4501 Forbes Boulevard, Suite 200, Lanham, Maryland 20706
www.rowman.com

Unit A, Whitacre Mews, 26-34 Stannary Street, London SE11 4AB,
United Kingdom

British Library Cataloguing in Publication Information Available

Library of Congress Cataloging-in-Publication Data
Names: Winzeler, Robert L., author.
Title: Popular religion in Southeast Asia / Robert L. Winzeler.
Description: Lanham : Rowman & Littlefield, [2016] | Includes bibliographical references and index.
Identifiers: LCCN 2015039825| ISBN 9780759124400 (cloth : alk. paper) | ISBN 9780759124417 (electronic : alk. paper)
Subjects: LCSH: Southeast Asia—Religious life and customs. | Religion and culture—Southeast Asia. | Popular culture—Religious aspects.
Classification: LCC BL2050 .W56 2016 | DDC 200.959—dc23 LC record available at http://lccn.loc.gov/2015039825

∞ ™ The paper used in this publication meets the minimum requirements of American National Standard for Information Sciences Permanence of Paper for Printed Library Materials, ANSI/NISO Z39.48-1992.

Printed in the United States of America

CONTENTS

PREFACE

This volume grew from work on previous books, one on the anthropology of religion and the other on peoples of Southeast Asia today. Much of it is heavily dependent on the work of others, without which it could not have been written. Though only about half of chapter 5 is based largely on my own research experience, it is all grounded in a long history of personal interest in popular religion in various places in Southeast Asia. I began studying religion and social change in the east coast of the Malaysian state of Kelantan in 1966–1967 as a graduate student, living in the town of Pasir Mas with my family for a year and a half—long enough to see and participate in the full yearly round of popular religious celebrations. I continued making subsequent trips there every several years through 1986, with a more recent return visit. Over the course of this twenty-year period I developed new interests, though my old concerns remained. By the middle 1980s the research I had been doing included surveys and interviews in different communities—urban as well as rural Malays, Chinese, Thai, and even refugee Chams from Cambodia who had fled the Khmer Rouge and had made their way to Kota Bharu, Kelantan, where many were living on rafts on the Kelantan River. By this time also I had been introduced to popular Hinduism through a summer of collaborative work with a Malaysian colleague concerning the migration of Indian laborers from declining plantations to squatter settlements in the west coast city of Kuala Lumpur. I was also able to see Thaipusan processions and celebrations on two occasions, one in Kuala Lumpur and a later one in Kuching Sarawak. As with many other things, such experiences alone did not come close to yielding publishable results, but they did leave me with vivid impressions and create an interest in the work of others on which I have drawn. I have also had a firsthand, if again limited, view of Balinese Hinduism on two occasions, the first in the 1970s, and the second in the 1990s. The first trip was extended to include far northern Sulawesi, a Christian area.

By the mid-1980s I began including Sarawak in a project on which I was working in Kelantan. I spent nine months during 1984–1985 in Sarawak, one of the two Malaysian states located in Borneo. Subsequently I returned many times over the next fifteen years to Sarawak and other areas of Borneo. In Sarawak my research similarly involved moving around and doing interviews among various ethnic groups. These groups included Malays around Kuching, the Bidayuh in eastern Sarawak, the coastal Melanau in central Sarawak to the north, the Iban in eastern and central Sarawak, and eventually the Orang Ulu or upriver peoples (mainly the Kenyah and Kayan) in central Sarawak. I also eventually extended my travels and inquiries on various matters to West and East Kalimantan in Indonesian Borneo. In Borneo I worked on various projects, but I could not have avoided religion and religious change if I had wanted to. This included patterns of religious conversion to either Christianity or Islam that I discuss in chapter 6. In Kelantan conversion had not been a very relevant matter since there was little or none occurring in the Kelantan plain where I was based. (There was some folklore about it I heard from my Malay friends, namely that there were rich Christian missionaries out there somewhere who would give large sums of money to any Muslim who would convert, but no specific examples of this happening.)

It was a very different story in Sarawak where conversion was an ongoing process in many areas and very much a major ethnological issue. Put simply, in terms of identity the Malays were by definition all Muslims; the Chinese were either adherents of Chinese folk religion, Christianity, or some of both; and the indigenous Dayak peoples were Christian, Muslim, or adherents of customary beliefs and practices—and sometimes referred to as pagans. As far as the indigenous peoples were concerned, the general pattern was that the coastal groups had converted or were converting to Islam, those upriver to Christianity, while some villages, especially in the upper reaches of inhabited rivers, had not yet converted. Beyond this general development, some of the Orang Ulu peoples in central and northern Sarawak had adapted Bungan, a reform movement (discussed in chapter 8) that was basically a renovation of the traditional religious system. In Kalimantan there were some differences. Here there appeared to be, due to Indonesian government pressure to convert to one or another acceptable world religion, fewer unconverted (at least in name) peoples. In addition, the Bungan reform movement (discussed in chapter 8) had died out in favor of Christian conversion.

In 2004, my wife Judy and I began a series of shorter trips to mainland Southeast Asia, including Vietnam, Laos, and Cambodia, combined with a longer stay in Chiang Mai, Thailand, in 2005–2006. I took my usual long-standing interests with me and was especially concerned with indigenous ethnic minorities and their different experiences in the socialist and non-socialist countries, including patterns of conversion. These groups included especially the Hmong in northern Vietnam and the Hmong, Yao, and Akha in both Laos and Thailand. In addition we also became acquainted with the Burmese Karen refugee community in Chiang Mai and came to be friends with several of their leaders who took us on trips to various Karen villages in the border area and arranged for us to spend four days in the Burmese Karen refugee camp at Mae Ra Ma on the border. Another year we were able to combine a conference on margins and minorities in mainland Southeast Asia with a trip to Ratanakiri Province, where many of the indigenous minorities of Cambodia are found. Here, judging from what I was able to do and see, there was little evidence of the penetration of Christianity or of ongoing missionary activity. The most recent of these trips was in 2010 to visit a student of mine doing PhD dissertation research in northeastern Laos among highland Tai, Hmong, and Khamu villagers on forest ecology and shifting cultivation. This included return trips to Sapa in northern Vietnam and to Chiang Mai as well as Udon Tani in eastern Thailand where Judy was involved with a school water project.

Over the decades, my interests in writing and publishing have changed. I decided to devote whatever energies and opportunities I had to larger, more comparative topics and to publish books that would reach a wider audience than only the usual one of academic specialists. I did this first with a book on the anthropology of religion, then one on the peoples of Southeast Asia today, and more recently with a revised edition of the first one. As a result of working on these books I was left with an interest in pursuing further the topic of popular religion. The strengths and weaknesses of the present book should therefore be similar to those of these previous ones. They have been a model for what I have attempted to do here.

Finally, a book needs an intended audience. This one has several, though I hope in this case they overlap to some extent. For college and university courses on comparative religion, or the religions of Asia and more specifically Southeast Asia, I see this book as an alternative or at least a supplement to the common treatment of religion as being a matter of doctrine and practice as set out in "bibles" and comparable texts that tell adherents what they should believe and do—even though this is at most only part of the story. For specialists and others with well-developed interests in comparative religion or some specific Southeast Asia religion in some particular country, this is a book that goes beyond their own specific ethnographic or historical interests. I also intend this book to be a conceptual contribution toward a fuller understanding of popular religion as a field of study. A book that attempts to do several different things and does not do them well can be said to fall between two stools. A book that does them well can be said to be a bridge over often turgid waters. This has been my goal.

ACKNOWLEDGMENTS

The photo on the cover showing a Dayak crucifix is used with the permission of the great Sarawak Museum, to whom I owe many thanks for support during my research between 1984 and 1999. All other photos are my own, as are the two maps that are modified versions of ones originally made for my earlier book *The Peoples of Southeast Asia Today*.

To the many friends, guides, assistants, officials and informants who have helped me in many places in Southeast Asia I also offer deeply felt thanks. The University of Chicago, the National Institute of Mental Health, the National Science Foundation, The Fulbright Program, The Luce Foundation and the University of Nevada have supported my research over the years. I have tried to document the essential use I have made of the published work of others throughout the book and hope that I have not missed much. Judy Winzeler has been a big part of everything from the beginning until the present.

1

INTRODUCTION

What is popular (or vernacular) religion? What makes it popular? How does it differ from the official doctrines and orthodoxy of the major religious institutions—referred to in Christianity, for example, as "the Church"? Those of us who do research and write about Southeast Asia commonly refer to "popular religion," but we have yet to systematically explore the differences between popular and elite, official, orthodox, and esoteric or (to use a term popular with some scholars) textual levels of religion. Westerners are not, in my experience, likely to recognize much distinction between ordinary and elite religion, or even to be familiar with the notion of popular religion. What does "popular" mean as applied to religion? I am often asked something like this when the topic of what I have been writing about lately comes up. In the context of Southeast Asia, at least, it is hard to understand religion writ large or even the flow of daily life without understanding how ordinary people in ordinary circumstances put their religious beliefs into practice.

Below I will begin to set out some of the general characteristics of popular religion as I have found them in my own research and in the existing literature. Half of the chapters in the book will concern specific named religions, and half will deal with other issues and developments that tend to cut across the various named religions of Southeast Asia. Because I have written this book for a broad readership I have tried to write it in ordinary language and to keep the jargon to a minimum. This is not to say that concepts are unimportant, only that they can usually be translated into plain English without great difficulty.

Map 1: Countries and Places Referred To

SOUTHEAST ASIA AND ITS RELIGIONS

Southeast Asia forms the southern and eastern corner of the Asian continent, plus the great, adjacent Philippine and Indonesian archipelagoes that lie just beyond it. Southeast Asia today is usually thought of and discussed in terms of a series of modern countries that include the Philippines, Indonesia, Malaysia, Thailand, Cambodia, Myanmar (formerly Burma), Laos, and Vietnam, plus the small nations of Brunei, Singapore, and Timor Leste. These countries are also commonly divided into mainland and insular zones, although Malaysia belongs to both. The present-day Southeast Asian countries are largely the crea-

Map 2: Peoples Referred To

tion of European colonialism rather than a reflection of natural geographical, cultural, historical, or linguistic boundaries.

Here and elsewhere I use the term *religion* to refer to supernaturally based or oriented beliefs and practices in general, rather than simply those that are organized or institutionalized. For Westerners and many others, the notion of religion usually implies a set of beliefs, doctrine, and liturgy, as written in books, institutionalized, systematized, organized, and collectivized. This view of religion is based on the model of the world religions, which include Christianity, Islam, Buddhism, Hinduism, and perhaps a few others. Religion in Southeast Asia includes those on this list that are practiced or identified as their religion by substantial numbers of people in the region. But it includes a great deal more as well.

The religious traditions of Southeast Asia, therefore, form two broad types.[1] One includes the various world religions noted above. These world religions consist of those organized and textually oriented traditions that both adherents and others identify by name. They all originated in other places and arrived in Southeast Asia at different times over the past two thousand years or so. To these can be added the religious traditions of the Chinese and the Vietnamese that lack the simple identity associated with the various world religions noted so far. A further complication here is that many Chinese as well as some Vietnamese have converted to Christianity.

With the partial exception of Christianity, the world religions in Southeast Asia are associated with lowland, agricultural, state-organized populations and with modern town and city dwellers. Today their adherents include the vast majority of the inhabitants of Southeast Asia, each moreover concentrated in a specific region. Buddhism is located mainly in the continental countries above Malaysia, and Islam in a zone extending from Malaysia and across Indonesia to the southern Philippines. Christianity is concentrated in the Philippines (the largest Christian nation in Asia) but otherwise scattered across both the insular and mainland region. Except in name, Hinduism is not a single religion in Southeast Asia and is therefore not found in a single place or zone. Chinese religion is also distributed across the range of places where most Chinese dwell, which is mainly in the towns and cities of Southeast Asia.

The second type of religion in Southeast Asia consists of those that exist beyond the bounds of the world religions. More specifically these are the religions that exist among the indigenous or tribal societies scattered across Southeast Asia. Such peoples have traditionally been either outside or on the physical margins of the civilized states of Southeast Asia. They are today generally under the control of the centralized modern states, although in some places (Myanmar/Burma, for example) such control has been weak, partial, rebelled against, or absent. In geographical terms they occupy the mountainous regions of continental Southeast Asia and the interior regions, also often mountainous, of the islands of insular Southeast Asia.

The number of people who adhere *only* to their own customary religious beliefs and practices has declined greatly since the nineteenth century. Many such people have by now converted to one of the world religions, especially to some version of Christianity, though usually without giving up all of their existing religious traditions. Such groups were formerly often referred to as "pagan" to distinguish them from those who had converted. The term *pagan* can probably be attributed mainly to missionaries, but it came to have an ethnological meaning as well. Although the word continues to be used in some regions (in the interior of Borneo, for example), anthropologists have generally gotten away from it because of its ethnocentric and negative implications. However, its abandonment has left some linguistic awkwardness in referring to the religious traditions of the non-adherents of the world religions. Today such non-adherents of the world religions are commonly referred to as "animists"—animism being the belief in spirits. While this term may be preferable to *pagan*, it is misleading. Most importantly, referring to some peoples as "animists" makes it sound like such people are unique in believing in spirits. In actuality, Buddhists, Muslims, and Christians in Southeast Asia are as likely to believe in spirits. Other terms that may be used are *customary* or *indigenous*. These, too, are problematic in the same way as *animism*. The religious traditions of the adherents of the world religions tend to include customary or indigenous beliefs and practices as well.

RELIGIOUS CONTENT AND RELIGIOUS IDENTITY

There are several further important differences between the indigenous and the world religions. Here it is useful to make a distinction between two fundamental dimensions of religion, or at least of the world religions. One of these is content, and the other is identity. The content of a religious tradition refers to what its adherents believe and do involving the supernatural and how such beliefs and practices are organized. The general Western (and not only the Western) view is that people who share a common religious identity—as Christians, Muslims, Buddhists, or Hindus in Southeast Asia—will share a set of core beliefs and practices because these are set out in foundational scripture in each instance. According to this view, religion is primarily a matter of belief or

Figure 1.3. Bidayuh Dayak shaman (Lundu, Sarawak, Malaysia, 1989).

faith based on texts, which in turn generate ritual practices, values, moral codes, and much social behavior.

This view can be disputed, however—as it has recently been, for example, by the Iranian-American Muslim scholar Reza Aslan (author of highly regarded popular books on both Islam and Christianity):

> No religion exists in a vacuum. On the contrary, every faith is rooted in the soil in which it is planted. It is a fallacy to believe that people of faith derive their values primarily from their Scriptures. The opposite is true. People of faith insert their values into their Scriptures, reading them through the lens of their own cultural, ethnic, nationalistic and even political perspectives.[2]

This quote is from a longer comment published in the *New York Times* that concerns the ongoing and currently very heated popular Western controversy over the inherent link between Islam and various evils (including the treatment of women) that continues to be a prominent topic in newspapers, the Internet, and political talk shows. If this contrary line of argument—that people find in their foundational relig-

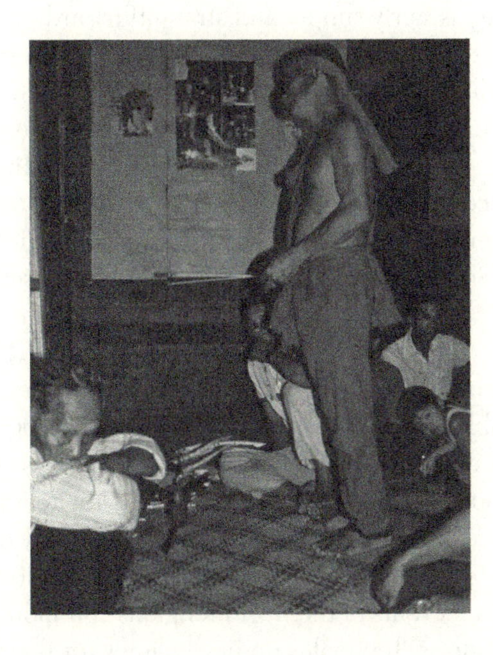

Figure 1.4. Chinese-Dayak spirit medium (Lundu, Sarawak, Malaysia, 1989).

ious texts what they want to find and ignore what they don't—is correct, then while scripture may be of great importance in its own right, it does not necessarily tell us much about the particularities of Malay or Indonesian Islam, Thai Buddhism, Filipino Christianity, or Balinese Hinduism, especially as believed and practiced at the popular level. In this regard, the author goes on to say that

> religion is often far more a matter of identity than it is a matter of beliefs and practices. The phrase "I am a Muslim," "I am a Christian," "I am a Jew" and the like is, often, not so much a description of what a person believes or what rituals he or she follows, as a simple statement of identity, of how the speaker views his or her place in the world.

To return to Southeast Asia (which Reza Aslan cites as an example of a region that contradicts popular Western assumptions about Islam), however well or poorly they may fit with what people actually seem to believe and practice, the adherents of the world religions here and elsewhere today have named identities known to everyone. But while religious identity is fairly simple and straightforward, there are complications. For one thing, religious identities do, however, have varying histories. Buddhism, Islam, and Christianity in Southeast Asia have probably been present as religious identities for long periods of time. In contrast, while some of the beliefs and practices of Hinduism have an ancient presence in Bali and elsewhere in Southeast Asia, the identity tends to be recent. In Bali, Indonesia—the most famous Hindu place in contemporary Southeast Asia—the Balinese came to see themselves as "Hindu" only in the twentieth century and have been officially recognized as such by the Indonesian government only since 1958.

Another complication is that explicit religious identities are nonexistent or problematic for people outside of the recognized world religions. Such peoples generally lack an explicit religious identity, a name for their "religion," or, for that matter, a word for religion itself. They certainly do have religion in terms of content, but they do not see their supernaturally oriented beliefs and practices as constituting a separate realm of life as adherents of the world religions commonly do. Today, as we shall see, some such peoples do have names for their traditional (or usually neo-traditional) religious beliefs and practices, but it appears that in all cases these names are recent developments that have been created after exposure to a world religion, missionization, colonialism, or modern nationalism and state policies and ideology.

POPULAR AND ELITE LEVELS OF RELIGION

A further distinction between the world religions and the indigenous religions of Southeast Asia concerns levels. The religious traditions of the indigenous peoples of Southeast Asia are, while diverse and localized, basically monolithic. The beliefs, practices, institutions, and notions of identity are not organized into those of ordinary and orthodox. Such societies are or were preliterate and therefore have no books and scripts in the first place and therefore are not divided into classes of those who could read and write and those who could not. In Southeast Asia and elsewhere, indigenous societies have religious specialists of various sorts but seldom if ever any real elites or separate institutions. In this sense the phrase "popular religion," which assumes such levels, is inappropriate for the fully indigenous religions. The notion of "popular religion" becomes applicable to the adherents of indigenous or tribal religion only when they convert or begin to convert to one or another of the world religions.

Unlike indigenous religions, the world religions are clearly differentiated, though not always to the same extent or in the same ways, a point recently made by several Southeast Asianists. The Singapore scholar Margaret Chan, whose field of study is Chinese popular religion in both China and Southeast Asia, attributes the existence of Chinese popular religion as a separate cultural domain from elite religion to the nature of the traditional Chinese state:

> Human agency is a tenet of Chinese popular religion; the people's will to control their own fate stemmed . . . from a historical response to the state cult of imperial China, which disenfranchised the common people. The worship of Tian . . . was a prerogative of the ruling elite, so the people had to create alternative avenues for commuting with their gods. Spirit medium worship was one such method.[3]

The Filipina scholar Cecilia De La Paz makes a similar point for the Philippines. Here ordinary people have constructed an alternative faith outside the purview of the institutional Catholic Church. They have done so by "developing various rituals centering on religious icons, such as public processions, community prayers, acts of devotion, and the celebration of feasts for town saints."[4] While the doctrinal and ethical teachings of the official church are supposed to guide believers in order for them to enter heaven, those at the popular level are replaced or adjusted to fit the circumstances of their earthly lives. The motives behind people's religious actions are aimed toward their everyday struggles and ambitions: finding a job, recovering from an illness, getting a successful harvest, seeking protection from natural calamities (volcanic eruptions, landslides, typhoons), traveling safely, or finding decent employment in a foreign country. "An example of an icon that promises mundane benefits is the virgin of Antipolo, who is considered the patron saint for travelers, especially of Filipinos employed abroad who frequently fly in and out of the country."[5]

In a third example, the Malaysian Chinese anthropologist Yeoh Seng Guan notes the difference between orthodox and popular attitudes and practices regarding "holy water" at a Christian pilgrimage site.[6] The place in question is Saint Anne's Church in Bukit Mertajam in northern peninsular Malaysia, founded as a French Catholic Mission project for local Chinese and Indian converts in the late nineteenth century. However its fame developed, the church became widely recognized as a shrine with a reputation for healing. The beneficial effects of its holy water are linked to Saint Anne and sought by diverse supplicants from near and far. The local priests who represent the official church are tolerant but ambivalent regarding the popular status of the shrine and its waters. Here the official concern is that the pilgrims seeking Saint Anne's water should understand that it is not "real" holy water that has been duly sanctified by correct Catholic ritual procedures. The water comes directly from underground sources beneath the church and is simply obtained without proper Catholic ritual action from taps outside the church. Pilgrims seek its benefits by drinking it, washing themselves with it, or taking it away in containers, much in the way that pilgrims do at the lingam fountain at the Hindu-Buddhist shrine at Phnom Kulen in northwestern Cambodia that dates to the Angkor period. The local church authorities are neutral with regard to the alleged spiritual powers of the water. The church sells bottles of the water as a convenience for supplicants who cannot come in person but does not endorse any extraordinary benefits.

The popular religious view of the Saint Anne's water is quite different. Whatever the official church may think of the water and its differences from official holy water, or of the eclectic religious identities or views of Saint Anne's supplicants, these are matters of little concern to the pilgrims themselves. Their interests rather concern the likelihood that the water has miraculous properties that will help them in some useful way. Though some church members and officials may be critical of the apparent syncretic nature of Saint Anne's popularity, the magical power attributed to the water is what is important to supplicants.[7]

PRACTICALITY AND OTHER CHARACTERISTICS OF POPULAR RELIGION

Although there is variation among the religions of Southeast Asia, the general points made in these examples have wide applicability. As they suggest, popular religion often tends to be concerned with the mundane. Though often also highly expressive and on occasion theatrical, popular religion is strongly oriented to the satisfaction of worldly wants and everyday needs—protection, relief from illness, making the crops grow in the case of farmers, finding love, fertility, and economic success, to name a few.

While common Western views of religion generally do not recognize a distinction between popular and elite sorts of religion, anthropologists and other scholars often do.[8] Sometimes these differences are phrased as "transcendental" versus "practical" orientations.[9] It is easy to understand what Americans and other Westerners recognize as the transcendental dimensions of Christianity, for example. These include what people variously believe as a matter of faith about God, the ultimate nature of the universe, human life having a divine purpose, the salvation and the afterlife, and the religious basis of morality. The behavioral or ritual counterpart of such concerns includes all of the prescribed and patterned things that people are supposed to do or not do as persons of faith. All of this forms what people regard as "religion," and not only in Christianity but in a general way in the other world religions as well.

On the other hand, Westerners do not usually think of religion in terms of its practical side. Indeed, the phrase "transcendental religion" as described above would seem to many to be redundant. Why bother with the *transcendental* part? Of course many Americans, for example, would say that religious faith and participation in ritual activities are very practical in the sense of bringing satisfaction and contentment in life even if, as some would readily acknowledge, the beliefs involved are a matter of faith that is quite remote from certainty. And the prayers typically offered during church for the recovery of the ill and afflicted are sometimes made in the hope or expectation that they will have some material effect. To go a bit further, there are the prayers for rain in Texas, which has been suffering from serious drought for several years, that have been in the news recently. Further still is the "prosperity gospel" (God and Jesus want you to be rich and will help you become so if you pray and make donations to the televangelist involved), but this tends to be shunned or rejected by mainline Christians, who see it as a fundamental contradiction of Christian doctrine. Other instances of what might be called practical religion (such as believing that a license plate or a fortune cookie may reveal a winning lottery number or a trial lawyer wearing a special suit or dress ensures good luck) are apt to be regarded by many people as amusing superstition rather than real religion.

While the differences between Western and Asian attitudes and practices that fall into the general category of practical religion are certainly not total, they are substantial. Nor are strongly practical religious orientations found only in the less developed countries in Asia. Margaret Chan notes various examples of the importance of practical religion in present-day Singapore (technologically and economically considered to be one of the most modern countries in the world). The Imperfect Deity, for example, "is worshipped for good health. His statue shows this god is willing to bear bodily imperfections, such as weak eyesight, an amputated leg, or a crippled hand, on behalf of his worshippers."[10] She notes also that as business developed in Chinese society in the Song era (960–1279 CE), the gods were quick to learn about it in order to make themselves useful and thereby gain popular support. Today an efficacious god is especially one who knows how to pick lucky numbers in the state 4-D (four-digit) draw.

In ultramodern present-day Japan, the story is much the same. Ian Reader and George Tanabe devote an entire book, *Practically Religious: Worldly Benefits and Common Religion in Japan*, to showing that Japanese popular religion is utilitarian in nature.[11] The new religions of Japan are geared above all to helping people to succeed in the modern corporate world, and there are many shrines devoted to various dimensions of technology, including one that provides airplane flight protection. Westerners, the authors argue, tend to mistakenly think that modern Japanese are not very religious; it is rather that they are just not very religious in the transcendental ways that Westerners consider being religious.

The Places of Popular Religion

In Southeast Asia as elsewhere, the places of popular religion tend to differ from those of the institutional or orthodox versions of religion. In the case of the world religions, the principal spaces of official or institutional religion tend to be interior ones—those of churches, mosques, temples, monasteries, schools, and universities, to name a few. The locations of popular religion, on the other hand, are apt to be external to such structures. Much of popular religion takes place in the household, on the public veranda of a longhouse in Borneo or on a street corner, beside a river, under a tree, in a rice field or a parking lot, or on the steps or the plaza of a modern hotel, such as the Erawan Bangkok. These are all common locations of popular shrines and ritual activities, and many others could be noted as well. While Saint Anne's Church in Bukit Mertajam is itself a shrine, the water that is the main object of pilgrims and supplicants is obtained from a line of taps on the outside of the building.

Of course, the distinction between the interior spaces of formal religion and external space of popular religion is, again, not a black-and-white difference. Some formal, institutionalized religious activity takes place or extends outdoors (or on the margin between interior and exterior space—as when the pope at the Vatican appears on a balcony of his palace and waves to the crowd below or drives through the streets in his Popemobile). Buildings of different types are linked to different levels of religion ranging from the most common ones of popular religion, such as the small locally built and used temples and prayer houses that are likely devoted entirely to popular worship, to the largest temples and mosques that are also institutional centers of orthodox religion.

There are probably several reasons for the association of different forms or levels of religion with different types of space. Buildings and monuments often symbolize power and authority in the realm of religion as in secular matters. In Southeast Asia, one way of elevating the status or dignity of a shrine is to enclose it in a building, especially one made of durable materials.

There are also practical considerations. Institutional religious authority or the state is better able to organize, guide, and control what goes on in and around official or dedicated buildings than what takes place in the street, in a private house, or at an open-air popular religious shrine. Here participants and onlookers are freer to do what they want, and crowds are harder to control. Streets taken over for popular religious celebrations are above all the places of "rituals of reversal" (e.g., Mardi Gras) that may include excessive, naughty, improper, amusing, or forbidden behavior at the very opposite extreme of what should take place in religious buildings. The activities that occur in street celebrations make it much harder to separate "religious" and "non-religious" behavior—to the extent that anyone involved is concerned with doing so.

Both the symbolism of official religious buildings and the greater control over behavior they afford also make them places of opportunity for government authority and political interest—both of which are more difficult to apply or control in the realm of more decentralized and egalitarian popular religious activity. During the early periods of my fieldwork in Kelantan, Malaysia, the national government and dominant Malay political party was generally assumed by everyone to be providing grants for the construction of mosques and *surau* (prayer houses) as a way of attracting Malay supporters. Conversely, when governments or political groups in power seek to control, diminish, or eliminate institutional religion, buildings become an easier target than the more decentralized spaces of popular religious activity. In contemporary Malaysia, non-Malay, non-Muslim critics of the Malay Muslim-dominated national and state governments complain of impediments placed in the way of the construction of Christian churches and Hindu temples.[12] The anti-Chinese Suharto regime in Indonesia forbade Chinese outdoor public religious celebrations. And from a different perspective, when the communist government was established in Vietnam in 1975, it closed village temples as part of its efforts to diminish, discourage, or eliminate religion, before beginning to permit their reopening after liberalization began in 1986. And as a major part of its attack on institutional Buddhism in Cambodia, the Khmer Rouge destroyed or closed temples and monasteries, or converted them to non-religious uses.

Boundary Crossing

The foregoing discussion points up another important and common characteristic of popular religion. This is its permeability or openness to outsiders or its lack of a distinction between members and nonmembers. According to Yeoh Seng Guan, while Saint Anne's in Bukit Mertajam is an official church, as a popular shrine it is something else—a place to which many non-Christians make pilgrimages to obtain healing waters—many of whom, it can probably be assumed, have never been inside the building. Some of the members of the church are not happy about the situation but are not in a position to do anything about it. One older Christian Indian informant estimated that 60 percent of those who came to the shrine for water were non-Christians, including many Hindus who regard Saint Anne as, in reality, a Hindu goddess in disguise who grants their every wish—for a husband or wife or a child, for example. According to this informant, supplicants also included many Buddhists and even Muslims. While such ritual boundary crossing may lead in some instances to conversion, this is certainly not seen as a requirement or a likely outcome of seeking practical help from a person or supernatural being with a different orthodox religious identity, or from participating in a religious festival or procession.[13]

Such popular religious mixing (which does not mean that those who engage in it do not also or mainly engage in the religious practices associated with their own religious or ethnic identity) is not uncommon in Malaysia or elsewhere in Southeast Asia, especially in urban areas. For instance, in another apt example provided by Yeoh Seng Guan, during the Hindu festival of Thaipusan, in the nearby state capital city of Georgetown, it is commonplace to see a significant number of (presumably non-Hindu) Chinese shopkeepers who reside along the processional route giving respectful recognition and obeisance to the male deity (Lord Murugan) by breaking coconuts and offering *archanai* (ritual gifts) in return for his blessings and boons.[14] And as I will note in more detail later, boundary crossing in the realm of popular religion was among the earliest things I learned about during my first phase of fieldwork among Malays in the east coast state of Kelantan. Here Malays often sought ritual help from Thai Buddhist practitioners without the slightest inclination or likelihood of ever converting to Buddhism.

Popular Religion and Folk Religion

Popular religion is closely associated with the notion of folk religion. The terms are sometimes used interchangeably. Both are based on the view that religions linked to literacy and civilization are not cultural monoliths but have different levels with differing characteristics. In the anthropology of religion, such ideas derive especially from the work of Robert Redfield in the 1950s. In *The Primitive World and Its Transformations*, Redfield made an attempt to grasp and explain the totality of civilizations, including their religions.[15] He did so by formulating a distinction between the "great tradition" and the "little tradition." Primitive religion (and culture in general) was unitary. The split came with the rise of states and empires where there had formerly been only tribes. Redfield stressed the importance of writing and literacy. Primitive peoples (as they were known then) were not illiterate; they were preliterate.

Civilization and its religions were different. With writing and literacy and the formation of cities, society became divided. There were basically two levels of religion and culture. At the top were the scholars and scribes, councilors, priests, and pedagogues. This was the overarching, more unified tradition of the cities, universities, monasteries, and literate elites who read and wrote in Latin, or Sanskrit, Arabic, Mandarin, and so on. Below was the little tradition of the villages where oral transmission and local religions, languages, and dialects prevailed. There endless variation existed from one region to another. The little tradition was a folk tradition, and its culture was folklore, meaning based on oral tradition, whereby people learned from one another rather than books. Unlike the culture of tribal society, folk culture was not totally separated from the great tradition; there was some interaction and exchange but also great differences. Folk culture was local whereas elite culture was translocal.

Though less well known, another concept of note is that of "restricted (or partial) literacy," as developed by the anthropologist Jack Goody and others.[16] The basic idea is that throughout large parts of the world where the various world religions are practiced, most of the people who practice them are (or until recently have been) unable to read or write. Though the sacred books are of enormous symbolic importance in these places, most religious knowledge is transmitted orally and through rote learning. And like the proverbial one-eyed man who is a king in the village of the blind, partial literacy gives those who could read and write, even if only a little, a special status and influence over those who could not at all. Less obviously, scripture gets turned into magic, and an important popular use of writing is the preparation of charms and amulets. In ethnically complex regions, where some groups have them and others do not, books and scripts become associated with power.[17]

Popular religion is close to folk religion or Redfield's little tradition, but there are differences. Popular religion can be defined simply as whatever ordinary people believe and practice as opposed to official, elite, or orthodox religion, in which case it can be said to have been around as long as have civilization or complex, stratified society. Recent scholars, however, have emphasized that popular religion in its current form also strongly reflects various modern developments. The Thai anthropologist Pattana Kitiarsa, for example, stresses that popular religion in modern Thailand has three related characteristics.[18] The first is that it has most fully developed in urban rather than rural areas—urban areas having increased greatly in size and number in the post–World War II period. It is true that urban spirit medium cults, amulet cults, fortune-tellers, and other common forms of popular religion have developed from older rural-based beliefs and practices. They are therefore not brand new religious innovations, but rather are the adaptation of pre-existing religious practices to the needs of the urban population.

A second characteristic both links modern popular religion especially to urban areas and distinguishes it more fully and clearly from traditional folk religion. This is the extent to which it is dependent upon modern mass media, including newspapers, magazines, radio, television, and now the Internet. This means that the audiences for popular religious activities are vastly increased—though it is also true that while the mass media generally have an urban origin, they also circulate in suburban and rural areas, and thus reduce the traditional separation of such zones.

The third characteristic is that markets and market forces have become a very important part of the environment in which most of the modern forms of popular religion have developed. "Through the process of commodification, religious symbols, rites, and places are converted into goods just like other commodities in the marketplace, resulting in the blurring of distinctions between a place of worship and a market."[19] Such references to market forces and popular religious activity are common in the literature and will be considered at some length in chapter 7. Much recent attention, for example, has been devoted to the rapidly developing urban context of popular religion in neo-socialist Vietnam. Here the resurgence of public occult practices, including those of spirit mediums, fortune-tellers, and visits to shrines in search of practical benefits has raised an important question. Was the resurgence—which came with the market liberalization after the state had for a decade sought to eliminate or at least repress supernatural practices—merely a return to the traditional status quo before the socialist unification of the country? Or did it represent a new level of popular urban religious activity, one beyond where it had been in the pre-socialist era. While it is difficult to know for certain (or to go from correlation to causation), the view appears to be that spirit medium practices and other popular religious activities are flourishing as never before.

Or here is a different sort of example from Malaysia. Johan Fischer reports that among middle-class urban Muslim Malays in Kuala Lumpur, proper shopping and consumption have become an expression of popular and politically correct Islamic piety. To appeal to religiously conscious Muslim shoppers (and to counter declining sales due to the relaxation of automobile import taxes), Proton, the national Malaysian automobile company, announced several years ago the production of a special Islamic car in association with manufacturers in several other Muslim countries. The special Islamic features were to include a compass that always showed the correct direction to Mecca and a special compartment for storing a woman's headscarf and a Koran.[20]

Social Characteristics

Two final and related differentiating characteristics of popular religion in Southeast Asia may be noted. The first is that popular religious practices and organization are more egalitarian than those of higher or institutionalized religion. Though some more than others, the institutionalized world religions are all, by their nature, hierarchical structures with well-delineated lines of authority, control, and often wealth. Generally also religious authority is integrated at least to some extent with that of the state. The popular religious activities discussed throughout this book that range from protective magic to curing, to spirit medium practices, to the search for other economic rewards, to ancestor worship, all involve egalitarian, volunteeristic transactions, or ones with limited authority.

The second and related social characteristic of popular religion that differentiates it from higher orders of religion is a combination of greater gender (in some instances transgender) neutrality and to some extent female predominance. Again, the usual qualification applies—that this characteristic is a matter of tendencies rather than absolutes—and counter-examples can be found. Spirit mediums in Southeast Asia are widely reported to be more often women than men.

There are several likely reasons for gender equality and the prominent involvement of women in popular religion. Most important perhaps are the barriers to women in the institutional and authority structures (as priests, monks, and ulamas) of all of the world religions in Southeast Asia (or more specifically in the case of Christianity, in Roman Catholicism, which includes a sizable majority of all Southeast Asian Christians). Of course in all of these religions, women are heavily involved in activities, but in supportive, subordinate ways. And probably because of this, female spirituality is expressed in more popular religious activities, including ones of a practical nature. In addition, among those peoples where women are responsible for the well-being of the family, this may include spiritual well-being.

THE CHAPTERS THAT FOLLOW

The book is organized in the following way. Chapter 2 provides historical background on the development of religion in Southeast Asia. It begins with the earlier period. Here note is taken of the contrasts between the interaction of religion and traditional states in Southeast Asia and what occurred in the far larger states of East Asia. It will be argued that these differences meant that the Southeast Asian states were also far more open to the penetration of new religions. The second part of this chapter deals with the development of religion under European rule. Here different colonial powers followed different policies regarding religion, but in general the newly established regimes were more careful about promoting religious change that might cause political problems than the earlier ones had been. The final part of this chapter considers the efforts of post-colonial governments to shape religion to fit with their notions of development, modernity, and identity. This was a matter of which mix of religions prevailed, but the main difference has been between developments in the non-socialist and the socialist countries. The non-socialist countries recognized or emphasized religion as a major part of the architecture of their society and culture, but adopted varying policies and goals ranging from religious pluralism to limited religious choices to a single official or quasi-official religion. Though varying greatly in severity, the post-colonial socialist countries in contrast to others began with efforts to reduce, deemphasize, or eliminate religion, though sooner or later all such efforts failed in one way or another. More generally, post-colonial religious agendas in both socialist and non-socialist regimes were easier to achieve in countries with a single world religion prevailing among the dominant ethnic community than in ones with greater religious and ethnic variation.

The middle section of the book consists of chapters (3–6) that examine popular religion in relation to each of the major world religions in Southeast Asia, including Hinduism, Buddhism, Islam, and Christianity. These chapters are not approached in a cookie-cutter fashion whereby the same themes or topics are covered in each. They are developed rather according to several considerations, including the specific problems posed by each religion, and to some varying extent my own particular experiences and knowledge, which means greater knowledge of Islam and Christianity than of Hinduism and Buddhism.

Chapter 3 deals with popular Hinduism and shows that except in terms of identity, there is no such single religion in Southeast Asia. In addition to discussing people who identify themselves as Hindu and describing popular practices of various forms of Hinduism, this chapter notes that there are some groups that engage in Hindu practices while not regarding themselves as Hindus. It also seeks to explain how and why some people have come to call themselves Hindu while having little to do with the beliefs and practices usually assumed to be a core part of Hinduism.

Chapter 4 concerns popular Buddhism but shifts the perspective. Here the focus is on the various ways that both Western and Southeast Asian scholars have sought to interpret the nature of popular religion among Buddhist peoples. All such scholars appear to agree that the popular religion of the Thai, Burmese, Khmer, Lao, and other Theravada Buddhist peoples includes far more than beliefs and practices based on textual or Great Tradition Buddhism, and that textual Buddhism itself tends to be reinterpreted at the popular level. But different scholars have formulated this acknowledged medley of popular Buddhism in various ways. These range from the position that Buddhist and non-Buddhist traditions are entirely separate and in conflict, to the opposite view that Buddhism is simply whatever those who identify themselves as Buddhist believe and do and for whatever reasons, including aesthetic ones—the diverse origins of their beliefs, practices, and preferences notwithstanding.

Chapter 5 is about popular Islam. It begins with an overview of the general development of Islam in Southeast Asia and then includes sections on Malaysia and Indonesia. In the section on Malaysia, the focus is especially on Islam in Kelantan, an east coast state in peninsular Malaysia. This section also adopts a distinct approach. Much of it concerns Islam in Kelantan as I first learned about it in the late 1960s and the changes I witnessed over the next two decades when I returned to work on various projects. Kelantan at that time was itself a very distinctive place, as it has continued to be—very different from the more urbanized, ethnically mixed, and development-centered Malaysian west coast. It also seemed to be a place of paradox. Southeast Asian Islam as a popular religion at that time was mainly known from studies done in Indonesia. These tended to present particular groups as being either very strongly Islamic or as having religious traditions that were more strongly syncretic. Popular religion in Kelantan did not fit either type in that it seemed to have some of each, and understanding how and why this was so preoccupied me during the early phase of my research. Over the years, however, the course of change was clear. Strongly affected by political struggles as well as state initiatives and policies, the direction has been toward greater Islamic fundamentalism or Islamism and the suppression of non-Muslim traditions.

The section on Indonesia is concerned with the problem of two different forms of popular Islam, specifically with what are referred to as an orthodox or standard version in contrast to a syncretic or nonstandard one. This section includes case studies of two instances that have been particularly important in the literature on Indonesian Islam, one concerning the island of Lombok and the other of Java. Both instances not only involve popular heterodoxy and syncretism but also differences in terms of identity, whereby adherents of the two versions see themselves in opposition to the followers of the other. It concludes with a discussion of the reported collapse of heterodox Islam and the reasons this has taken place.

Chapter 6 is about popular Christianity and the consequences of conversion for those who have become Christian. Beyond overseas immigrant populations, conversion in general has occurred mainly among indigenous peoples as opposed to existing adherents of world religions. The conversion of indigenous peoples has involved all of the world religions, depending upon the area, though Christian conversion has been the most widespread across both island and continental Southeast

Asia and has probably also been more common than conversion to Islam, Buddhism, or Hinduism.

The last section of the book (chapters 7–9) returns to more fully comparative issues. Chapter 7 is about what is now sometimes called the "occult economy." This somewhat awkward label refers, in brief, to the mixing of rational social and economic knowledge and behavior with popular religious or magical beliefs, practices, and explanations. Though not necessarily or even frequently identified as such, the specific topics that fit the general notion of occult economics have been a major concern in studies of popular religion in recent years, especially regarding Vietnam and Thailand.

Chapter 8 is about religious movements, specifically those that belong in the realm of popular religion. This means that while some occur among indigenous peoples who have not yet converted to a world religion, they have in all the instances developed where such influences have been present. The movements considered in this chapter are linked to either Christianity or Islam, but others linked to Buddhism and Hinduism are noted elsewhere. After describing a variety of movements, the chapter concludes with a more comparative discussion of how movements can be interpreted. Chapter 9 offers a concluding discussion.

2

THE DEVELOPMENT OF RELIGION IN SOUTHEAST ASIA

The lands of Southeast Asia form a region of great religious diversity. All four of the largest world religions are present in a major way. And in addition to several ethnically particular religious traditions, there are also innumerable local, indigenous, or tribal religions, though these are in decline as their adherents are converting to one of the world religions. The various world religions are mainly distributed in particular areas, but there are zones of overlap in many places, and the cities of Southeast Asia have generally been centers of ethnic and religious diversity and mutual tolerance or pluralism.

But how can we account for the long-term religious diversity of Southeast Asia? For example, was European colonialism responsible? Various parts of the region were colonized at various times and in different places by six different colonial powers (Spain, Portugal, Great Britain, France, the Netherlands, and the United States), which undoubtedly had some effect on its religious development. Colonialism was responsible for (or contributed greatly to) the introduction and spread of only one new major world religion—Christianity—to Southeast Asia. It was also, however, linked to the large-scale immigration of a great many Chinese and their popular religions into the region, and to a much less extent the immigration of South Indian Hindus as plantation laborers into British Malaya. With the exception of the addition of Christianity, the fundamental religious diversity of Southeast Asia formed long before the arrival of European colonialism, but this brought a new phase of complexity and differentiation.

Geography offers another line of explanation. The islands of Southeast Asia lie along the sea route between India and China and contained the Spice Islands that once were an international obsession. The Malay Peninsula, and the Indonesian and Philippine archipelagos, have long been open to penetration by traders, adventurers, missionaries, and colonizers. But the mainland above the Malay Peninsula was a corner of the vast Asian continent and therefore was much less accessible beyond the coastal areas—hence, for example, its much later colonization. The region, however, is tropical as well as mountainous, which made possible a variety of modes of adaptation. Geography also protected and encouraged people who wished to live their own way of life to do so in close proximity to others who adhered to one or another of the world religions, or at least did so until recently.[1]

RELIGION AND STATES AND EMPIRES IN ASIA

Beyond the general importance of geography, the religious diversity of Southeast Asia is closely associated with the political development of the region. This can be seen through comparisons with developments in East Asia, specifically in China and Japan. While there are similarities between East and Southeast Asia, these (except to some extent for Vietnam) are outweighed by differences.[2]

In both East and Southeast Asia the development of religion has been inseparable from the development of the state and national ethnic culture. Throughout East and Southeast Asia the political strength of institutionalized religion and the state have been inversely correlated: the larger and more culturally powerful the state, the weaker or more politically subordinated that of institutionalized religion, and vice versa. The pattern in Southeast Asia was mainly the opposite of the one that developed in East Asia.

In China and Japan, state power enabled it to create, control, or influence the development of national ethnic culture that reached from the highest to the lowest levels of society. Once established, the state-based cultures of China and Japan were not easily penetrated or transformed by external religious traditions. China and Japan were not fertile ground for religious change, or at least far less so than the lands of Southeast Asia. Religious conversion was slow and did not involve the abandonment of existing religious beliefs and practices. Except on the margins, the world religions thrived only to the extent that they fitted into the framework of existing religious traditions.

In both regions, religious development has also been inseparable from state ethnicity or national culture. In China and Japan the state was large and powerful, and culturally dominant over the various institutionalized religious traditions that entered or developed within them. In Southeast Asia the relationship between religion and the state was more the opposite. Here the development of traditional states tended to be limited in size, complexity, and duration, while (and consequently) the political importance and cultural power of the world religions has been strong. Note that such an equation says nothing about the matter of the content or "purity" of the religious traditions involved, or about the differences between textual, elite, or official religion and popular belief and practice. It is rather the independent political or institutional strength of religion that has been important.

China is the most striking example of powerful state development in Asia over a long period of human history. At an early point—well before the Common Era—China developed centralized states that eventually expanded to become a vast, enduring empire. Dynasties of course rose and fell, invasions occurred, and disruption and periods of chaos prevailed, but an administrative, elite, culture-bearing bureaucracy remained. Regional or ethnic dialects and local folk traditions also continued and evolved. But over these there developed a national culture and language based on a common script, a common elite philosophy of social and political organization, a common aesthetic, and a common elite religious culture that surmounted local and regional spirits, gods, and rituals.[3]

In terms of ethnicity, the vast majority of Chinese thus came to know themselves as "Han" to distinguish them from the various ethnic minorities. Many of the latter were tribal people, some of whom are adherents of one or another of the world religions (mainly Buddhism or Islam) and are often speakers of non-Sinitic languages. China remains very ethnically diverse in terms of the number of languages spoken or ethnic groups identified within its borders. But the total numerical size of the minority populations in comparison to the Han is far smaller.

Moreover, the ethnic minority populations are concentrated in the geographical margins of China, the north, west, and south on the mainland, and in Taiwan and some of the other islands. While some minorities (most recently the Manchu) arrived later and conquered the Han Empire and established new dynasties of their own, others have been present for as long as or longer than China has been a country. Some ethnic minority groups exist on the margins because these are the places where they have been able to survive on their traditional ways of gaining a livelihood. In other instances they have been pushed into zones where they could survive but that were not suitable for traditional Han agricultural practices, but where either animal herding or slash-and-burn cultivation could provide a living and a measure of autonomy in deserts or rugged mountains. Such groups were generally able to maintain some degree of linguistic, political, and cultural-religious autonomy from the Han monolith.

In the mountainous region of southwestern China, for example, the ethnic minorities are "hill tribes" that generally practice shifting cultivation, traditionally have shamanistic religious practices, and are now inclined to become Christian if given the opportunity. In the adjacent regions of Southeast Asia, many of the hill tribe populations of northern Burma (now Myanmar), Thailand, Laos, and Vietnam have been migrating for centuries from China as a result of pressure from the expanding Han population and government. As is the case elsewhere on the ethnic margins of China, the various non-Han ethnic groups are also the bearers of their own cultural and religious traditions. In the Southeast Asian countries, they have sought to retain autonomy, this time from the dominant Buddhist, lowland states of Laos, Thailand, and Burma, in part by converting to Christianity.

The situation in Japan was somewhat different than in China. But here again a single, all-powerful ethnic group coalesced and expanded throughout Japan, either absorbing the aboriginal and other non-Japanese ethnic groups or pushing or limiting them to marginal areas in the north (including the Ainu in Hokkaido) and the south (including the Ryukyu peoples of Okinawa). And, though often strongly influenced by China, the Japanese majority again developed a powerful national ethnic culture based on common written traditions that again transcended the frequent feudal divisions and struggles that constituted much of the political history of the country. And also again the national ethnic culture had religious and aesthetic as well as philosophical and practical social and political dimensions.

The strength of the state and the pervasiveness of a highly developed national ethnic culture in both China and Japan served as a filter if not a barrier to the penetration of external world religions, one that absorbed and limited their impact. Though to a lesser extent, this is true of Buddhism as well as Islam and Christianity.

Buddhism had a great and enduring impact on the state religion of China, but its independence and institutional structure was attacked and persecuted and its political force destroyed. By a thousand years ago, "Buddhism became acculturated to the Chinese social milieu both in its theology and in its organizational relationship to secular authority."[4] Today Islam in China is mainly limited to the Turkic-speaking ethnic minorities of far western China. And while some ethnic Han Chinese have in the last century or so become Christian, the number in proportional terms has been very small. Missionary Christianity in China has had its greatest proportional appeal among the ethnic minorities, though its spread anywhere in the socialist mainland has often been severely curtailed. In Japan, Christianity had some early success in a few places but was brutally eradicated or driven underground during the Tokugawa Shogunate. Christianity returned to Japan in the more recent past with the Meiji Restoration.

In contrast to Islam and Christianity, Buddhism spread widely in East Asia. It has been an extremely important religious tradition in both China and Japan for a long period of time. But the development and influence of Buddhism in both countries has been constrained and fitted in with other existing religious traditions rather than dominating them. In terms of identity, scholars of comparative religion would probably agree that it would be incorrect to say that either country is (or, in mainland China, was before the revolution) simply Buddhist. Some Chinese and Japanese would certainly identify themselves as Buddhists, especially if they were members of monastic orders. But most would evidently see their religious traditions and loyalties as mixed or multiple. People in both countries recognize major, named, non-Buddhist traditions, including Shinto in Japan and Daoism and Confucianism in China. The matter of content of Han Chinese religion is even more complicated. Here there are a great many notions, doctrines, and activities that are not necessarily lumped into any of the named traditions.

These include spirit medium practices, fortune-telling, agriculture fertility cults, and many other popular forms of religious practice, sometimes referred to as Daoism.[5] In the modern period in both places the long-existing monolith of national ethnic culture has been shattered, though more so in China than in Japan.

Southeast Asia

It might seem at first that the religious situation in Southeast Asia is not much different from that of China and Japan. But nowhere in Southeast Asia was state formation and development of a national ethnic culture the equivalent of what took place in the large countries of East Asia. The Indonesian archipelago and the adjacent Malay Peninsula contained numerous small, mainly coastal states that were open to the spread of Islam, as were the trading centers of Java's northern coast. Eventually the Muslim states succeeded in gaining control of Java and destroying much, though not all, of the old Indic-Javanese culture. All but a handful of highland communities accepted Islam, at least as a matter of identity. Elsewhere, it was mainly Bali that held on to a form of what later came to be called Hinduism.[6]

In contrast to what occurred in East Asia, one or another of the world religions has become dominant in each country or region of Southeast Asia except Vietnam. Most Filipinos identify themselves as Christians and see the Philippines as a Christian country. Although post-colonial Indonesia has no official religion except for monotheism, most Indonesians identify themselves as Muslims and regard Indonesia as a Muslim country, though there are also enclaves of Hinduism (centering on Bali) and Christianity in various places.

In the mainland above Malaysia (which is officially Muslim), the dominant lowland ethnic groups (the Thai in Thailand, the Burmese in Burma or Myanmar, the Lao in Laos, and the Khmer in Cambodia) identify themselves and their country as Buddhist. In all of these places the association of a country or dominant ethnic group with a particular world religion is long-standing and pervasive. The political and cultural influence of the various world religions and their role as cultural features in civilization have been commensurate with their identity.

One question is whether the mainland of Southeast Asia was as open to the penetration and domination of external religion as were the peninsular and insular regions. There certainly were differences, which are reflected, for example, in the earlier and more complete establishment of European colonial rule and the beginning of conversion to Christianity in the islands and peninsula of Southeast Asia. The European colonial takeover in the latter region began in the early sixteenth century. In contrast, colonization did not occur in the mainland above the Malay Peninsula until the nineteenth century. Yet, these historical differences notwithstanding, the religious development in continental Southeast Asia was not very different from that of the island region, at least in terms of comparison with China and Japan. The anthropologist Lucien Hanks has observed that for one thousand years or longer mainland Southeast Asia (beyond Northern Vietnam) consisted of a great forest scattered with occasional savannah-like areas, lightly sprinkled with villages and an occasional walled city. There are grass- and jungle-covered ruins of past capitals strewn up and down the Irrawaddy, Chao Praya, and Mekong Rivers. Capital cities like Pagan in Burma, Angkor in Cambodia, and Ayuthia in Thailand rose and then fell into decay. Only a few lasted longer than one or two centuries. Ayuthia, which lasted three centuries, was a remarkable exception.[7]

This overstates the small, limited, and relatively brief endurance of the continental states over the past thousand years (before which time, less was known about them). For example, the Khmer state centered at Angkor was certainly at its peak more than a walled river town with a small population and limited shelf life. It was twice or more the size of present-day Cambodia. It encompassed the present part of southeastern Thailand and the southern parts of modern Vietnam and Laos. It lasted for considerably longer than two centuries, and while the government was organized around the usual cult of a divine ruler and had the usual limited range of interests, abilities, and institutions, it was able to mobilize a large labor force and create some of the most impressive pre-modern architecture in the world.

But the Khmer do not disprove the generalization that countries of Southeast Asia have been more open to the penetration of external world religions than the much larger and culturally more powerful states of China and Japan. For all of its world-class architectural achievements and the size of the labor force they required, the Khmer empire at its height would fit into a small corner of China, and the ethnic high culture of the Angkor state seems to have been limited to

Figure 2.1. Angkor Wat (Siem Reap, Cambodia, 2008) was originally built as a Hindu temple in the early twelfth century but was subsequently Buddha-ized, though some original Hindu carving and statuary remain and continue to be venerated.

the Khmer, though it probably influenced the Thai and other groups that were part of its empire. The institutionalized religion of the Khmer during the Angkor period was Indic, meaning that both Hindu and Mahayana Buddhist traditions were present, though the former were predominant. With the collapse of the Angkor state, the Khmer became Theravada Buddhists, though without abandoning their older Indic divinities (which are still venerated, for example, at Angkor Wat and at the major shrine of Phnom Kulen) or its folk religious, magical, and animistic traditions.

Siam (as Thailand remained known until 1939) provides a more recent example. The still existing Chakri dynasty became the basis for the strongest traditional state to develop anywhere in Southeast Asia in recent centuries, and the only one to avoid colonization by a Western power. The Chakri dynasty may have been founded by another upstart warlord who built a walled city on the river, but it continued to grow by innovation and modernization as well as by absorbing the other regional

Figure 2.2. A large and elaborately decorated stone statue of Vishnu in Angkor Wat (2008).

Thai states, part of the Khmer empire, and other foreign ethnic territory. The reasons Siam escaped the colonial fate of all other parts of Southeast Asia are various. It formed a buffer zone between the British Southeast Asian empire in Burma to the west and Malaysia to the south, and the French one to the east in Indochina. Also, however, the Chakri dynasty had or acquired internal strengths, including its openness to Western innovation and to economic development.

But Thailand, like the Khmer empire, is at most only a partial exception to the general thesis that the Southeast Asian countries were, unlike East Asian ones, open to the expansion of the world religions. In the case of the ethnic Thai, this meant Theravada Buddhism. The history of the conversion to Buddhism is far from clear or known in detail, though it seems to have been peaceful and voluntary. The anthropologist Charles Keyes reports that in the eleventh century the Thai were still barbarians who existed on the peripheries of the Indic states of Southeast Asia.[8] The Thai were not at that time Indianized, although older traditions are visible in present-day Thai religious practices, for example, the popularity of Shiva, Vishnu, Brahma, and Ganesha in local business and household shrines. The Thai were Buddhist before the creation of Siam/Thailand.[9] But the totality of religious beliefs and practices among the Thai consists of much more than Buddhism, and Thai Buddhism consists of much more than textual Buddhism. What is not present in Thailand or most of the other countries in Southeast Asia is an identity or label for any of the non-Buddhist or semi-Buddhist religious beliefs and practices comparable to Confucianism and Daoism in China and Shinto in Japan.

Colonialism and the Development of Religion

The world religions grew up within and among states and empires of the Old World. They spread through trade, conquest, colonialism, or peaceful missionary activities. Conquest and colonialism were largely responsible for the establishment of Christianity throughout the New World. It is therefore not surprising that when, a few decades later, the Portuguese and Spanish arrived in Southeast Asia they attempted to do what they had already been doing in the New World. They were, however, able to do so only to a comparatively limited extent. For one thing, in Southeast Asia they faced competition from other world religions, especially Islam, which did not exist in the New World. For their part, the Portuguese were too few in number, and Asia too far from home, to expand beyond trading enclaves to develop large, enduring colonies like Brazil. Their ability to spread Christianity beyond such enclaves was similarly restricted. The Spanish were more successful. The only real equivalent of Iberian Latin American religious-political colonialism in Southeast Asia was therefore limited to the Philippines.

A second phase of European colonialism in Southeast Asia began in the eighteenth century with the expansion of the Dutch, who took over the Portuguese trading enclaves at Malacca and (with the exception of East Timor) in eastern Indonesia and then proceeded to add to them. Colonialism greatly expanded in Southeast Asia in the nineteenth century with the expansion of the English and the arrival of the French and, finally, the Americans, each of which came to control sizable chunks of territory and rule over large numbers of people. Though the forms of colonialism that developed in the second phase also clearly facilitated Christian missionary activities, these were mainly limited to the indigenous minorities outside of the existing world religions. Whatever the religious views and loyalties that individual colonial authorities may have had toward Christianity (probably mixed in most cases), its widespread establishment through the conversion of Buddhists or Muslims was clearly not part of the agenda. In their earlier phases, both Dutch and British colonialism involved charter companies aimed at making profits rather than saving souls. Nor were there Christian European settler populations of the sort that formed throughout much of the New World and some other regions where geographical conditions were more similar to those of Europe.

During the mercantile period and after, colonial rule was often "indirect" in many regions. This meant that government was supposed to be limited and administered through traditional indigenous rulers, with European authorities providing advice and expert guidance rather than directly issuing orders. The policy of indirect rule was also supposed to minimize official interference in matters of custom and religion, especially where Islam or Buddhism was concerned. Indirect rule was not intended to inhibit the development of European capitalist exploitation and ownership of opportunities in mining, plantation agriculture, trade, and forestry. But in general such developments did not have major religious implications.

Colonial attitudes toward Christian missionary activity began to change in the nineteenth century. The expansion of European pacification made mission efforts possible in areas where they had previously not been. The groups targeted were the adherents of indigenous religious traditions rather than Buddhists or Muslims, few of whom were willing to convert. Colonial authorities and other Europeans in some places feared the possibility that Christian missionary efforts would cause unrest among nearby Muslims. In other instances they thought the natives would be better off and more useful or less trouble if they were Christianized.[10]

For the officials of the Netherlands East Indies, the initial decision to encourage the spread of Christianity among the highland peoples was rooted more in political concerns than in distinctly religious ones. By the end of the first decade of the twentieth century, the Dutch were finally ending a costly war of forty years with the anti-colonial Acehnese on the northern tip of Sumatra. There was widespread concern about the further resurgence of militant Islam throughout the Indonesian islands and therefore a strong desire to minimize this development by inhibiting the remaining "heathen" peoples from Muslim conversion. There was special interest in doing so among the groups in the interior or highlands of islands where the coastal peoples had already become Muslims and were beginning to seek the conversion of the tribal peoples of the interior. There was some irony in the situation that had developed. Before Dutch pacification, the warlike nature of the highlanders had restricted the entry of the coastal Muslims into the interior, although trade took place along the interface of the two ethnological zones. Dutch pacification of the interior therefore opened it up not only to developments they sought but also to ones they did not favor—namely the encroachment of the coastal peoples or lowlanders into the highlands and the threat of their complete Islamization, and with it likely further opposition to colonial authority.[11]

On the positive side, among both the Dutch and other colonial regimes, Christians came to be seen both as political allies and, in the case of those who learned to read and write in mission schools, as useful clerks and office workers and lesser colonial officers. Christianity came to overlap to a considerable extent with the ethnic boundaries that formed in the colonial plural societies—a development that eventually had serious negative consequences in some places (especially Indonesia and Burma) in the post-colonial period. What would have happened to the spread of Christianity in Southeast Asia beyond the Philippines or at all without colonial rule as well is a question that cannot be answered. Thailand, however, which remained free of colonial control, was nonetheless eventually opened to Christian missionary efforts and today has seen extensive conversion among its hill tribes.

THE MODERN PERIOD

The independent governments, political parties, and religious movements that came into existence in Southeast Asia in the modern period with the end of colonial rule became involved in religious matters to a greater extent than the colonial regimes had generally been. Religion became a major consideration when countries sought to establish what sort of nation they were to be and to chart a course forward to development and modernization. Indonesia, for example, enshrined monotheism (liberally interpreted) as the first of the five basic principles (*pancasila*) of its constitution. Most or all of the modern countries of Southeast Asia have constitutional or other provisions guaranteeing freedom of religion for everyone, though these are sometimes qualified, offset, or largely negated by other laws or provisions. "Religion," moreover, has tended to be defined as meaning Christianity, Buddhism, Islam, Hinduism, or some other named religion, and not to include animism or indigenous religions. While most or all of the Southeast Asian countries today officially endorse religious pluralism, there are in reality considerable differences in the extent to which tolerance is practiced. Often religious identity maps ethnic identity, and therefore tolerance or hostility in one is projected into the other.

The development of religion in Southeast Asia in the modern period has varied most importantly between the non-socialist countries and the socialist states, specifically those of Vietnam, Laos, and Cambodia. This does not mean that what happened in the countries of each type was uniform, for it certainly was not. But there have been general differences between the two. One such difference is that the non-socialist countries have attempted to change the development of popular religion in less radical ways than did the socialist ones. The non-socialist governments' approaches ranged from religious pluralism to efforts to control and shape religion. In contrast, the socialist states—initially at least—took a negative view of religion, though they had less ability to affect popular religions practices than institutionalized religion. Another difference is that the pace of religious change has also been, overall, less abrupt and less coercive in the non-socialist countries. Comparing religious developments in three of the non-socialist countries with what has occurred in the three socialist ones shows these differences.

The Non-socialist Countries of Thailand, Malaysia, and Indonesia

We begin with Thailand, Malaysia, and Indonesia, which reveal something of the range of what occurred in the non-socialist states.[12]

Thailand

In the recent period, the Thai state has sought to create a national ethnic culture that includes Buddhism, the Thai monarchy, and the Thai language. But the acceptance of this has spread beyond the ethnic Thai only to a limited extent. The fullest acceptance of national Thai culture has occurred among the various Tai ethnic minorities such as the Tai Dam, Tai Lu, and Shan, and among other Buddhist people such as the Mon. Among the non-Thai minorities, including the Chinese, Malays, and the many different hill tribes, as they are known, the acceptance has been varied. Even among the Thai themselves, a national culture has not always brought political stability or unity, as can be seen in the long and continuing history of military takeovers and political turbulence.

Of the non-Thai groups, the Chinese have by far gone furthest in accepting national Thai culture. This is probably especially because of extensive Chinese–Thai intermarriage and the Chinese familiarity with Buddhism. The Chinese in Thailand are not or were not generally Theravada Buddhists, at least in the way the Thai have been for a long period of time. But many Chinese have become Buddhist and contribute to and participate in Thai Buddhist temples, into which various Chinese deities have sometimes been incorporated. Of the Chinese who have been in Thailand for several generations or longer, many see themselves as Thai with Chinese ancestors, or as mixed (Thai-Chinese). Many have become full cultural citizens of Thailand.

The Malay Muslim minority is at the opposite extreme. The Malays in Thailand have been on bad terms with the Thai state for many generations. They are part of Thailand because of the southward expansion of the Thai state and the incorporation of the old Malay Muslim state of Pattani and other ethnically Malay and religiously Muslim areas in the far south of the modern country. Such Malay Muslims accept as little of national Thai culture and religion as possible, and instead identify with

Malay Muslim culture to the south in Malaysia and beyond this to the wider Muslim world.

The various indigenous non-Thai tribal minorities are yet another matter. As in China, these minorities dwell on the margins, often both geographically and culturally. Until the recent past, their existence was of relatively little concern to the Thai rulers and population. In Thailand, as in other continental countries, the indigenous minorities are mainly highland peoples, referred to as hill tribes. In recent decades the Thai government has made some effort to convert the Hmong and other hill tribe populations to Buddhism, but with little success. The main tendency has been for these groups to become Christian.

Malaysia

Malaysia has also sought to develop a national culture and identity involving religion but has had only little success in doing so. The basic problem is that colonial rule left the country with an ethnically and religiously mixed and divided population. The majority are Malays who are all Muslims. But the non-Muslim Chinese community is also both economically very powerful and well developed in terms of modernization. There is also a smaller but still sizable, mainly Hindu Indian population. While Malaysia isn't officially an Islamic state, Islam is the national religion, and all Muslims are subject to some religious (or sharia) as well as secular laws and forbidden to convert to other religions—a set of provisions that does not apply to non-Muslims (except where Muslims are involved). More generally, Malaysia has remained a plural society, even at the level of ethnic identity. When Malaysians go abroad, they are "Malaysians," but within the country they are Malays, Chinese, Indians, Orang Asli, or Dayaks, as the case may be, each with its own religious practices, festivals, and celebrations—a continuing plural society in spite of the desire of most of its citizens to move beyond this.

Indonesia

Indonesia chose yet a different course. Before the coming of Dutch colonial rule, the countries of what became Indonesia included many scattered, small agricultural and trade-based states, some of which (especially in Bali and Java) had Indic or "Hindu-Buddhist" religious traditions, while others were more distinctly Muslim. Most of the indigenous tribal peoples of the various islands adhered to their own religious traditions before, in many cases, converting to Christianity in the twentieth century or earlier. By the time of independence, the largest number of Indonesians by far were Muslim, though some much more completely and militantly so than others.

While both the numerical size of and proportion of its Muslim population (about 87 percent) is far larger than that of Malaysia, at the time of independence in 1949 Indonesia did not become a Muslim state or declare Islam to be the national religion. This was partly because by then the inhabitants of many of its far-flung islands and ethnic groups were already Christian, and in some cases had been for a long period of time. In addition, the small but densely populated and important island of Bali was Hindu, while the much larger core island of Java was divided between those who saw themselves as true or orthodox Muslims and those who identified themselves as non-orthodox "Javanese" Muslims. In order to better unify the diverse peoples of the former Dutch East Indies, Indonesia therefore instead became an officially "monotheistic" country. This constitutionally based policy was pluralistic. It meant that all Indonesian people should belong to a religion deemed to be monotheistic but had a choice among several. Therefore since monotheism is not a religion of identity, a national religious culture has not developed here either.

The society and culture of Indonesia is divided along ethnic as well as religious lines. And these do not overlap to the same extent as in Malaysia, Thailand, or many other Southeast Asian countries. Inhabitants of Indonesia recognized their religion as Muslims, Christians, Hindus, or Buddhists as a part of their national Indonesian identity that they shared with other ethnic communities. Until recently ethnic differences were emphasized. But with increasing globalization of Islamism and the reactions to this by adherents of other religious traditions, religion has tended to increasingly transcend ethnic differences. Muslims have sought in some instances to be ruled by Islamic law, and Muslims have increasingly sought to emphasize the Islamic rather than the pluralist nature of the country.

The Socialist or Neo-socialist States

Three countries in Southeast Asia are or have for a time been committed to Marxist-socialist governments: Vietnam, Laos, and Cambodia. Of these, Vietnam and Laos remain officially socialist while having shifted in the late 1980s to mainly capitalist market economies and liberalized state attitudes and policies toward religious practices. Socialism is gone entirely from Cambodia, and religion (at least Buddhism) has been more fully embraced than in the neo-socialist countries of Vietnam and Laos. The effects of Khmer Rouge rule and its aftermath, however, had a far more severe effect on Buddhism than anything that occurred elsewhere.

In terms of pre-socialist characteristics and developments, there are again similarities and differences among the three countries. In both Cambodia and Laos the dominant lowland population is Theravada Buddhist while the highland minorities are either Christian or in most cases continue to adhere to indigenous beliefs and practices. In both of these countries Buddhist religious institutions and practices are similar to those of Thailand and Burma/Myanmar. Cambodia, Laos, and Vietnam together formed the Southeast Asian French colonial empire of Indochina. At least in the latter phase of colonial rule, the French supported Buddhism along with monarchies in these countries as a conservative counter-force to socialism and nationalism. This worked (and then only for a brief time) in Cambodia, which was granted independence on peaceful terms, in a way that had no parallel in British, Dutch, or American colonialism elsewhere in Southeast Asia.

The differences are also important. While the lowland Khmer and Lao are Theravada Buddhists, traditional religion in lowland Vietnam is more like that of China—a combination of Mahayana Buddhism, Daoism, ancestor worship, and other popular religious practices. The French succeeded in introducing Catholicism into Vietnam among the lowland ethnic Vietnamese at an early point as well as subsequently among some of the highland peoples in southern Vietnam. Elsewhere in Indochina, Christian conversion was limited mainly to the highland minority peoples.

Though they varied greatly in their application, the attitudes of the socialist countries in Southeast Asia were based in part on the examples of anti-religious ideology and policies set by previously established socialist regimes going back to the Russian Revolution and the formation of the USSR. With the exception of northern Vietnam, which has had a socialist regime since 1954, the socialist states in Southeast Asia came into existence in 1975 (the last of all countries in the world to do so).

This was the time of the Cultural Revolution in neighboring China, the period in which anti-religious political sentiment, policy, and attacks were at a peak. Although anti-religion or anti-clericalism had a presence in social revolutionary movements going back at least to the French Revolution in the eighteenth century, such attitudes and practices were most fully developed as part of the communist revolutions of the twentieth.

Here official mistrust and hostility toward religion were a matter of doctrine and policy based upon several objections. One was that in general philosophical or doctrinal terms, Marxist socialism is atheistic and materialistic. It denies the reality of all supernatural beings, places, and processes, and of all supernatural forms of agency or causation. It holds that all religious beliefs and practices amount to superstition, although some forms of superstition are more foolish or objectionable than others. In place of supernaturally based religion, it offers scientific materialism as the basis of progress to a better life. A further objection is reflected in the famous iconic phrase "Religion is the opium of the masses," although there are earlier versions of this aphorism as well.[13] This phrase means that religion dulls a society to the wrongs and inequalities to which the masses of people are subjected. The people are therefore distracted from seeking improvement through rational change. At least at first, most or all revolutionary socialist leaders subscribed to such doctrines.

There are also practical economic and socialist objections to religion. Religious expenditures are often costly, therefore a burden especially for the poor, and a waste of resources needed for national development. In addition to being an economic waste, religious ceremonies—for example weddings and funerals—tend to serve as displays of wealth and social status and therefore run counter to the cardinal socialist principle of equality. Also, the practices of specialists who claim supernatural powers, such as spirit mediums, shamans, or fortune-tellers, are forms of economic exploitation that take advantage of those who are superstitious.

In addition to such social evils, religion was also believed to pose various political problems for the implementation of the revolution and the governance and preservation of the socialist state. Organized religion in a society is often seen as being "feudalistic," that is, closely linked to and supporting the pre-socialist feudal regime or ruling class, and all the more so where monarchs were believed to be in some way divine. On the other hand, religious movements or newly formed sects may be thought to be counter-revolutionary or associated with opposition to the Communist Party or state and treated accordingly—Falun Gong in China is a well-known recent example. And finally, though not exclusively so in socialist countries, religious identities are often seen as leading to or worsening ethnic conflicts between the state and minority groups.

In Southeast Asia the full implementation of Marxist religious doctrine took place over a relatively brief period. The countries of Vietnam, Laos, and Cambodia did so fully only in 1975. In Vietnam and Laos the relaxation of restrictions on religion began in the late 1980s. In Cambodia the brutal and devastating policies of the Khmer Rouge lasted only a few years, though their effects continued far beyond this time. In Laos and Vietnam, by the time that people had only begun to cope with socialist restrictions on religious practices, they were being abandoned or relaxed.

Vietnam

In Vietnam there were also historical differences from one region of the country to another. The north had been governed by a communist regime since the French defeat and withdrawal in 1954, while the south only since the end of the civil war and unification of Vietnam in 1975. This means that the communist regime began to implement its policies concerning religion and other cultural matters twenty years earlier in the north. In addition, many Christian Vietnamese moved south after the partition in 1954 (and some of these left the country after the socialist unification and became refugees in the United States and other Western countries).

Even in the north, however, regardless of possible preferences, the revolutionary government of Vietnam never attempted to eliminate all religion per se. It did attempt to redefine legitimate religion, to eliminate or diminish various practices, and to introduce new ones in their place. Some practices were deemed objectionable for reasons involving public health, most notably, the exhumation and reburial of the dead in secondary mortuary rituals. The latter practices were not banned but over time were subjected to increasing restrictions.[14]

More generally the Communist Party objected to traditional popular religious activities for the usual Marxist reasons. They involved backward superstition, waste, exploitation, and in some instances the display of differences in social status. Added to such criticism was the potent nationalist objection that most of the common religious practices were not only feudal superstitions, but they were also (and perhaps even worse) imports from China and therefore a dilution of Vietnamese cultural purity, and, further, encouraged by the Americans in the south to weaken the spirit of resistance.[15]

The reaction to party and government criticisms of traditional religious practices varied. Women (especially older women) were mainly responsible for the well-being of their families, and this included their spiritual well-being. Such women were therefore less willing to give up traditional beliefs and practices than were men. There were also differences among men. Soldiers and party members, who had been extensively exposed to party education and doctrine, were more apt to agree with government efforts to eliminate, diminish, or alter religion than were ordinary men.[16]

Efforts at secularization were at most only partially successful. Some people never accepted the revolutionary religious changes, and some of those who at first accepted the changes eventually reverted to prerevolutionary practices as the state and party came to care less what individuals and families actually did, or at least to give up on doing much about it. The liberalization of party and state attitudes and policies regarding religion appears to have been linked especially to the official *doi moi* reforms of 1986 whereby much of the socialist basis of the economy was abandoned in favor of market principles, private ownership and trade, and interaction with non-socialist countries. The loss of confidence in socialism appears to have brought a more general willingness to favor openness and heterodoxy in other matters, including religion.

The question of how far to go in religious permissiveness, however, remained. And here what happened to Ho Chi Minh is notable. Following his death, an official effort was made to commemorate Ho's standing as the central revolutionary hero of Vietnam. This was in keeping with a well-developed tradition in Vietnamese history whereby cults form around deceased military heroes, especially ones who have defended the country against foreign invasion and control. The state and party encouraged an ideological cult of Ho but did not want this to be a traditional religious cult of the nationalist warrior hero. Deification at the level of popular religion practices could not always be controlled, however, and in places Ho became a god.[17] Eventually the state intervened after authorities had decided that the cult of Ho was getting out of hand. In one version Ho was being worshipped as the eighteenth king in a dynasty of rulers said to have founded Vietnam.[18] Here the state cracked down and banned such veneration in 1995, though again whether this was effective is another matter.

The government and party hard-liners who opposed resurgent popular religion, however, fought a losing battle. Unable to eliminate or suppress popular religion, the state began to change its view of some things. Many of the beliefs and practices formerly condemned as backward and harmful superstition carried out by disreputable people came to be seen as authentic traditional examples of local culture and therefore as deserving of some respect.[19]

Restrictions on religious activities by the state continued to relax over the years. The government promulgated new enactments, including a lengthy one in 2004. This guaranteed the right to practice any religion—or none—although this is qualified by various restrictions included in other laws. In addition, the state has created a list of officially recognized religions, one that includes local named religions as well as world religions. Such recognition means that these religions were permitted to operate as organizations within the country. The world religions on the list include Buddhism, Catholicism, Protestantism, and Islam. The Vietnamese ones are Cao Dai and Hoa Hao, both of which began as syncretic religious movements under colonial rule and were opposed to the socialist revolution.[20] Confucianism, however, was not on the Vietnamese roster. Its absence left the minority Chinese community without an official religion, except for Buddhism. Nor were the religious traditions of the highland ethnic minorities recognized except where people had converted to Catholicism, Protestantism, or Buddhism. Being on the government's list of approved, identified religions may have been important in some respects, but the practical significance of the difference between recognized official religion and popular religious activities waned. Shrines and spirit mediums, fortunetelling, and other occult practices formerly labeled as superstition reemerged or increased.[21] Although it is not listed as a religion, the practice of ancestor worship has come to be officially regarded as at the center of Vietnamese national religious traditions and culture and is practiced by adherents of all religions.[22] Even popular ritual practices that involved lavish spending eventually also came back into vogue.[23]

Laos

Put in very general terms, the socialists in Laos began by accepting and to some extent acting upon the general attitudes of communists about religion noted above. But what occurred was a different matter, and again what occurred at first changed over time. The revolutionary religious policies previously put in place in North Vietnam in 1954 had a strong influence on those implemented in the Lao People's Democratic Republic after the establishment of the communist government in 1975. The religious situation in the two countries, however, had never been the same.

The most important difference concerns Buddhism. While Buddhism was present in both countries, it was different and more important in Laos than in Vietnam. Buddhism in Laos is Theravada and dominates the popular religious life of the ethnic Lao, whereas Buddhism in Vietnam is Mahayana and is but one of several organized religious traditions that reflect the Chinese model. The matter of how to deal with popular Buddhism was therefore a much larger issue in Laos than in Vietnam.

Buddhism presented both problems and opportunities to the new socialist government in Laos. After the socialists came to power in 1975, Buddhism ceased to be the official state religion. The socialist government, however, never set itself against Buddhism or attempted to destroy it as the Khmer Rouge did in Cambodia.[24] Monks were occasionally arrested or defrocked for engaging in animist or superstitious activities or for opposition to the regime. The numbers, however, seem to have been small, and no monks appear to have ever been executed, unless this was done in secret. In its early manifesto, the Communist Party had affirmed the right of men to enter the monkhood and were not prevented from doing so. After 1975, the *sangha* (monks) were also included as an official part of the National Front. In terms of ideology, Buddhism was always declared to be at least compatible with socialism. Beyond the occasional deviant or troublemaking activities of monks, a problem with Buddhism was that it had been traditionally closely associated with the monarchy, which, along with feudalism and elitism, had been the central and popular reason for the revolution. This, however, was eventually accepted.

The policies of the party and government had two somewhat seemingly contradictory goals or strategies involving Buddhism. One was to use it as a means of increasing the party's popularity and support, and so further legitimize the new regime in the eyes of the population. The other was to gain control over Buddhism and make it more compatible with the principles of socialism. The achievement of the first goal was mainly a matter of symbolism, such as including monks as a prominent visible presence in public state ceremonies and incorporating Buddhist icons into the central ideology and iconography of the state. Although this strategy had a downside, it grew in importance over time, especially as socialism retreated or collapsed elsewhere. The second goal was more complicated and was eventually mainly abandoned.

Buddhism had a name, an identity, a mythology, and organized institutions, all focusing on the monasteries, temples and shrines, and festivals—and therefore great popular meaning and prestige among its lowland Lao adherents. While retaining these, the party and government sought to change Buddhism in a number of ways. They wished to see less money spent on popular celebrations and festivals so that more could be devoted to material improvement and development. They wanted to place the *sangha* under their control, and to turn Buddhism into something closer to socialism. In terms of doctrine and worldview, it wished to shift the traditionally otherworldly orientation of official Buddhism to worldly practical social concerns. Monasteries were to become cooperatives, and monks were to plant their own food or receive rations of rice for teaching rather than be dependent on alms from the laity. But such efforts were not well received by the Buddhist Lao. In popular religion, festivals and celebrations were very important, and supporting monks with daily gifts of rice and other contributions were the fundamental means of earning merit, which was viewed as contributing to well-being in daily life as well as in transcendental terms.

Over time, the attempt to socialize Buddhism was deemphasized. And therefore the goal of using it to strengthen the legitimacy of the government became the more dominant concern. Increasing the identity of the government with Buddhism did not work well with the entire ethnically diverse population of Laos. A large minority of the population of the country consisted of non-Buddhist highland peoples, some of whom were well represented in the party and in the revolutionary struggle against the monarchy. And for these people, Buddhism—which had been the state religion under the monarchy and was associated with the assumed cultural superiority of the lowlanders—had little positive appeal.[25]

The limits of its appeal notwithstanding, the link of Buddhism with the new Lao state grew and became more formalized. Government officials and party functionaries emphasized public acts of Buddhist piety, merit making, and interaction with monks. Eventually the famous Buddhist shrine of That Luang near the capital of Vientiane was designated as the official national monument and was included on all currency and official documents in place of the hammer and sickle. And when Kaysone Phomvihane (the Ho Chi Minh of Laos, who had led the Communist Party since its founding in 1955 and served as prime minister since independence) died, he was given an elaborate Buddhist state funeral conducted by eighty monks.[26]

The Buddha-ization of socialism in Laos was also partly an assertion of lowland Lao nationalism. As signified by the inclusion of three women dressed in tribal costume in the new national seal of the country, the socialist government had retained the prevailing distinction among ethnic population types. All the inhabitants became "Lao," meaning "Laotian," to emphasize common citizenship, cooperation, and equality, but diversity is also emphasized according to where people lived, specifically the lowlands, the midlands, and the highlands. As in northern Vietnam, the socialists saw success in their revolutionary struggle as requiring the unification of all the ethnic groups and therefore (and beyond this) the emphasis on equality among all. Nonetheless, the ethnic categories in Laos have retained an important subtext of inferiority and superiority in terms of which elevation negatively correlates with prestige (whereby the low are high and the high are low). And here religion has been an important consideration. The lowland Lao Lum are Buddhist and see themselves as bearers of civilization and the other groups as more backward. The midland Lao Theung and highland Lao Sung peoples in turn tend to resent this. In religious terms these latter groups were inclined to conversion to Christianity (or to religious movements) rather than to Buddhism, though conversion to Christianity was inhibited by the war and then suppressed by the socialist state that restricted missionary activity. In the earlier years following the socialist victory, the government and party had hoped and assumed that the non-Buddhists would evolve from animism to atheism. This expectation was not realized, however, either in the case of the non-Buddhist minorities or in the popular religious animist beliefs and practices of the Lao Buddhists.

Non-Buddhist forms of popular religion also posed a problem. After the socialists came to power in Laos they, like the Vietnamese socialists, objected to animism and superstition, in part because they involved expenditures that should be reserved for more useful things, and also because they were simply backward. Occult activities have a range of traditional concerns including protection through amulets from physical harm, curing, sorcery and counter-sorcery, fortune seeking, and the problems of love and marriage. But the activities of spirit mediums and fortune-tellers also posed political problems as well. Troublesome spirits might make an appearance at a séance and say embarrassing things about the new regime. Such spirits might include the ghosts of past kings—traditionally popular characters at séances—or of recently deceased politicians of the previous regime. Such spirits might even speak through the medium and say that the present communist regime would soon fall.[27] Although it was superstition, there was the risk that some people might believe such things if they were spoken through the mouth of a reliable medium.

As elsewhere, popular religion was harder to control than institutional Buddhism. Monks wear orange robes as their daily dress and shave their heads, and therefore they are highly visible. Some monks were hermits, but most lived in monasteries and followed well-known routines where they were part of an institutionalized hierarchy and subject to discipline. Monasteries could be closed and monks defrocked, as the Khmer Rouge did in both instances in Cambodia. Again, none of this is really true of spirit mediums and other practitioners of occult services, unless they are also monks. Costumes, if any, are worn only during performances, and rituals are often in ordinary houses; organization and hierarchy are limited to a practitioner (or a loose association of practitioners) and clients; activities are usually sporadic rather than routine; and discipline is at most informal.

A problem here was that while party leaders and intellectuals might be convinced of the falsity of both spirits and the powers of mediums to give them voice, ordinary people (including some ordinary party members) often accepted these things. In addition, the government had little to offer in the way of practical help as an alternative to the information and advice offered by spirit mediums or monks. Here monks might be all right, but the well-publicized early campaign against superstition made them less willing to provide their customary forms of practical advice and ritual assistance to people with personal problems. This reluctance, based on the fear of being attacked by the government for engaging in superstitious activities, promoted greater use of the services of the mediums who operated more privately and informally.[28]

The socialist government fairly quickly decided that Buddhism, including the questionable or deviant activities and reputations of well-known magical monks, were things better supported and utilized than opposed. It eventually also decided that the belief in spirits and related notions of the occult should not, or at least could not, be eliminated. By the time I was in Laos in 2010, *baci* or soul-tying ceremonies had become national in scope, performed by monks among Buddhists and by village officials among non-Buddhists. The *baci* ritual, in which cotton strings are tied around the wrists of honored guests to secure their souls, are otherwise used to bring luck and protection. The blessings that are typically invoked include good luck, becoming rich, and winning the lottery. Such ceremonies can also be simply rituals of solidarity, inclusion, and good as well as acts of benevolence by those holding them. Nor have the spirits disappeared. A story that was circulating in 2010 when I was in Luang Prabang—a World Heritage site and major tourist center—was that a resort recently built by the government was failing. Guests were not coming because it had been built on an inauspicious site, one said to be haunted by the ghosts of the many patients who had died in the hospital that had previously occupied that spot.

Cambodia

Some socialist revolutionary regimes in the world took a much harder line against religious beliefs, practices, and institutions than did others. In Southeast Asia the Khmer Rouge, who ruled in Cambodia from 1975 to 1979 (when they were driven from power by the Vietnamese-backed socialists), appear to have acted with unprecedented anti-religious virulence against Cambodian Buddhism. Here the goal was not just to weaken and control or exploit Buddhism but to destroy it.[29] This was a part of the broader goal of completely transforming Cambodian society and culture by emptying the cities, ending traditional cultural performances, and liquidating teachers and intellectuals outside of the Khmer Rouge themselves. The effort to eradicate Buddhism consisted chiefly of several policies, one of which was to force the closing of monasteries. These policies had begun earlier during the civil war in areas under Khmer Rouge control and were completed by 1978. They were also preceded by the curtailment of many kinds of Buddhist ceremonies. Some monasteries, especially in eastern Cambodia, had in fact already been destroyed by indiscriminant American bombing, and of those that survived some were simply left empty as the cities were abandoned; others were closed and their statues and paintings, manuscripts, and records destroyed; and yet others were turned into storehouses and many to centers of detention, interrogation, torture, and execution. Large numbers of human skeletons and skulls were later recovered from *wats* used for the latter purposes.

Beyond closing monasteries, the decimation of the *sangha* was achieved mainly by issuing orders that all monks were to disrobe and join the laboring population in general, and by prohibiting further ordinations. The Khmer Rouge in some cases required monks not only to disrobe but also to marry in order to ensure the dissolution of their vows. For their part, some monks did not accept that defrocking ended their status as monks, especially insofar as it was forced, for this did not conform to any of the orthodox ways in which a monastic bond could be severed.

Some monks were executed.[30] Here a relevant distinction was made by the Khmer Rouge between "base" or "rank-and-file" monks and "new" or "imperialist" monks who were deemed anti-revolutionary troublemakers. Such a distinction had evolved out of an earlier one between more traditional rural monks and less traditional urban ones. Such labels aside, few monks were executed for simply being monks and performing their religious duties. Those who were executed were mainly monks who refused to disrobe or to obey other orders, or who encouraged others to resist. Many others died, however.[31] Some monks who disrobed and took up the work of ordinary people perished, like lay Cambodians, from forced labor, malnourishment, sickness, and harsh living conditions, which were especially hard on older people.[32] Some monks or ex-monks were protected by Khmer Rouge cadres who were former students who held them in respect or fond regard.

Less is known about the practice of popular religion under the Khmer Rouge, their attitudes and policies toward occult beliefs and practices, such as the activities of spirit mediums, offerings to altars and shrines for spirits, fortune-telling, or the wearing of amulets for protection. Some of this would be hard to control even if the Khmer Rouge did object and punish those involved. Further, recourse to supernatural protection and other help would have undoubtedly had a stronger appeal than ever under the harsh and dangerous circumstances.

As elsewhere, monks and their robes were associated with magical powers. These were popular religious attitudes held by ordinary Cambodians and, evidently, never entirely abandoned by Khmer Rouge cadres themselves. It was supposed that certain monks escaped death by execution by magically disappearing. The orange robes had great symbolic importance and were sometimes kept in secret, whole or in fragments, or dyed black. Only a few monks in all of Cambodia appear to have survived the rule of the Khmer Rouge while still wearing their robes. But while the Khmer Rouge disavowed Buddhism and sought its annihilation, some respect for—or fear of—monastic robes remained. In at least some instances, monks who were executed were not permitted to wear their robes but were forced to first change into other clothing.[33]

After the Khmer Rouge were overthrown in 1979, a new Vietnamese-dominated socialist government (the People's Republic of Kampuchea, or PRK) was created. Under this regime political attitudes and policies toward religion and other matters were closer to those in Laos and Vietnam and evolved accordingly. Buddhism was found to be compatible with communism.[34] The partial restoration of Buddhism was quickly undertaken, though the new attitudes and policies did not simply revert to those of the pre–Khmer Rouge period. Buddhism was to be rebuilt as one of the cornerstones of the new society, though not without restrictions. Some monasteries were soon reopened, but others continued to be used for other purposes, a great many as garrisons for Vietnamese troops. New or reordination began, while some defrocked monks simply put on their orange robes and returned to a monastery. Ordination was declared to be subject to government approval, and many ordinations were not approved. Some monks that had not been officially sanctioned were defrocked, or re-defrocked. Assistance from

Buddhist organizations elsewhere was limited to those in other communist countries.[35]

Then there was the issue of how monasteries, monks, and their activities were to be supported. The government disapproved of the traditional monastic practice of begging and dependence on charity, the most common way for laymen and women to earn merit. Instead monks were expected to grow vegetables on the grounds of *wats* and to earn their way through teaching and other practical contributions. Such policies, however, ran against popular sentiment, since the daily feeding of monks and other forms of charity were the principal means by which lay Buddhists earned merit.

The more complete liberation of Buddhism and the return to traditional monastic procedures did not come until the withdrawal of the Vietnamese and the end of socialism in 1989.[36] The traditional attribution of magical powers to certain monks and the importance of this as a basis for monastic fame and fortune began to reemerge after 1993 with the support of wealthy and ambitious patrons, including ex–Khmer Rouge communists. But rebuilding would be a long-term process in impoverished and institutionally devastated Cambodia. A traveler on the roads of Cambodia in the late 2000s (as I was in 2008) would see many fewer *wats* than in Laos, let alone Thailand.

THE REDUCTION OF RELIGIOUS DIVERSITY

The religious diversity of Southeast Asia is the consequence of interacting geographical and historical patterns and developments. The seas, rivers, lowland plains, and trade routes made the islands and coastal areas of the mainland open to penetration by the various world religions brought by traders, colonialists, and missionaries, though seldom if ever by conquering armies. The fuller penetration of Hinduism, Buddhism, Islam, and Christianity was restricted in the often rugged or mountainous and densely forested interior areas of the mainland and the larger islands. Such conditions served to protect the traditional ethnic and religious diversity of the peoples who occupied these regions. The development of world religions was linked to the formation and expansion of states among coastal and lowland, wet rice cultivating populations. But in comparison to what occurred in East Asia, the Southeast Asian states were relatively small and limited in their political and cultural development. The result was that religious change was generally more a matter of syncretism than the complete replacement of one religion by another. At the same time, religious institutions gained a political power and cultural influence in the lowland and coastal countries that they lacked in the great states of China and Japan.

European colonialism, which began five hundred years ago, had various effects on the development of religion, in some ways enhancing diversity and in others reducing it. Most importantly it contributed to the religious diversity of Southeast Asia by in effect adding a whole new world religion, that of Christianity. This, however, was a slow and limited development, one that began with colonialism and continues into the present. Also, the efforts and effects varied. As they did in the New World, the Spanish made conversion to Christianity a major part of their colonial project in the Philippines and created what became the only large Christian-majority country in Asia. The American takeover of the Philippines added to its religious diversity by encouraging and facilitating the introduction of Protestant forms of Christianity as an alternative to the existing Catholicism. The Portuguese also established Christian colonies in Southeast Asia but succeeded only to a limited extent and eventually lost these all except for part of the small island of Timor in present-day eastern Indonesia. For the other European colonizers (Dutch, French, British, and American), spreading Christianity was never a comparable goal, especially among the lowland and coastal peoples who were already Buddhist or Muslim. The eventual extension of colonial authority over the interior and highland regions enabled missionization in places where it would have previously been difficult or impossible, for example the vast interior of Borneo.

Colonial rule also enhanced religious diversity by encouraging or creating a new level of ethnic pluralism, especially involving Chinese and Indian immigrants. Both Chinese and Indians, who brought their own popular religions, had been present before colonial rule, and some would have come anyway (as the Chinese did in modernizing but noncolonized Thailand). But the economic opportunities and protections afforded by colonial rule greatly, if not evenly, enhanced immigration and therefore the presence of different religious traditions—popular or folk versions of southeastern Chinese and Indian religions, above all South Indian Hinduism in the Malay Peninsula. Many of the members of these ethnic communities have retained versions of the popular religious identities, beliefs, and practices brought by the original immigrants, but some have converted to other world religions—mainly Buddhism and Christianity in the case of the Chinese, and Christianity in the case of the Indians.

In another sense, however, colonialism reduced diversity or set its eventual decline on track. Here the pacification and the extension of colonial control over the highlands and interior regions of both the islands and the mountainous areas of the mainland were very important. This development, which came often in the late nineteenth and early twentieth centuries, enabled the penetration of world religions (above all Christianity). This eventually led to the decline of the diversity of localized indigenous religious traditions in the interior and highland regions that had formerly been beyond the scope of expansion of the world religions. Again, however, this was a long-term development. By the end of colonial rule many indigenous minority peoples remained unconverted. And, as suggested by what has occurred in Thailand, conversion to Christianity or another world religion would likely have taken place anyway, at least outside of the socialist and neo-socialist nations.

The effects of developments under colonialism on diversity have again been mixed in the post-colonial period. But the main thrust of religious change has been in the further reduction of religious diversity, above all as a result of the increases in conversion to Christianity in many areas. Here religious diversity occurs mainly in the varieties of Christianity—Catholic versus Protestant, fundamentalist or evangelical versus mainline, and so on—found in different areas, villages, or neighborhoods. In the mainland countries, however, there is a striking difference in developments in the socialist or neo-socialist states and the others. Much of the limited conversion that has taken place among the indigenous minorities in Vietnam and Laos, for example, appears to have occurred during the colonial period. While present governments of these countries have relaxed, altered, or abandoned their earlier efforts to reduce or eliminate religious practices and "superstition," they have continued to block or discourage further conversion, at least to Christianity. Wars and government policies in these countries have served as a buffer against the trend toward the reduction in indigenous religious diversity that is occurring elsewhere across much of Southeast Asia.

Outside of the socialist countries, the most authoritarian and sustained effort to reduce diversity has been the Indonesian effort to persuade or pressure all inhabitants to have a monotheistic religious identity as Muslim, Protestant or Catholic Christian, Buddhist, Hindu, or Confucian (the latter two being later additions). The requirement has most strongly affected the previously unconverted highland and interior peoples. Those who have converted in accord with the official pressures and opportunities have chosen Islam in some instances, and Buddhism and Hinduism in others, but most frequently Christianity.[37]

3

THREE VERSIONS OF POPULAR HINDUISM

Hinduism has the distinction of being at once among both the oldest and the newest of the major world religions. The gods, rituals, laws, social conventions, art and architecture, and sacred texts of Hinduism have ancient roots, as ancient as any of the existing religious traditions in the world. At the same time, the name Hinduism and the pan-Hindu identity it created among hundreds of millions of people are recent. The term probably came into use only around the turn of the nineteenth century. It is true that the word has been around much longer as a geographical reference to the people of the Indian Subcontinent who were followers of many different traditions or religions that shared various elements. But in terms of its current meaning, *Hinduism* is a fairly modern term. Nor does this seem to have been a matter of replacing an older term of identity with the recent one.

The recent development of Hinduism as a named religious tradition is sometimes attributed to the British colonization of India. It would probably be most accurate to say the term is a product of the interaction of colonial influence and Indian culture and society. Exposed to Western colonial Christianity (and before that to Muslim conquest and domination), Indian intellectuals and elites sought a unifying religious identity that put their own ancient but endlessly localized and varied sacred traditions on par with the other named religions while at the same time seeking purifying reforms that would encourage a return to older practices.[1] The lack of an earlier unifying term of identity may also be due in part to the absence of a single defining iconic central figure or doctrine of the sort characteristic of other world religions, including Christianity, Buddhism, and Islam.

The religious traditions of "Hinduism" as well as Buddhism also have an ancient presence in Southeast Asia. Hinduism spread as early as two thousand years ago, probably mainly by trade, first to the coastal areas of the western area of the islands of present-day Indonesia, the Malay Peninsula, and other southern areas of the continent. Hinduism (or Hindu-Buddhism) reached its peak in the thirteenth and fourteenth centuries in the inland states of Java and the Khmer empire centering on Angkor in Cambodia. After this, both rapidly declined with the advent of Islam in the Malayan Peninsula and archipelago and Theravada Buddhism in much of the mainland. Hinduism never entirely disappeared, however.[2] It has remained and has been replenished by more recent immigrants from India as well as recreated in several new ways, to be discussed below.

Ancient Hinduism as a popular religion in Southeast Asia is far from clearly understood. The use of the modern term of identity incorrectly implies that those who participated in the cults of Shiva, Vishnu, Brahma, Ganesha, and other Indic divinities considered themselves at the time to be "Hindus." But beyond that, while the presence and influence of Indic cults of various divinities are indisputable from archaeological evidence from many sites, though especially ones in ancient Java and Cambodia, the place of Hinduism in the popular religion of these and other regions remains a matter of some doubt. Archaeological and historical attention to both Buddhism and Hinduism in earlier periods has understandably focused on the cult centers that abound with the ruins and relics of Indic temples, statuary, carvings and inscriptions, and art motifs. These indicate a sophisticated great tradition in which clear distinctions were probably made by religious and political elites between Hindu cults and Mahayana or Theravada Buddhist ones.[3] Ordinary people, on the other hand, probably understood or cared little about such distinctions, seeing them mainly as varying sources of pageantry and festivity or sacred power and magic related to fertility, protection, healing, and other practical considerations, as opposed to doctrine or philosophy. Elite religion was carved in stone and cast in brass, some of which has survived to be studied. That of ordinary people was carved in wood or made from bamboo, leaves, cloth, and other perishable materials, little of which has survived over time. Not unexpectedly, Hinduism as a popular religion today is much better understood than what it was like in the past.

Here it is useful to keep in mind that when Westerners and perhaps many scholars of comparative religion think of Hinduism, they have in mind what can be called the classic or textual model of religion, which anthropologists have called the Great Tradition. From this perspective and in terms of general understanding, Hinduism can probably be said to include the following:

1. Polytheism, the worship of many gods and goddesses, of which the most important are presumed to be Shiva, Vishnu, Brahma, and Ganesha, followed by others including Kali that, taken together, are not unlike those of the ancient Greeks, Romans, and Egyptians.
2. An architectural tradition of temples and shrines where images of the gods and goddesses are placed and worshipped with offerings as acts of devotion, requests for favors, or in payment of vows.
3. Two great classic mythical stories, the Mahaberata and the Ramayana, which tell of the adventures and struggles of the gods and goddesses and other characters, again not unlike Greek and Roman myths, performed in dances and dramas.
4. A vegetarian diet, based on the belief in the sanctity of all forms of life. In particular, this includes the abstention of cow slaughter and the consumption of beef.
5. Rapid cremation after death and the belief in reincarnation.
6. A caste system based on (a) extreme notions of purity and pollution; (b) hierarchy, ranging from Brahmans at the top to untouchables at the bottom; (c) endogamy, or marriage within the caste; (d) particular occupations or types of occupations (e.g., Brahmin priests, untouchable sweepers); and (e) the exchange of ritual and other services between castes based on obligation.
7. At the popular level a great emphasis on pilgrimages, festivals, and processions.

Our concern in this chapter is mainly with the popular forms of Hinduism as practiced today by people in Southeast Asia who identify themselves as Hindus. This kind of Hinduism exists in several quite different versions. One of these can be called "ethnic Hinduism"—that followed by peoples of recent ethnic descent from Indian immigrants, though as we shall see this itself is not a simple or unified tradition. Another version is the religious tradition of the Balinese and perhaps of a few other groups in which Hindu-based beliefs and practices have been long present but not identified as such until the twentieth century.

There is also what is best termed "neo-Hinduism." This refers to religious traditions that have only recently become identified or created as Hinduism—in some instances by peoples who had previously probably seldom heard the term, let alone used it as a name for their religion. All these instances appear to involve peoples in Indonesia, and most are a consequence of government mandates and policies concerning acceptable religions. Neo-Hinduism itself exists in several forms. These include the "invention of tradition" of a neo-Hindu religious identity among various Indonesian peoples that had little or nothing in the way of "orthodox" or Indic Hinduism in their traditional religious practices or history. Such people have sought to become officially Hindu in order to achieve legitimacy for their indigenous or customary religious practices. And finally there are Hindu converts. These are people who, once Hinduism became a government-approved national religion, were able to become officially Hindu and did so, as some Javanese in particular have done.[4]

SOUTH INDIAN HINDUISM

The form of popular Hinduism in Southeast Asia that most fully approximates that of the Indian Subcontinent and Ceylon (now Sri Lanka) is that found in Malaysia and Singapore. It was brought directly to Southeast Asian countries during the colonial era by immigrant Indians, above all Tamil groups from South India who were recruited mainly in the first part of the twentieth century.

Hinduism was part of the cultural makeup of the ideal Malayan plantation and public-works labor force. The Indian population that developed in Malaysia during the period of peak immigration was about 80 percent Hindu, and that of recruits for plantation work was even higher.[5] The main object of recruitment during this period was to secure workers for the rubber estates of western Malaya to serve as tree tappers and laborers. The colonial European plantation owners and managers whose views influenced the composition of the migrant population probably had little interest in religious beliefs and rituals per se. Religion, however, was a part of the specific identity that was considered to be ideal for plantation labor. The association of religion with certain occupations in the colonial plural society could also be seen elsewhere. Many Sikhs from the Punjab who came to Malaya became policemen and guards. In the case of Hinduism the connection was the caste system, one of the basic parts of traditional Hindu religion and society in India. Low caste standing was considered to be a desirable trait in plantation laborers because it was linked to servility and to the probable view that life could only be better than what had been left behind. The Hinduism of an early twentieth century Malayan rubber plantation in some ways accurately replicated that of the villages in South India from whence the immigrants came. It did not, however, reflect the social and cultural totality, let alone the vastly wider geographical, ethnic, and cultural range of Hinduism in India.

Plantation Hinduism

Beyond the matter of caste, plantation owners and managers accepted the practice of religion by the migrants on the plantation for several reasons. Management saw religion as a source of contentment and, periodically, entertainment and a relief from the routine of daily work. The plantation was a "total institution" where workers not only performed their assigned tasks but also lived and spent most of their time. They were not forbidden to leave and could visit other plantations or other places for religious celebrations or other purposes. But one of the main cultural principles of the organization of an efficient estate was that the needs and interests of the workers, including religious ones, could and should be largely satisfied within its bounds. The ideal estate was a little world in itself.

Every "standard estate" based on Indian workers therefore had at least one Hindu temple, and a large estate with divisions would have more, plus lesser shrines. If a plantation had been in existence for a long time, it might have an older partially or completely abandoned temple as well as a newer one. The temple was often a basic utilitarian structure provided by the management, built of wood or cement, with a tin roof and minimal decoration. Sometimes a temple was upgraded with religious statues and paintings or a cement-floored porch. Some were more impressive buildings. In any case, the temple was usually located in the central area of the plantation near the "labor lines" (as the workers' living quarters were generally known) and the estate store, which sold provisions as well as snacks and drinks and was where male workers spent a lot of their leisure time. There would also likely be smaller shrines.

Each plantation temple was devoted to a particular god, but shrines for other divinities were often located nearby. While there are well-known urban temples in Malaysia devoted to the major divinities, including Siva and Vishnu, these were not the gods usually found on a rubber estate. The latter are rather the local ones favored by Tamils and other South Indian peoples from the areas whence the migrants came. On the estates the main gods tend to be Murugan, Mariaman, and Muniandi, and if there is more than one temple or a shrine, two or three deities are likely to be present. These gods are Tamil and South Indian versions of Great Tradition deities of antiquity, but this connection was generally left out in popular plantation Hinduism in Malaysia. Murugan, who is probably the most popular of all, is known in Hindu mythology as Subramaniam, one of the children of Siva and Paravathi, but this, to the extent that it is even known, is of little importance, at least to estate Hindus. Mariaman is the goddess of smallpox (and various other rashes and poxes) but also of rain and fertility. She is prayed to for the prevention of disease, for help with school exams and for other practical purposes relating to pregnancy and childbirth, and for having a good marriage and children. By way of specific examples, on the estate studied and described by Paul Wiebe and S. Mariappen in the 1970s, there were three temples, including an older, mainly abandoned Mariaman one; a newer main temple, also for Mariaman; and a third and smaller one devoted to Muniandi.[6] On the Pal Melayu estate as studied by the Indian anthropologist Ravindra Jain in the 1960s and described in his lengthy ethnography, the main temple was also devoted to Mariaman, while there was a smaller Muniandi shrine nearby.[7] These gods remain the main ones of the present-day popular religion of working-class Hindus, including the many who are now long gone from the plantations and living in cities.

The Later Development of Hinduism

The Hindu religious beliefs and practices brought by Indian communities over several generations continued to be practiced (if in evolving ways) by their descendants. As a popular religion practiced in Malaysia and Singapore, this Hinduism still has much in common with that of their ancestors who immigrated in the last decades of the nineteenth century and the first of the twentieth. In some ways the contemporary popular Hinduism to be described here is not very much like that of the classic or Great Tradition model noted earlier. This is because the Hindu Indian immigrants who came to Southeast Asia were, for the most part, a highly selected group. And also, the circumstances in which they came to live in Southeast Asia were, especially for the first one or two generations, generally very specific and highly constrained.

While the South Indian religious practices (especially those related to caste) on rubber and other estates changed over the generations, the larger changes in Hinduism in Malaysia have taken place within the wider, developing context beyond the plantation. By the 1970s, the estate sector was also changing. Rubber was being widely replaced by more profitable oil palm. The older standard or classic colonial estate had begun to wane or had already done so. Larger, more highly mechanized plantations, increasingly corporately owned by Westerners or local tycoons, did very well. But smaller or older, sometimes subdivided, less well-capitalized estates often failed and were abandoned, or were sold off to make room for housing estates, factories, airports, and other new purposes in the booming areas of the west coast. Indian estate workers left plantations in large numbers, either because they had become redundant or their plantation had gone out of business or because they sought a better life. Many former estate workers moved into squatter settlements in Kuala Lumpur and other cities and found employment in factories and in other laboring occupations, and a few became upwardly mobile.

Over time, therefore, Indian society became increasingly fragmented, though not along traditional caste lines but into separate socioeconomic classes. There was first a large lower class, often impoverished by Malaysian standards, of minimally educated and marginalized estate (or former estate) workers and urban laborers. Then there was a middle class and an elite one of much better educated, urban professionals and businessmen who had done well in the post-colonial period. This group had formed from the descendants of Indian migrants who had migrated to become clerical staff on estates and in colonial government offices, or had become successful traders and businessmen. It also included the smaller numbers of descendants of estate workers who had been able to move up in the world. The presence of this successful, developing sector notwithstanding, Indians remained at the bottom of the west Malaysian plural society—one in which, it is said in an oversimplified but not completely inaccurate way, Malays have political power, Chinese have economic power, and Indians have neither. Indians, it is also said (by Indians themselves), are factionalized and therefore unable to effectively assert their interests in Malaysian politics as well as they otherwise might.

The development of Hinduism in colonial and post-colonial Malaysia expresses these divisions. Here the anthropologist Andrew Willford, who has written the most extensive account of this development, makes a number of points.[8] While most Tamil and other Indians remained Hindu, some have converted to Christianity and others to Islam. Muslim Tamil television programs and Tamil Christian missionaries highlight the backwardness of Tamil culture and popular religion and therefore the role of Hinduism in perpetuating a culture of poverty. Such ideas are also shared by middle-class and elite Indians, including those who themselves are Hindu. In terms of religion, the latter have sought to develop a more elite, great-tradition version of Hinduism. Hinduism in Malaysia has thus divided into two subtraditions.[9]

One of these, already noted, is rooted in the popular religion brought by mainly low-caste Tamil plantation workers and other laborers from South India. It was nurtured on the rubber estates and other plantations, complete with local temples and caste-based ritual interaction. As many plantations ceased to exist or were consolidated and workers left them for urban areas, they again brought their religion with them, but (also again) not without change. While this popular religion has a problem-solving, practical help orientation, some of its traditions also have a strongly expressive dimension as well. Urban festivals and devotional and penitential processions have increased and become a larger part of popular Hinduism. These have developed to their greatest extent in Kuala Lumpur and other cities with large Indian populations, including Singapore.

The largest and most publicized (and tourist attracting) of these festivals is Thaipusan, the yearly celebration of the god Murugan. This festival culminates in a great procession to a Murugan temple or shrine, the most important of which in Malaysia is at Batu Caves in Kuala Lumpur. Its best-known feature is the carrying of *kavadi* (a large and sometimes heavy wheel-shaped edifice carried on the shoulders and often attached by skewers into the chest and back). Other participants walk with trident skewers through their cheeks, and limes and other objects hung from hooks that pierce the flesh of the chest and back, or pull a cart that is attached to hooks in the flesh of the back of their shoulders. Such participants are believed to be strengthened and protected from pain by their devotion but also by being in a state of trance.

Those who undergo the ordeal of the *kavadi* or other forms of sacred mutilation (mainly younger men) do so in association with a request for help from Murugan or as the fulfillment of a vow. They do so for a specific purpose and as a display of both devotion and spiritual and

Figure 3.1. A devotee in the Thaipusan procession (Kuala Lumpur, Malaysia, 1980) with a steel trident skewered through his cheeks.

Figure 3.2. Devotees in the Thaipusan procession ascend steps to the Hindu temple complex at Batu Caves on the outskirts of Kuala Lumpur, 1980.

physical strength. The procession is also, however, a display of ethnic and ideological themes. Kuala Lumpur, where the largest of the Thaipusan celebrations in Malaysia are held, is the capital of the country and a place where ethnic and religious traditions (which largely overlap) and symbolism are on competitive display as an expression of ethnic and religious identity and solidarity. But Thaipusan and other public ceremonial displays involving feats of mutilation and apparent suffering may also dramatize other and darker themes—the alienation and despair felt by many lower-class Indians because of growing national Islamism and their own continued poverty and marginality.[10]

Figure 3.3. Devotees dancing around a *kavadi* carried during Thaipusan (Kuala Lumpur, Malaysia, 1980).

Indian Elites and Reformed Hinduism

The other version of Hinduism that has been developed is very different. It began to form very early in the twentieth century as a result of the migration of educated, English-speaking Ceylonese Tamils and South Indian Malayalees who were hired as Asian staff on estates and in government offices because they could read and write and because they could serve as mediators between the British managers and Tamil workers. They were oriented to a very different form of Hinduism. They sought English educations for their children in multiethnic schools often operated by Christian missionaries, but this brought the threat of a loss of Hindu identity or, worse still, conversion to Christianity. To counter this while still seeking the achievement of middle- or upper-middle-class status in the colonial Malayan plural society marked by English language and literacy, they sought the development of an *agamic* (orthodox), elite, or Great Tradition version of Hinduism. They built large, ornate temples in Kuala Lumpur and other cities that were very different from the often simple, inexpensive shrines and small and crude temples of the plantations. Such urban temples had Brahmin priests and conducted orthodox ritual activities rather than those that were typical of lower-status plantation workers and other laborers, such as fire walking, ancestor worship, animal sacrifice, ritual public body mutilation, trance states, spirit medium practices, and the emphasis on seeking practical assistance from supernatural sources.

There was more, however, to both the elite and the Little Tradition popular versions of Hinduism. Both were open to reform or revitalization movements that began in India. The lower-caste, laboring-class Tamils (or more specifically the intellectuals and leaders that had emerged among this sector) were drawn to anti-Brahmin movements associated with Dravidian or Tamil nationalism. For their part, middle-class and elite adherents of orthodox or Brahminist Hinduism were attracted to various Hindu reformist organizations and movements such as Sai Baba. In the post-colonial period the gap between high and low forms of Hinduism increased, as did antagonism between middle-class and elite Hindu Indians and lower-status Tamils. With the breakup of many estates and the movement of plantation laborers into urban areas, often into squatter communities, what were seen to be their social pathologies and religious excesses increased, or rather became more apparent to other Indians and the public.

HINDUISM IN INDONESIA

Before its independence in 1949, Hinduism in Indonesia had an ancient and culturally important but limited existence. There are ancient Hindu as well as Buddhist monuments in Java and elsewhere, and over the course of the first half of the twentieth century Hinduism has come to be recognized as the religion of Bali, already Indonesia's most famous tourist destination. In addition, elements of Hinduism remained in the popular religious beliefs and practices of the Javanese and other groups, though not generally as a matter of identity.

After independence, and with the ensuing formation of national religious doctrine and policies, the place of Hinduism changed, though not immediately. It eventually became and remained an important national religion, even though, while its numbers of adherents increased, the totality is relatively small (currently Hindus are listed as forming about 1 percent of the population). At the popular level these developments have meant that ordinary people in various places have had to decide if they were or should be Hindu (or members of another approved religion), and if so to convince the government of this. At one point (the mid- and late 1960s), such decisions about Hinduism acquired a seemingly life-and-death significance.

The story here begins with Pancasila, the founding doctrine of the Indonesian constitution, the first principle of which is "belief in one god." It continues with the elaboration of the legal policies that were implemented to put this principle into effect. Indonesia is and has long been a country in which a large majority identify themselves as Muslim. Many Indonesians also saw themselves as following their own localized version of Islam and favored a pluralistic and tolerant approach to religion, taking pride in a country with "unity in diversity." While some Muslim elites favored the formation of an Islamic state, others did not. On the other hand most did not want a Western-style secular (meaning insufficiently religious) state. The country should be religious, more specifically "monotheistic," but not a religious state based on Islam or any other particular religion.

The basic idea here was that certain religions would be acceptable. The main characteristic was monotheism (liberally conceived), but there were others as well. The religion should not be particular to one ethnic community, and it should be based on a book or books. The religions that were accepted as meeting these criteria were distinguished from those that did not. The Indonesian language already had a word for religion, which was *agama* (from Sanskrit). It was decided to reserve this venerable term for the officially approved religions and to refer to the others as *relig*, a Dutch linguistic import that approximates the generally Western notion of religion in the broad sense.[11] Not all of the religions of the various peoples of Indonesia were to be recognized as legitimate *agamas*. Those that were not were referred to as simply "beliefs" or *kepercayaan*. This included the animistic beliefs and practices of the various isolated tribal peoples of the Indonesian archipelago and the mystical cults of the non-orthodox Muslim Javanese.[12] The acceptance of Hinduism as an officially monotheistic religion, in turn, enabled various non-Christian, non-Muslim groups to have their indigenous beliefs and ritual practices pass go and be officially declared as acceptable forms of Hinduism.

The significance of the distinction between *agama* and non-*agama* religion had various implications, including prestige. The indigenous peoples who had only "beliefs" were regarded as backward and were urged to become modern and civilized. This included proselytization as well as education. Having only animistic religions was similar to living in pre-modern kinds of housing (such as communal longhouses in Borneo, which should be abandoned in favor of modern single-family dwellings), hygienic forms of burial, and other customs that had been tolerated by the colonial government. People who were outside of the officially recognized religions were subject to efforts at conversion by those within them. Religious status also became a crucial part of official identity, required for the completion of all documents and included on all identification cards and therefore for full citizenship.[13]

During the darkest period of post-colonial Indonesian history, religious status came to be perceived in some places as a matter of life and death. This began with the military coup of 1965 and the ascension to power of the Suharto regime and involved the mass killing of hundreds of thousands of alleged communists in Java and Bali. The connection to religion was that people of non-*agama* status were in danger of being identified as atheists, who were in turn equated with communists. Since communists were known to be atheists, atheists were also considered to be communists, and hence a dire threat to society as well as simply politically incorrect.

The initial religions accepted as *agamas* were Islam, Buddhism, Protestantism, and Catholicism.[14] The list of acceptable religions changed somewhat over subsequent decades. One change involved Confucianism, which stood for the religion of the Chinese (an ancient but non-indigenous community in Indonesia) who otherwise had no official religion, unless they declared themselves to be Buddhists or had converted to one of the other approved *agama* religions.[15]

Hinduism was left off the original list of approved religions but was subsequently and permanently added. Hinduism as well as Buddhism, which was accepted initially, was part of the glorious past of pre-colonial Indonesian civilization, though the practice of both had either disappeared or greatly waned in the present era. Hinduism lived on in the syncretic popular religious beliefs and values of the animistic and mystically oriented Javanese Muslims; and Hinduism did as well as a part of Balinese religion. Both religions were represented by monumental relics—above all in Java (especially the ninth-century Mahayana Buddhist Borobudur, second only in grandeur and size to Angkor in Cambodia).

The issue of Hinduism was decided initially with reference to religion in Bali. During the initial formulation of religious law and policy in the new Indonesian state, Balinese religious leaders sought recognition of their religion as a form of Hinduism. This, however, was rejected because Balinese religious practices were held to be endlessly localized forms of *adat* and animism. The Balinese persisted and eight years later succeeded in having what was initially declared to be an *aliran kepercayaan* accepted as Agama Hindu Bali.[16]

The acceptance and development of Balinese Hinduism opened other doors. Since one of the official criteria of an *agama* was that it had to be more than a local religion of a particular community (in this case the Balinese), Hinduism needed to be recognized as a national religion to which, therefore, anyone in the country could convert. It also brought a whole new strategy for local ethnic communities whose beliefs and practices had not been recognized as making the grade as *agamas*. Before the recognition of the Balinese as Hindus and of Hinduism as an *agama*, people seeking to upgrade their religious status had only one way of doing so, which was to convert to one of the recognized religions—mainly to Islam or some form of Christianity (which often meant Christianity in the case of interior peoples, and Islam in the case of coastal ones).[17]

The acceptance of Balinese religion as Hinduism and the recognition of Hinduism as one of the acceptable national religions created a second possibility. This was for people whose religious traditions did not qualify as an *agama* to follow the path of the Balinese and have their own indigenous beliefs and practices recognized by the government as a form of Hinduism. This was a somewhat more difficult task than it had been for the Balinese, but some groups had already decided their religion should be accepted as Hinduism and had been developing their case. The actual content of their religious beliefs and practices was less obviously Hindu than that of the Balinese. It took longer, but a precedent had been set and a door opened, though some groups were more interested in being recognized as Hindus than others—usually less so if many people had already converted to Christianity or Islam. But in any case, Indonesian religious authorities in charge of these matters had come to see "Hinduism" as a broader category and more a matter of self-identity than a highly specific set of beliefs and practices. Or, to put it another way, they seem to have decided that if the Balinese could make themselves into Hindus, anybody else was welcome to do so as well if they were willing to work at it. This could, therefore, be seen as a triumph of religious identity over actual content.

Balinese Hinduism

The addition of Hinduism as an official *agama* religion resulted from the successful campaign of Balinese leaders to have their religious status recognized as "Hindu Bali." They had sought such acceptance in 1950 when the original policy of recognizing and developing *agama* religions was initiated, but were unsuccessful. The Balinese effort succeeded in 1958, and then led to further developments. Initially Balinese Hinduism was accepted as such, but since *agama* status was supposed to apply to religions that were national in scope rather than of particular ethnic groups, Hindu Bali was merged into Hindu Drama. This became an Indonesia-wide *agama* to which non-Balinese could also convert.

While they had the best case for having their religion recognized as Hinduism (and Hinduism therefore recognized as an official *agama*), the Balinese had not in the past, especially at the popular level, recognized themselves as Hindus, or as a people having Hinduism as a religion—or even as having a "religion" or, for that matter, as being Balinese rather than something more localized. All of this developed later, mainly in the twentieth century, according to Leo Howe and others.[18] As we have seen, Hindu or Hinduism as a specific religious label and identity for India itself dates only to around the turn of the nineteenth century, and the Balinese came to apply the name to their own religious beliefs and practices only considerably later than that—though just how much later does not seem to have been established.

To put this again in terms of content and identity, Balinese religion is ancient, while identity as Hinduism is much more recent. This change began to emerge before Indonesian independence and the formation of national religious policies regarding *agama* versus lesser forms of religion; however the fuller development of Hindu identity occurred only after that time. When the Dutch colonized South Bali in 1906, the Balinese had no word for religion as a distinct domain of belief and activity, let alone a particular name for such a domain. They included their ritual practices and other religious activities—like many other religiously pre-modern peoples in Southeast Asia—under the widespread rubric of custom, that is *adat*, instead of anything like the Western notion of religion or even culture, a term for which they also lacked. Dutch colonialism and tourism both encouraged the Balinese to discover or create a religious identity that they had formerly lacked, something that then took on added importance after independence. Eventually, however, a Hindu identity itself became problematic, because it brought the issue of what sort of Hindus they wished to be.

But if Hinduism is complicated as a matter of identity in Bali, the actual content is no less so. Though the Balinese did add to and develop the Hindu content of their religion as they came to see themselves as being Hindus, they did not make up or invent everything. There was something Hindu there to begin with—something more explicit and substantial than there was in Malay or even Javanese culture and religion. The problem was just what and how much.

Some things seem clear. Unlike the island of Java and the coastal regions of the Malayan Peninsula, Sumatra, Borneo, and elsewhere, the island of Bali was never Islamized. This in turn was consistent with the

Figure 3.4. Children at a temple festival, Ubud, Bali, 1971.

Figure 3.5. A temple festival in Ubud, Bali, 1971.

absence of Bali's involvement with trade and interisland commerce that were characteristic of the places where Islamization occurred, including the northern coast of Java. The ecology of Bali was based on intensive wet rice cultivation practiced on steep, terraced mountainsides and small but intricate systems of irrigation. Centers of political power and culture were inland rather than coastal. The absence of centers of commerce and the potential for plantation agriculture meant less attraction for colonial development, which came late. While the north was taken earlier, the Dutch did not annex the heartland of Bali in the south until 1906, and then only through military conquest that was resisted through incidents of mass suicide at the various royal courts. Once in control, the Dutch developed a strongly paternalistic attitude and fondness for Bali as a very special place. They kept the traditional ruling courts and encouraged the highly developed artistry, culture, and religion, as well as the forms of social stratification of Balinese society. The Dutch saw Bali as a living museum, of what Java was like centuries earlier before Islamization and colonization, and sought to preserve it as such.

This raised the question of the basic nature of Balinese religion. Was it a form of Hinduism, or simply animism and magic, in terms of which the Balinese were mainly interested in ancestors and other local spirits rather than Hindu divinities? The Balinese had a sort of caste system, which is an integral part of Hinduism, but the four Balinese castes were more like named status categories than numerous economically and ritually interlocking groups found in Indian religion and society. The practice of cremation was important to the Balinese as well as the Hindus of India but very different. While Indian Hindus cremate the dead soon after death, the Balinese practiced a form of "secondary burial" that is also traditional in some "non-Hindu" places, including central Borneo; but here the dead are first interred for up to several years before some form of secondary treatment, including cremation.

And if the Balinese had Hinduism, how had it developed? Here matters become even less clear. According to Howe, the pre-twentieth-century history of Balinese Hinduism cannot be readily separated from myth, which reflects the competing interests of different status groups in a highly stratified society.[19] He argues that the development of Hinduism in Bali is currently subject to several somewhat different myths, one older and favoring the place of traditional high-caste groups and a second one, probably more recent, favoring the commoners. Put very briefly, the older myth explains Balinese Hinduism as the result of the fall of the Javanese empire of Majapahit in the fourteenth century before the onslaught of Islam. The nobility of the various Balinese kingdoms claim their status on the basis of their descent from rulers of Majapahit who invaded Bali as refugees and there reestablished themselves and their religion. This transfer also included Brahmin Hindu priests who in turn founded many of the most famous temples of Bali, thus establishing the high status of the present-day Balinese priesthood.

The contemporary low-caste (*sudra*) version of the myth that Howe found in the all-commoner village he studied and throughout the Gianyar region of central Bali generally has, not surprisingly, prominent egalitarian features.[20] This version of the myth may have developed as part of the competition and controversy over cremation ceremonies, an important part of Balinese ritual life. Over the course of the twentieth century, cremation became a struggle for status, a Balinese version of the potlatch—the more elaborate and expensive the cremation, the higher the status it verified or established. But as the richer, higher-status Balinese increased the elaboration and expense of their cremations, the wider effect was also inflationary. The ordinary Balinese, moreover, who became less willing to accept the prerogatives of the higher castes, sought to increase the scale of their own ceremonies and came to more openly resent what the elite were doing. The commoners thus tell a version of the story that establishes their own origins as preceding those of the high castes and as therefore more authentic. In this version, the ruling elite of Majapahit came to Bali as refugees from encroaching Islam and recreated their Hindu-Javanese civilization at the court of Gélgél, which became the place of origin for the entire Balinese gentry. From there they spread throughout Bali to build temples and palaces, hold elaborate ceremonies, and make the ordinary, previously free Balinese into subjects, dependents, and slaves.[21]

However it had developed in the ancient past, the acceptance of Balinese religion as Hinduism had several effects. It created a name for their religion that gave it a crucial identity more comparable to Christianity or Islam. In addition, the success of *agama*-ization was assisted by the central importance of some spectacular ritual activity. Such a core ritual was all the more important if it had the potential to help attract tourists and thereby hopefully transform a meager, subsistence-oriented local or regional economy. As elsewhere in the world, money is important in Indonesia, and people and places that had been looked down on as backward, poor, and primitive came to be seen in a new light as they began to attract tourists. This can be seen with Bali itself, which began the process of *agama*-ization through Hinduism. Throughout much of the twentieth century, Bali had been attracting tourists—first elite European tourists, then backpackers, and finally mass tourists seeking cheap vacations as much as exotic culture and beauty. There were a number of things that have attracted tourists to Bali, including the natural volcanoes and especially the human-created beauty of the spectacular rice terraces, as well as the artistry and cultural performances of the Balinese. Tourists were also, however, attracted to Balinese ceremonies, which were generally open to viewing and photography. As well as religious performances staged for tourists and temple festivals, these included cremations, especially the spectacular royal versions that could involve thousands of participants and spectators.

Neo-Hinduism: The Development of Agama Hindu beyond Bali

The acceptance of Balinese Hinduism as Hinduism, and Hinduism as a national *agama*, enabled official Hinduism to spread to other regions of the country. This occurred in several different ways, one of which was that many Balinese themselves left Bali in the government transmigration program to be relocated in Kalimantan (Indonesian Borneo) and to other less densely populated islands. Another was that non-Balinese, non-Hindus became free to convert to Hinduism in the same way that they could convert to Buddhism, Catholicism, Protestantism, or Islam.[22]

The expansion of Agama Hinduism took place in a somewhat different way from what occurred in Bali. This involved small-scale or tribal ethnic groups that had been put in the category of "remote and isolated" (*suku suku terasing*) peoples. They were located mainly in the upriver (*ulu*) or interior highland areas of larger islands including Borneo, Sumatra, and Sulawesi and on many smaller remote ones in eastern Indonesia. Since their indigenous religions were classed as "beliefs" (*kepercayan*) rather than *agama*, they were placed under the authority of the Ministry of Education and Culture rather than that of religion. Many of these groups had been exposed to the efforts of Christian missionaries, sometimes over a long period of time. Many had often converted, either during the colonial period with the encouragement of colonial officials or after this in the face of pressure by Indonesian government officials. Others—usually in fewer numbers in the interior at least—were exposed to the influence of coastal or upriver Muslim enclaves. After 1965 the situation changed. With the onset of the Suharto era, government pressure to get all such peoples into one or another of the (at the time) five approved *agama* religions greatly increased.

The traditionalist holdouts in a few places in Sulawesi, Borneo, and Sumatra, however, sought a different solution to their problem. This involved trying to have their own religious traditions recognized as a legitimate *agama* rather than simply as beliefs, specifically as Agama Hindu, as had the Balinese. The groups that made such efforts included the Toraja of central Sulawesi, the Karo Batak of the highlands of northern Sumatra, and the Ngaju and other Dayak peoples of the interior of South Borneo. As with the Balinese, these groups were not initially successful, but all eventually gained *agama* status as variants of official

Hindu Dharma. By the time the advocates for the recognition of their traditional beliefs and practices had achieved success, they had created a named identity for their religion and themselves. The name chosen by the Toraja was Aluk To Dolo (the way of the ancestors), or simply Aluk.[23] The Ngaju named their traditional religion Kaharingan (from the phrase "water of life"), which can be traced back to the 1940s.[24] The Karo traditionalists identified their religion as Agama Pemena (the "first" or "original religion") although Christian Karo referred to it derisively as Perbegu or "ghost keepers."[25]

The Toraja of Sulawesi

Several scholars, including the anthropologist Toby Alice Volkman, who did fieldwork among the Toraja of central Sulawesi in the 1970s, and the historian Terrance Bigalke, provide an incisive account of religious change.[26] Here the story of the developments that finally led to the Hinduization among the Toraja (or some of them) goes back to the earliest phase of colonialism and missionization. This began with the extension of Dutch control over the Toraja highlands in 1905–1906 and the ensuing effort to promote the conversion of the Toraja to Christianity.

As noted earlier, the initial decision to encourage the spread of Christianity among the highland peoples was rooted in concerns about countering the spread of Islam. There was special interest in doing so among the groups in the interior or highlands of islands where the coastal peoples had already become Muslims and were beginning to seek the conversion of the tribal peoples of the interior. Before Dutch pacification, the warlike nature of the highlanders had restricted the entry of the coastal Muslims into the interior. Dutch pacification of the interior therefore opened it up not only to developments they sought but also to ones they did not favor—namely the threat of further Islamization and opposition to colonial authority. In central Sulawesi, the coastal lowlanders were Bugis Muslims who were eager to expand into the Toraja highlands. Here the creation of a barrier through Christian proselytization became a Dutch priority.[27]

This, however, was more easily said than done. The Dutch authorized the establishment of a Calvinist mission, and the first missionary arrived in 1913. This was A. A. van Loosdrecht, who was confronted with the problem of how to encourage conversion and how to approach existing Toraja ritual, especially the great death ceremonies. His initial response was to avoid this problem, establish good relations with the nobility, and develop mission schools that would promote conversion. This accomplished little, and so he chose a more direct attack, which involved appealing to the poor against the interests of the nobles, trying to convince them that the lavish expenditures for death ceremonies were the reason they had lost their lands to the rich—apparently true enough in some instances. He also began to oppose the popular blood sport of cockfighting.

This effort ended badly, at least for van Loosdrecht. Rumors spread among the Toraja that the Dutch were going to force everyone to convert to Christianity, and plans were formed for a rebellion to overthrow and expel the Dutch. Van Loosdrecht was attacked and speared to death on his front porch. The Dutch arrested those responsible for the rebellion, which brought an end to Toraja resistance. It also led to the realization that Toraja religion and their conversion to Christianity presented complex and difficult problems.[28]

By 1923, when more missionaries and native Christian teachers from elsewhere had arrived, a mission council was formed. The council took on the task of deciding what parts of their beliefs and rituals Toraja could keep and what would have to go if, as the council wanted, they became Christian. This involved some fine theological hair splitting concerning the division of belief and ritual between what was to be considered religion, or *aluk*, and what was custom or *adat*. While most *adat* practices were acceptable, religious ones were further divided into those that had to go for Christians and those that could be kept. Here they followed the Toraja distinction between "rising and descending smoke" ritual and worldview categories, which are similar to other cultural dichotomies found elsewhere in the region—for example, upper world and lower world and upriver and downriver in Borneo. In this case, rising smoke was associated with fertility, sunrise, and life while descending smoke was associated with the opposite, which therefore included the great funerals. The Dutch here banned most of the rising smoke beliefs and practices while permitting the retention of the falling smoke ones. Since van Loosdrecht had been martyred for his opposition to the funerals, the Dutch reasoning behind the decision is not fully apparent, though it may have something to do with the bleak Calvinist worldview as well as the long European religious history of finely tuned religious disputation of the "how-many-angels-can-dance-on-the-head-of-a-pin" sort. In any case, the approval of the death celebrations was qualified with regard to what could be done and believed by Christians. The Dutch edict held that the large-scale animal sacrifices and feasting was acceptable as an *adat* practice of providing and sharing food with family, kin, and fellow villagers. But this could not include ancestor spirits or others that were central to the traditional ceremony, for this was a heathen custom. The extent to which the Toraja at the time understood or cared about the theology involved, as opposed to the practical consequences, is questionable. The decision, however, set a long-term precedent that enabled subsequent Toraja Christians to continue with animal sacrifice and massive funerals, whatever they chose to believe about the existence of the spirits and their participation in the activities.

The early Dutch missionaries may have hoped that grandfathering in the traditional funerals—with appropriate changes in belief and behavior—would open the door to conversion, but if so, few Toraja walked through. By 1930, seventeen years after the opening of the first mission, 1,700 Toraja—or less than 1 percent of the estimated population—had become Christian; by 1938 this had increased to more than 8,000, though this was still only 5.5 percent. Nor, therefore, had the elementary schools that the missionaries had begun partly in the hope that they would encourage the spread of Christianity had much immediate effect. The mission schools did have a secular consequence of enabling those boys who had attended and learned to read and write to gain employment as clerks and other lower-level office workers—an important consequence given the many poor and landless among the highland Toraja. Early conversion took place mainly on the margins of the highlands where lowland Bugis Muslims were encroaching on the Toraja.[29] Extensive conversion to Christianity did not begin until the 1950s. This involved the combination of mission education and the government downgrade of non-*agama* religions and other pressures that increased Toraja perception that a choice would have to be made between Christianity and Islam—Hinduism was not yet an option.

Not all the Toraja became Christian, and, of those that did, some reverted to the Aluk. Toraja aristocrats were inclined to be traditionalists and therefore to support the customary funerals. Since the early period of mission activity, Christianity and Aluk religion had been mixed as a way of encouraging conversion. With the resurgence of the aristocracy, however, the Aluk was more desired by traditionalists. After the government acceptance of Hinduism as an *agama* based on Balinese religion, having Aluk recognized as a form of Hinduism became a possibility. This was supported by traditionalists and came to pass in 1969 when Alukta was officially declared to be a sect of Hindu Dharma.[30]

By this time other forces of social and cultural change had already begun to sweep through the highlands or were about to begin. Many Toraja had begun to work for wages on the coast or further away in Indonesia. As usual, this involved the remission of wages to families back in the villages. One main purpose in this instance was to enable families to hold expensive funerals that would otherwise not be possible or would require selling ancestral land or indebtedness. Another change that overwhelmed others was tourism, which began to boom in the late 1970s and had strong implications for traditional (or neo-traditional) practices, especially funerary ones. As in Bali, tourists were attracted to Toraja country by a number of things, including the spectacular beauty and an interest in the cultural landscape, especially the strikingly exotic Toraja houses. But again, the Toraja funeral celebrations—in this instance involving the large-scale sacrifice of water buffalos—were a special draw.[31] Toraja country was much less accessible than Bali, which had long been drawing visitors with similar appeals, but it was also more primitive and exotic. For the Toraja, tourism meant money to be made at home rather than in distant places, as guides and drivers; as owners and workers at hotels, guesthouses, and souvenir shops; and as street hawkers. The tourist boom motivated the Toraja to take a new look at their religion, or more accurately religions. Tourists were not coming to view modest European-style churches or Calvinist or Catholic funeral ceremonies but spectacular, exotic, indigenous ones, or what could pass as such.

In the decades following the recognition of Aluk To Dolo as a Hindu sect, the Toraja came to adopt various attitudes toward the old religion, or what was left of it. For reformist-minded Protestants, the original synthesis of Christianity and Aluk beliefs and practices was no longer viable, if it had ever been. It would never be possible to put custom and religion into suitably separate compartments as the early missionaries had attempted. Of those non-Christians who favored the Aluk and its acceptability as official Hinduism, there were those who still believed in the old gods and rituals as such. There were also those who valued the old religion in a poetic rather than a literal way. Then there was a third group. This included both Aluk adherents and pragmatic Christians who saw the old ways—especially the funeral ceremonies—as worthwhile and highly valuable tourist attractions, whatever compromises this required with either indigenous culture or Christianity.[32]

Of the several religious paths such orientations suggest, official Hinduism did not become the main choice, or even a close second. For one thing, the importance of having a legitimate religion as protection against being accused of being an atheist and therefore a communist had waned. But aside from this, Christianity was more compatible with some of the other modern developments in which the Toraja became caught up. To the many Toraja who lived and worked outside of the Toraja highlands, the world consisted of people who were adherents of one of the world religions and mainly either Christianity or Islam. And of these two choices, as elsewhere for ethnic minorities in Southeast Asia, Christianity was best associated with the retention of a Toraja identity. Young people who were educated in schools or who worked abroad were inclined to become or remain Christian, and they in some instances influenced older Toraja who had lived as adherents of Aluk to do so as well. As important as having their officially non-religion become an approved religion seemed at the time it was accomplished, the number of adherents of Hinduism declined to 13 percent of the population by 1984. The older adherents died off and their children and grandchildren did not want to be associated with the old religion.[33]

The Ngaju of South Borneo

The fullest account of neo-Hinduism outside of Bali is provided by Anne Schiller's account of religious change among the Ngaju of South Borneo. Following the Toraja, the Ngaju and other related groups of the interior of south Borneo also succeeded in achieving religious *agama*-ization. Like the Balinese, the Ngaju had made an earlier attempt at simply having their neo-traditional Kaharingan religion recognized as an *agama*. This again had failed for the usual reasons, leading to the subsequent successful effort via the road of Hinduism.[34] As had the Toraja, the Ngaju had had a long experience with Christianity; missionary efforts had begun in the nineteenth century and gained momentum in the twentieth. In addition, however, many Ngaju had also converted to Islam, giving rise—after the acceptance of Kaharingan—to three *agama* religions rather than two, though tripartite religious divisions are not an unusual situation in the coastal–interior interface of Borneo.

By the time (1980) that the Ngaju proponents of Kaharingan had succeeded, the political momentum toward the Hinduization of indigenous religious traditions was already strong since it provided a ready solution to the official desire to see these religions replaced in one way or another with a certified *agama*. There were, however, again special circumstances that promoted both the desire of the Ngaju to have their indigenous religion recognized, and the willingness of the government to agree. One of these was that Ngaju supernatural beliefs had been the subject of a well-known book by the colonial missionary Hans Shärer, making Ngaju indigenous religion among the better known of all those of Indonesia. This book described the classic Indonesian dualistic view of the universe as divided into an upper world (symbolized by the hornbill bird) and the lower world (symbolized by the water serpent, or dragon).

The other circumstance again involves traditional funeral ceremonies or *tiwah*. These were not important because they helped attract tourists, as in Bali or Tanah Toraja. At least in comparison to either of these places, the interior of southern Borneo has little to attract on a large scale either local tourists (other Indonesians tend to consider upriver Borneo a frightening place of ferocious headhunters and other dangers to be avoided at all costs) or foreign ones.[35] However, the Ngaju tend to see the *tiwah* as very important, at the heart of their traditional religion and culture.

To understand this, it helps to know that *tiwah* are a form of two-stage mortuary practices often known to anthropologists and archaeologists as "secondary burial," though this label is somewhat misleading in that interment in the ground is not necessarily involved in either stage. Two-stage funerals are common (though not ubiquitous) throughout the interior of Borneo and occur elsewhere in Southeast Asia and the world, including among both the Balinese and the Toraja. The basic practice involves an initial, rapid, little-ritualized, temporary disposal of the body of the deceased either above or below ground followed some months or years later by a second, much grander ceremony in which the bones of the deceased are recovered, cleaned, and then either cremated (as in Bali), buried, or placed permanently in some aboveground container (as is common in Borneo).[36]

As elsewhere, the acceptance by the Department of Religious Affairs of Kaharingan as a legitimate form of Agama Hinduism came with strings attached. Hinduism was supposed to be improved and made more orthodox—meaning based in textual sources. The characteristics of the Indonesian notions of a proper *agama* were to be developed and stressed. There had to be monotheism, meaning at least a high god of some sort. Books setting out doctrine, requirements, and ritual procedures needed to be obtained or written, and these taught and understood by anyone rather than only members of the local cultural community.

All of this, however, was more readily begun than achieved. Leaving aside the question of whether the Ngaju Kaharingan adherents had any desire to become "orthodox" Hindus (about which they knew little) or were simply seeking a way of gaining *agama* status, becoming Hindu in an orthodox sense would not be easy. Kaharingan was not an Indic religion but an entirely Bornean one. Unlike the Balinese—whose religious beliefs and practices were a mixture of ancient Indic and indigenous Indonesian ones—the Ngaju do not appear to have had any of the classic religious or social features of Hinduism. Shiva, Vishnu, Ganesha, Brahma, and the other divinities had no existence and do not appear to have been introduced, nor were the Hindu epics or caste practices. The Ngaju did not cremate their dead at all, let alone soon after death. And lacking these, there was little to build upon. The representatives of Balinese Hinduism had encouraged and helped the Ngaju Kaharinganists become officially Hindu, which furthered the national development and political strength of the religion. But Balinese or other teachers of Hinduism were reluctant to undertake missionary work in upriver South Borneo. Books on Hinduism were scarce, so the Ngaju who were able to read and write had to produce their own in a vocabulary based on Indonesian texts.

The terms they used say something about the influences that were in operation. In creating Kaharingan Hinduism, the Ngaju thus drew upon what they knew, and "orthodox" or Great Tradition Indic (or even Balinese) Hinduism appears to have had little role. Many Ngaju having converted to Christianity and some to Islam, the architects of Kaharingan Hindu looked to these religions as the main examples of what an *agama* religion should be like. In addition to Christianity and Islam, they also drew upon their experience with the Indonesian government and military, which was hierarchical, bureaucratized, and authoritarian, and therefore provided a model of how supernatural power was organized and administered. The new version of Kaharingan had five pillars, as in both Islam and the Indonesian Pancasila or the principles of state. The chief god of the upper world in Kaharingan (Ranyit Hatalla Langit) became the more monotheistic "Almighty God." God, however, was often compared to "the president"—at the time General Suharto—who exerted power through other upper-world authorities that the Kaharinganists referred to as prophets (*nabi*) and angels (*malaikat*).

The organization, activities, and material structure and notions of Kaharingan Hinduism otherwise drew heavily on Protestant Christian elements, or a combination of these and Islamic ones. The basic religious activities include weekly *services*, ideally held in a special building or *church* (rather than a temple). Services include an *offering* or collection, a *sermon*, the singing of *hymns* from hymnals, a *recitation*, and various *prayers* from prayer books. There were also lessons based on a lesson book, and over the years various efforts were made to create a Kaharingan *bible*.[37] In terms of theology, a major innovation has been the addition of "sin" (*dosa*) and the forgiveness of sins—neither of which existed in the traditional religion. Here there were only taboos and sacrifices to spirits and divinities that had been offended or from whom help was sought. With the acceptance of sin and its forgiveness, sacrifices in general were downgraded.

The new or *agama* version of Kaharingan also complicated and required some revision of funeral practices. Two-stage mortuary practices had no apparent model in Hinduism, or for that matter in Islam or Christianity. The *Burial Book* advised what amounted to a more Christian-like funeral during the initial interment, including prayers for the soul of the dead, something not traditionally practiced, and made little mention of the secondary funeral or the *tiwah*, the major ceremony in the old religion. *Tiwah* continued to be held (elsewhere in Borneo, the major secondary funeral has generally been eliminated entirely with conversion to Christianity). But the importance of kin making sacrifices and following other ceremonial practices in order to ensure the deceased a comfortable existence in the afterlife was diminished. Not everyone was happy with the requirements set out in the *Burial Book*.

Some tried to ignore it and follow more traditional practices, but here new authority and bureaucracy triumphed again. The official *Kaharingan* council wanted to standardize funeral practices, and the police would not issue a festival permit for a *tiwah* until the council had signed off on what was to be done.[38]

What is not apparent is the likely outcome or trend in Ngaju religious change. Will Kaharingan continue, and if so, more in the direction of more orthodox Hinduism or on its own? Or will the Ngaju be more apt to follow the same path as the Toraja and prefer to become Christians or Muslims and a part of a much larger national and international community of religious identity?

HINDUISM IN SOUTHEAST ASIA

To sum up a complicated matter, whatever it may have been in the distant past, Hinduism in present-day Southeast Asia is not a single religion except as a term of identity. At the popular level it exists in several different forms or ways. It is an integral element in the religious and cultural traditions of many Southeast Asian peoples who were once participants in "Hindu" or "Hindu-Buddhist" civilizations in the region, or who were indirectly influenced by these. Language is one of the main forms of evidence for such influence. Many words in Malay/Indonesian and other languages in Southeast Asia are known to be of Sanskrit origin—including *ugama/agama*, the modern term for religion itself (or in Indonesia as a government-approved one) as in "Ugama Islam."

Present-day or recently practiced customs have also been cited (especially by colonial scholars) as the residue of Hinduism. There is little reason to suppose that Southeast Asian peoples themselves in the past knew or cared that some or many of their religious and cultural customs had Hindu origins before colonial and local scholars and political leaders and intellectuals (most notably in Malaysia the long-serving Malay prime minister Mahathir bin Mohamad) made an issue of these things.[39] But over the past half century Hinduism has become an important religious-political issue in some places. This is so, for example, in both Indonesia and Malaysia, though in rather opposite ways. In Indonesia, at least for ethnic groups seeking to have their own religions officially recognized as Agama Hindu, evidence of past or ancient Hindu religious practices is regarded very positively. In Malaysia, on the other hand, especially for Malay Islamists, evidence (or assertions) that customary practices have a Hindu origin is a very negative consideration, a reason to stop practicing or banning anything so tainted. The traditional popular Malay *bersanding* (wedding ceremony, in which the bride and groom dress as royalty and are seated on thrones on a dais) was condemned as non-Islamic and unacceptable because it was held to be a Hindu practice. Over the years fatwas (binding religious opinions) and government edicts have been issued condemning practices simply because they have Hindu origins or associations, even though nothing else about them is shown to violate religious law. In Kelantan, Malaysia, traditional Malay forms of drama were banned because they were based on the Hindu epics, though this became a matter of considerable political controversy because it involved the loss of cherished Malay culture. And several years ago even secularized yoga was negatively fatwa-ized, including the modern secularized and globalized version performed as a form of exercise, because of its Hindu derivation. We shall return to this issue in chapter 5.

4

BUDDHISM AND POPULAR RELIGION

Buddhism is the national religion of identity of the largest number of countries and dominant ethnic populations in continental Southeast Asia. Christianity is geographically widespread across both continental and insular Southeast Asia. Among the larger countries it is, however, the predominant religion only in the Philippines, while elsewhere it is mainly limited to ethnic minorities, especially to indigenous peoples living in mountainous and interior regions of both the mainland and insular Southeast Asia. Islam is a dominant or official religion only in Indonesia and Malaysia and a regional minority religion in the southern Philippines and in the far south of Thailand, although there are pockets of Muslims elsewhere as well. Hinduism, at least as a religion of identity, exists mainly in Bali and a few ethnic enclaves as discussed in the previous chapter. Theravada Buddhism, in contrast, is the national or majority religion in four of the mainland countries of Southeast Asia. Buddhism is also present in Vietnam, though mainly in the form of Mahayana rather than Theravada and as part of a Chinese-style religious collage. During the colonial era, the French ruled two of the four Theravada Buddhist countries (Cambodia and Laos) and the British ruled one (Burma), while one (Siam/Thailand) remained independent.

There are also smaller numbers of Buddhists in other Southeast Asian countries, including Malaysia and Indonesia. In Malaysia most Theravada Buddhists are ethnic Thai who live in Kelantan and other northern states near the southern border of Thailand. The presence of

Buddhism in Indonesia in its current form is more complex and recent and will be discussed at the end of this chapter.

In accord with the size and ethnic and historical diversity of the Theravada peoples, Buddhism has probably been subject to the greatest amount of scholarly attention and controversy of all the world religions of Southeast Asia. This complexity has been further complicated by the variety of perspectives involved, ones ranging from history to religious studies to the social sciences, especially anthropology, not to mention the accounts of travelers, missionaries, and colonial officials. Most modern studies, moreover, have had a country focus rather than a Southeast Asia–wide one. Few scholars have therefore been in a good position to say with much certainty how similar popular Buddhism is in different places, for example, in Thailand and Burma/Myanmar.

Nor have studies of Buddhism been distributed evenly across Southeast Asia, especially in the modern or recent period. During this time, as colonial rule was ending and new nations were forming in the postwar era, Burma was the main focus. Most of the scholars involved were anthropologists, including Melford Spiro, Manning Nash, June Nash, and Michael Mendelson. Their interests where not so much with Buddhism per se or even popular Buddhism as with the totality of Burmese religion that included the famous *nat* cults and their spirit mediums.

With the military coup of 1962 and the decline or closure of Burma as a site for foreign research, attention shifted above all to Thailand where it has largely remained. This situation is not unique to studies of Buddhism and Thai religions but is true of many other topics as well. It is not hard to understand given the recent history of mainland Southeast Asia. Thailand is the geographical center of the continental countries. It is large in area and in population and the most economically developed and prosperous of the wholly continental states. While avoiding colonial rule, it has been open or even eager to accept Western influences, economic ties, and modernization. Most importantly, perhaps, Thailand has been more welcoming to foreign researchers and scholars, as well as to Westerners in general than has any other of the continental countries. In particular, Thailand remained open and accessible during the latter part of the twentieth century when a great deal of research was done and many works were published, while the other mainland countries to the north of Malaya were closed or at least difficult and dangerous to enter as a result of warfare or government restrictions.

BUDDHISM AND POPULAR RELIGION IN BURMA AND THAILAND

While Thailand has been the main focus of research and scholarship on Theravada Buddhism in Southeast Asia, Burma/Myanmar has also had a prominent, if now mainly a historical, place.[1] Unlike in Thailand, anthropological and other fieldwork-based studies of Buddhism and popular religion in Burma were done mainly during a limited period of time. This period of time (from the late 1950s through the early 1960s) was a consequence of developments in the anthropology of religion, on the one hand, and political changes in newly post-colonial Burma, on the other. Before the 1950s, anthropological studies of religion were in general focused on the non-world religions of small-scale or tribal peoples. During and after the 1950s anthropologists became increasingly interested in local or village-based studies of the various world religions, including Buddhism in Southeast Asia and elsewhere. In Burma a number of such studies were carried out but then were largely brought to an end by the military coup in 1962, which discouraged further foreign research for a long period of time. In Thailand, on the other hand, where anthropologically oriented studies of Buddhism and other dimensions of Thai religion began at about the same time as in Burma, they have continued long after such research ceased or greatly diminished there.

Beyond Burma, field research in other mainland Southeast Asian Theravada countries (that is, Laos and Cambodia) has also generally been much more limited than in Thailand and has so far produced less work of comparative significance. In these countries also, research was soon blocked after anthropological interest had begun to be focused on Buddhism, this time by post-colonial wars involving Western governments and socialist regimes and their aftermath. The main recent interest in Buddhism in both Laos and Cambodia has concerned recent developments under socialism, as already discussed in chapter 2.[2] The following are the main ways that Buddhism has been interpreted in Burma/Myanmar and Thailand.

Figure 4.1. Monks on their early morning begging round (Pakse, Laos, 2006).

Southeast Asian Buddhism Is Syncretic but Changing

The first interpretation, that popular Buddhism is syncretic, requires only brief attention, for it was offered in earlier periods. It has sometimes been made in brief comments that introduce a fuller discussion of Buddhism. For example, writing in a 1950s overview of contemporary village life in Thailand, the sociologist John de Young begins a chapter on Thai religious beliefs and practices with the following generalization:

> The Thai peasant practices Hinayana [a now seldom used term that has been replaced by Theravada] Buddhism which, through the centuries has become so blended with Brahmanism and with earlier elements of animism that have become so closely interwoven as to be impossible to segregate pure elements of each. . . . As a means of storing up merit for life in the next world the villager turns to Buddhism; for protection in the present world, the peasant looks to the host of good and evil spirits that affect his every undertaking.[3]

Note also here the functional distinction made between the different uses of Buddhism and animism. Buddhism addresses otherworldly concerns while animism and Brahmanism address the practical concerns of this life, including protection from harm and success in cultivation, and so on.[4] Most of de Young's chapter discusses Buddhist beliefs, practices, and institutions, but in the final section he returns to animism in daily life and to religious change. While non-Buddhist traditions are still pervasive, he assumes the direction of change is toward their decline as Thai society undergoes inevitable modernization, and as the Buddhist hierarchy discourages animism and magic and promotes a purer form of Buddhism. Notably, this does not seem to have occurred.

In Burma, Two Religions in Conflict?

The second interpretation is anti-syncretic, at least as far as Buddhism is concerned. This interpretation, by the psychological anthropologist

Figure 4.2. Young Thais making offerings to a Buddhist saint at Wat Phra That (Doi Suthep Mountain, Chiang Mai, Thailand, 2010).

Melford Spiro, presents the most radical and schematic interpretation of Buddhist and non-Buddhist religious traditions in Theravada Southeast Asia. Spiro's account of Burmese religion was developed in his *Burmese Supernaturalism*. His argument consists of three parts. The first is that not only do the Burmese have "two religions," but they clearly recognize an explicit distinction between them. The first, not unexpectedly, is Buddhism, and the other is "animism," especially the worship of *nats* (*nat* meaning "spirit" in Burmese), which he calls supernaturalism. The latter term (and therefore Spiro's argument) is somewhat problematic because it appears to have no Burmese equivalent term, and because it implies that Buddhism lacks animistic beliefs—which he assures us it does in fact have.[5] The second part of his argument is that, while animism endures, Buddhism is dominant, though he does not go so far as to say that it is the "real" religion. And the third is that the Burmese have two religious traditions because they have two different kinds of needs, even though they also recognize that Buddhism and supernaturalism—though not identified—are in conflict.

The non-Buddhist part of Burmese religion involves *nat* worship. While *nat* is the general term for spirit, of which there are, as usual in Southeast Asia, many types, the main focus is on the Thirty-Seven Nats. This is a set of named spirits or deities, which is recognized by all Burmese, with a royal mythological charter going back to the tenth century. All of these *nats*, also known as the "upper *nats*," died by execution or other forms of bad (or "green") death, and the best known seem to have been connected to the royal family in one way or another. The spread of the cult has also been linked to the Burmese consolidation of power. Spiro points out that efforts to classify, clearly identify, or sort out the Thirty-Seven Nats have generally been confused, though this is not surprising or of great importance from the perspective of his argument; nor is the question of whether or not the cult preceded the arrival and spread of Buddhism in Burma, whenever exactly that was.

The *nats* in Burma, like spirits elsewhere in Southeast Asian Buddhist countries, are propitiated in various ways. Shrines in the form of spirit houses (as they are generally known to Westerners) are erected and provided with offerings. Some of the Thirty-Seven Nats are also worshipped at special festivals, the largest of which attract many people. The main practitioners of *nat* worship are persons Spiro refers to, for want of a better term, as "shamans," though they might more properly be called spirit mediums. Once initiated or spiritually married, the shaman will participate in organized séances and become possessed by one of the *nats* while dancing to music. This is done both at the *nat* festivals and for private clients seeking supernatural help for one or another practical problem.

Spiro's interpretation of the relationship of Buddhism and animism is that they are both complementary and in conflict. The complementary part is that the two separate religions exist because they meet two different kinds of psychological needs. Buddhism is otherworldly and addresses concerns about death, reincarnation, and salvation, which are matters beyond the scope of animism. The concerns of *nat* worship and other animistic beliefs and practices are worldly and practical in nature, matters to which Buddhism is not oriented and for which it is not adequately prepared. As we shall see, at least where Buddhism is concerned, this sort of interpretation is open to question. While perhaps true of textual Buddhism, what occurs in actual practice is a different matter.

Beyond the otherworldly/inner-worldly difference, the complementariness of Buddhism and animism is also a matter of ethos, values, or psychological dispositions. Through its emphasis on reflection, meditation, and rhythmic chanting, Buddhism is intellectualistic and values harmony and tranquility. *Nat* worship, exorcism, and the ethos of animism in general is the opposite. At least in shamanism and exorcism, the emphasis is on the display of emotion, rapture, and ecstasy. *Nats* can be angry, greedy, and vengeful.

Here Spiro invokes a well-known dichotomy between two extremes of religious sentiment and behavior. This is between Apollonian and Dionysian, named after the worship of the two Greek gods, noted by Friedrich Nietzsche and famously applied by the anthropologist Ruth Benedict to different modes of ritual behavior and satisfaction among Native Americans. Buddhism is thus Apollonian and animism is Dionysian. In Benedict's application of the dichotomy, Native American peoples were either Apollonian (the Pueblo groups of the Southwest) or Dionysian (the Plains peoples in particular and other Native Americans in general). In Spiro's interpretation, the Burmese (like the ancient Greeks) have both Apollonian and Dionysian needs and satisfy them accordingly. However, though they are opposite sides of the same coin, Buddhism and supernaturalism are in conflict.

Spiro claims that Buddhism and the *nat* cults are in conflict in several ways.[6] First, there is a conflict in doctrine. Buddhist belief emphasizes the law of karma as a complete explanation of causality in human life, rebirth, and salvation. The *nats* can have no significant role, except perhaps as agents in the working out of karma. Like most others, this conflict is one-sided. The persons who participate in the *nat* cults and in other animistic and magical activities do not dispute the Buddhist doctrine of karma but simply act on the belief that, for better or worse, animism and magic are significant causal forces in human life—for example in gaining wealth. The question, therefore, is how concerned Burmese, including Burmese Buddhist monks, are about the conflict, and here the level of concern would appear, for most people, to be low. In other words, nobody cares much, or at least enough to change their animistic religious practices.

A second conflict concerns ethos. This covers several matters, one of which is morality, which is fundamental to Buddhism but lacking in animism and magic. The *nats* are motivated by lust, greed, anger, and vengeance rather than by a desire to earn merit by doing good and not doing harm, and magic is simply amoral supernatural power or energy. Another is sensuality, Buddhism being asensual and ascetic, for suffering is caused by desire, and passion is to be avoided in favor of rationality, while the *nats* are, like humans, creatures of desire and passion. In terms of personality, the ideal Buddhist is one who develops a serene personality in contrast to the turbulent one of a *nat* or most humans. And finally, the Buddhist social value is to minimize participation in society. To become a monk is to withdraw from normal society. In an ordinary urban or rural monastery, this is not total withdrawal, for part of the monk's role is to help others in their journey through life and in their progress toward salvation. Some monks, however, withdraw from society more completely by moving into the forest and leading a life of meditation—though, paradoxically, the reclusive forest monks are regarded as the most spiritually or magically powerful.

Spiro's contrast between the two forms of Burmese religion has an apples-and-oranges quality. Although an anthropologist, his interpretation of Buddhism seems to be based heavily on doctrinal interpretations or ideals rather than popular or actual religious behavior. In contrast, while Burmese animistic beliefs and practices (at least those involving the Thirty-Seven Nats) have an important mythological dimension, they lack a scriptural or doctrinal one. Therefore, when it comes to animism, Spiro's interpretation is based on what the Burmese actually say and do whereas his interpretation of Buddhism is based on what they are textually supposed to believe and do.

A second problem concerns gender. Whether Buddhism and animism are regarded as "two religions" or as simply two dimensions of a single complex religion to be called "Burmese religion," gender would seem to be important. As part of his discussion of the contrasts between Buddhism and the *nat* cult, Spiro might have said that Buddhism is mainly male while animism is mainly female. However accurate, such an observation would have been consistent with the other sorts of categorical generalizations he makes. But gender is simply left out of his concluding discussion of the differences and conflicts between Buddhism and animism.

Elsewhere, however, his discussion points to important differences in gender. His description of "shamanism" includes gender issues. Burmese shamans are nearly always women. Spiro begins by noting that the Burmese term for what he calls a shaman can be more literally translated as "*nat* wife." This is because becoming initiated as a shaman is accomplished by undergoing a marriage to a *nat*. Careful empiricist that he is, Spiro notes immediately that not every shaman is a woman. He cites experts he consulted at one of the major *nat* festivals as saying that 4 percent are male. These 4 percent are not ordinary males but, with a few possible exceptions, are homosexual, transvestite, or excessively effeminate—or as it might be put today, "LGBT." Their *nat* spouses are, therefore, always female. In performing, the rare male shaman always dresses in a women's costume and is satisfying the female components of his personality. And, although male shamans always have female *nat* wives, some of the *nats* who possess them take the form of "mothers" or even "sisters." In other words, some strong sexual crosscurrents are at work.

Though less explicit, an opposite pattern of what Spiro interprets as female homosexuality may be found in female shamans. He reports that he never encountered homosexuality or transvestism among women shamans. Female shamans have only *nat* husbands and do not engage in cross-dressing. While performing, however, many female shamans become highly masculine in their behavior or are married (in real life) to weak, ineffectual men. Such shamans, therefore, seem to be satisfying homosexual or transsexual urges by identifying with their spirit husbands and acting out their male personalities. "At the very least the shamanistic role enables a latent lesbian, one with a strong masculine component, to act out her masculine impulses."[7] Again, not all women shamans are latent lesbians, but Spiro suggests that those who are heterosexual may also become shamans for sexual reasons. Burmese women are forbidden to engage in either premarital or extramarital sexual activity (though he does not attempt to say how fully this is adhered to). Such restrictions, however, apply only to human partners, not *nat* ones.

Shamans are not the only Burmese practitioners who deal with spirits. There are also *ahtelan hsaya* or "Masters of the Upper Path," whom Spiro refers to as "exorcists," though exorcism is only one of their activities. The most important characteristic of such exorcists from the perspective of the matter at hand is that they are men rather than usually women. This means they form an exception to the generalization that Burmese animism tends to be female in contrast to male Buddhism. The qualification, however, is less significant than it would first appear. For one thing, exorcists are less common than shamans. And, for another, all such exorcists must be males because they must be members of *gaings* or "quasi-Buddhist sects," to which only men can belong. Such *gaings* must observe Buddhist discipline and seek Buddhist salvation, although they also engage in alchemy and pursue other forms of magical power. Spiro sees such groups (which have also been referred to as "messianic Buddhist associations") as a middle ground between animism and Buddhism, which would seem to negate his main argument that these are separate religions, but he does not appear to think this is so or acknowledge the problem.

However this may be, the nature of the quasi-Buddhist *gaings* suggests that a further part of the explanation of why women in particular are associated with shamanism is that their involvement in Buddhism is limited in Burma (and elsewhere in Southeast Asia as well). Most importantly, women cannot become monks, the most important position for a Buddhist. The exclusion of women from Buddhism is not total. Older women may become religious devotees (who are referred to sometimes as "nuns," but this term is misleading in that such a status is not the equivalent of the recognized orders of women in the Roman Catholic Church, for example). Women can and do make merit by preparing and giving monks food and by helping them in other ways. Women may gain religious help from monks, but there can be no direct physical contact between them. Monks must be celibate and should not be tempted. But beyond this women can diminish the spiritual strengths through simple physical proximity (discussed further below). Boys are welcome and encouraged to spend time in monasteries and become helpers and acolytes of monks, but girls are not. The more limited possibilities for the involvement of women in Buddhism may help to channel their interest toward animism.

Buddhism and Other Traditions Are a Single Magical Religion for Most People

By the time that Spiro's book was published in 1967, studies of the overall nature of Burmese religion based on anthropological research that led to significant publication had ceased. Challenges or qualifications that might have been made to his interpretation based on further fieldwork were not forthcoming. This was partly because after the initial wave of research and writing on Buddhism and animism in Burma, attention shifted to Thailand, where it has remained centered. For the most part, the studies of Thai religion do not engage those done in Burma. By and large these studies also reject or avoid the emphatic distinction Spiro makes between Buddhism and animism as separate types of religion.[8]

Here an early anthropological study offers a clearer overall interpretation of the main contours of Thai religion. This was B. J. Terwiel's account of monks, magic, and animism, based on fieldwork in central Thailand in the late 1960s.[9] Terwiel himself became a monk (though he does not say whether he did so as a form of anthropological participant observation, or for personal religious reasons) in a small rural monastery, and his interpretation is offered as an inside story. Although his book *Monks and Magic* has been published in three editions, the last advertised as "thoroughly revised," the study is essentially an account of Thai religion in the 1960s, with only limited and occasional references to changes since that time. Subsequent field research, if any, is not mentioned.

Terwiel argues that the overall nature of Thai religion can be readily stated. Buddhism is central to Thai religion but is far from being the whole of it. But beyond that, Buddhism takes two forms among the Thai. Members of the elite—well educated, mainly urban—understand and practice a different form of Buddhism than do the ordinary people, that is, mainly villagers. Western and other scholarly observations and interpretations about the nature of Thai religion are often based on the views of elite or educated Thai. As do all Burmese, according to Spiro, such educated elite adherents of Buddhism in Thailand recognize a distinction between Buddhism and non-Buddhist traditions in Thai religion. They see themselves as grasping the philosophical and doctrinal messages of the Buddha while regarding ordinary or rural Thai as people who do not understand these things. They hold that while ordinary Thai also see themselves as Buddhists, they actually practice an animistic and magical form of Buddhism.

But non-elite Thai do not recognize a distinction between what they believe and do and orthodox Buddhism. The notion of syncretism as applied to Buddhism or anything else has no meaning for them. When Terwiel began his research he tried to get the rural Thai he studied to analyze their religious beliefs and practices according to Buddhist and non-Buddhist traditions. But this did not work. His informants were either confused and gave different sorts of answers at different times or could not even attempt to separate out the Buddhist from the non-Buddhist elements. There were, of course, individual variations and qualifications among both classes of Buddhists. And while elite Thai recognize the doctrine of the central causal role of karma in the good and bad things that happen to a person, they may also seek the same forms of supernatural help as do ordinary people. Conversely, while ordinary Buddhists may know something about the doctrine of karma, they see it as not only relevant to reincarnation into the next life but also as something that can be altered to protect or help them with the practical activities of their immediate existence. The main purpose of making merit for ordinary Buddhists, at least before they grow old and became concerned with their next life, is to help and protect them in this life, to have a good crop of rice, to stay healthy, to be happy, to be lucky, and to avoid misfortune. Buddhism for such ordinary Thai Buddhists is above all a superior form of magic, a view that is not totally lacking from the outlook of elite Buddhists as well.[10]

One way to accept a compartmentalized interpretation of Thai religion is to assume a diachronic explanation of its development. Thai religion and culture, in this view, are formed in layers. Magic and animism represent a core of popular religion that had been created before the Thai came under the influence of Hindu and Mahayana Buddhist traditions, followed by Theravada Buddhism. Such a view derives in part from archaeology, which, however, has been focused mainly on royal and cult centers. Here what has remained has been mainly stone or brick buildings, murals, the occasional inscription, and stone or bronze statues. Such centers show obvious and indisputable Indic influences, but also a better picture of the religion of the ruling class or elites than of the entire population. The nature of the original religious beliefs and practices of the masses of village dwellers are much harder to know because the material culture in which they were expressed was largely limited to cloth, wood, bamboo, and other perishable materials. Village temples in present-day Thailand and other Buddhist countries in Southeast Asia are made of bricks and mortar, but this is recent. They were until recently, like other short-lasting village buildings, made of wood, bamboo, and thatch.

But even the religion of the elite is not well understood in earlier periods. Unlike in Cambodia and some other places where Hindu-influenced cults seem to have been predominant, Buddhist and Hindu ones were mixed in what became central Thailand. Further, Buddhist and other Indic cults were probably not separated into distinct religious traditions before Theravada Buddhism became the dominant religion of elite and popular identity. Nor was Hindu-Buddhism clearly distinguished from more localized gods and spirits, spirit mediums, shamans, and other religious practitioners of animism and magic.

Terwiel argues that Buddhism developed in the Thai countryside not through a rapid conversion but gradually as villagers became convinced of its superior utilitarian value.[11] Over the centuries, pre-Buddhist magic and animism became magical-animistic Buddhism. Other types of offerings slowly replaced animal sacrifice. Buddhist monasteries were built outside of villages in the same locations as older shrines. As elsewhere, Thai Buddhism had the same characteristics of restricted literacy. Scripture was turned into magic. Those who learned to read a little gained influence over those who could not at all, and those monks who acquired a reputation for supernatural powers were venerated and sought out to give advice, make charms, and bless amulets. Some monks learned to read and became interested in the philosophical doctrines of Buddhism, but this was optional. To the present day some men become monks as a result of vows made in the face of mortal danger.

More rapid change in Thai Buddhism took place in the nineteenth and twentieth centuries as the state established more effective authority over rural areas. The government sought to standardize the Pali texts and therefore textual Buddhism, distributed textbooks to newly ordained monks, and sponsored the development of an elaborate set of exams for certifying knowledge of Buddhism. This probably increased the prestige of monks and promoted the expansion of monasteries throughout rural society to the point that no village is without one, or at least access to one.

Eventually more educated Thai came to recognize and practice a more textually oriented form of Buddhism (though always more in the abstract than the actual). For their part, the village populations, including those who entered the monasteries, became in their way devout Buddhists. But in doing so they adapted and interpreted Buddhism to their own long-standing religious needs, views, and practices. Terwiel stresses that popular Buddhism in Thailand has been reinterpreted by turning it into a system of practical magical (or magical-animistic) beliefs and activities.[12] The many different objects and images that form the material culture of Buddhism, up to and including images of the Buddha himself, are above all symbols of power. Buddhism, as Terwiel found it in the monastery he joined in the late 1960s, still had this magical-animistic orientation.

The popular interpretation of Buddhism and its incorporation into a worldview dominated by magical and animistic thought includes but subsumes the core Buddhist principles of karma and merit. Thai Buddhists know these doctrines but depart from the textual principles in several basic ways. One is that karma is not really the first line of mystical interpretation in dealing with success or misfortune. The first recourse is rather to magic or animism. With misfortune, the initial assumption is that the right ritual steps were not taken or the right spirits were not correctly propitiated. It is only a longer streak of bad luck or a larger pattern of misfortune that is likely to raise the issue of karma. In addition, the core principles of merit and sin are also changed from a long- to a short-term process of causality. In popular Buddhism, acts of merit are expected or hoped to have an immediate practical benefit. This also means that something of importance should be attempted soon after some quantity of merit has been acquired, before its strength has been dissipated.

The tendency to reinterpret and reshape Buddhist doctrine and ritual practices in magical terms continues. Terwiel goes on to document this claim at length through discussions of the role of Buddhism and magic in various spheres of life. His examples include notions of gender and the body, financial good fortune, the rules of house building, and spatial orientation. In some matters their practices are more stringent than orthodox Buddhist rules would seem to require while in others they are less so.

Some Principles of Buddhist Magic: The Human Body and Gender

In the traditional popular Thai view, the human body is endowed with magical properties. Such properties develop as persons mature, but need to be protected. Tattooing and the carrying of amulets are among the means of enhancing and protecting the spiritual dimensions of a person. Sleeping in the correct position—with the head to the east—is also important.

There are also important variations in the distribution of magical energy. One is that males have more than females, and another is that monks have more than laymen. Yet another is that higher parts of the body, above all the head, have more than lower parts—the feet having none at all. Here the waist is the main dividing line, not only because the part below it is simply lower, but also because it is the location of the sexual and excretory organs. Actually, the lower part of the body including the excretory organs also has magical potential, but this is associated with darker or more aggressive forms of magic, or sorcery.

A second important principle is that the spiritual properties of the body can be diminished as well as enhanced. An amulet should not be carried in a pocket below the waist, for example. And for men in general, and for monks in particular, one of the main threats to personal magical power comes from women. Compared to peoples in other parts of the world, the Thai (and other peoples of Southeast Asia) have a high degree of gender equality and gender integration in everyday life. Thus Thai men are clearly not obsessed with the threat of female pollution to the same extent as men are in some cultural settings. Men and women thus sleep together in the same room, both with their heads to the east, the auspicious direction.

But there are certainly concerns. A woman must never sleep on a higher level than a man, or assume a superior position during sexual intercourse. Either would seriously diminish male spiritual energy. Like men, women are capable of engaging in dangerous and aggressive forms of magic, that is, sorcery. Love magic that is deployed to attract or control a man commonly makes use of ingredients involving the genitalia. Aside from the assumption that this enhances the sexual attraction of the woman, it is also thought to work by lowering his resistance by weakening his male magical power.

Both the spiritual strengths and vulnerabilities of males are magnified in the person of a monk. Simply putting on the robes of a monk increases a man's magical power, but threats to it are also enhanced. While these threats are various, the Thai place special emphasis on those posed by women. Women make offerings of rice and other food to monks on their begging rounds and at other times, and thereby earn merit or, as it could also be put, are the recipients of spiritual energy from monks. But while this need not involve much physical separation, this exchange takes place without direct physical contact.

There are orthodox Buddhist strictures governing the monk's relationship with women, but these are enhanced according to Thai magical principles. Women are seen as having their own forms of magical power, and these are regarded as antithetical to those of monks. This is partly related to menstruation, which implies that post-menopausal women are less a threat than pre-menopausal ones. This may be part of the reason that the activity of providing food for monks on special occasions at the temple tends to be in the hands of older women, though the experience and authority of such women in household kitchens and management in general is probably also involved.

In general the interaction of monks and women is not completely avoided, but it is carefully regulated. Monks learn to avoid moving and sitting in ways that might result in accidental contact with a woman. The prohibition on female physical contact even extends to animals. A monk should not stroke a female dog or cat and should therefore check before touching the animal. Women as well as men need to interact with monks in order to earn merit and receive blessings, but such interaction should never be in private, even if the woman is the mother or grandmother of the monk. Here also the exchange of a gift to a monk and the receipt of his blessing are accomplished through a special transaction. In order to receive food from a woman kneeling before him, a seated monk places a piece of cloth on the floor. The woman places her bowl of food on the cloth and the monk picks it up. This apparently neutralizes the transmission of harmful energy from the woman while facilitating the flow of the blessing from the monk to her.[13]

The practice of using cotton cord or cloth to transfer or contain magical energy in Thai and other Southeast Asian ritual contexts is very common. Monks together will hold on to a cord in order to facilitate the transmission of spiritual energy. Buildings will have a length of thread or string tied around them in order to contain magical energy. In Laos the national blessing ceremony (now practiced by both Buddhists and non-Buddhists) is the *baci* ritual in which honored guests have pieces of cotton yarn tied around their wrists to secure their souls and bring them rewards.

Monks, Money, and Wealth

If the Thai popular magical version of Buddhism tends to overstress Buddhist strictures limiting the interaction of monks with women, Terwiel argues, it tends to take a more relaxed view of the monks' relationship with money.[14] Although monks are not supposed to touch money or gamble, both prohibitions are interpreted somewhat loosely. The orthodox rules under which Thai monks live include the prohibition on handling money, keeping it themselves, or having it kept for them by others. In theory it would be possible to adhere to this rule. In Theravada Buddhism there are legitimate ways of receiving and holding financial donations for a monastery and other charities, and all of the basic living requirements of monks are provided for without the need for them to spend money. If a monk does need to spend money on bus or taxi fare, it can be carried by a temple boy or someone else on his behalf.

"In practice, however, there are few rural monks who do not regularly break this rule. A monk handling money is a common sight."[15] In addition to paying directly for taxi or bus rides, monks can be seen paying for a morning meal in a restaurant. In a rural monastery, many monks buy tobacco, Ovaltine, or tea. Monks customarily also directly accept money from laymen for performing blessings and other ceremonies. Even if a monk would prefer not to receive such money directly, the layman giving it believes that the correct transfer of merit from the monk to him requires that the monk accept the gift—and that the bigger the gift the larger the allocation of merit. Although the giving of money to a monk in return for merit appears to involve a magical transaction from the perspective of the layman making the gift, the acceptance of money by the monk does not seem to involve a flow of negative spiritual energy as would direct contact with a woman, for example. While morally and legally problematic, money seems to be magically harmless. More positively, it appears to be ritually auspicious. The presentation of "money trees" (paper money fastened to a tree-like frame so that the bills look like leaves) is a very common part of popular Buddhist ceremonies.

Monks are best known as a means for laypersons to earn merit—merit that is thought of in magical terms as a form of protection and a source of good fortune. However, monks also transfer magical power in other ways. Blessings by monks, as noted above, commonly include a wish that those being blessed will become rich. Amulets are another example. They are an extremely important form of magical power and protection. Like rare coins or stamps, they can be worth large sums of money and are avidly sought by collectors. One of the ways that famous monks raise money is by having metal amulets cast for sale. The amulet will commonly have an image of the monk, which transfers some of his magical power to the person who acquires and carries it on his person or puts it in his car or on his motorcycle to protect against road accidents, and in the case of a taxi driver, to also increase tips. But the transfer of power is not accomplished until the amulet has been held and blessed by a monk.

Buddhism, Magic, Ghosts, and Shrines

Terwiel's detailed account of Buddhist magic in rural central Thailand in the late 1960s provides a good background for the much more recent treatment of Buddhism, magic, and animism provided by the American scholar Justin Thomas McDaniel in his book *The Lovelorn Ghost and the Magical Monk*.[16] Terwiel and McDaniel are Western scholars who have other things in common. Most importantly, both spent time as Buddhist monks in Thailand and, as such, learned things they would probably otherwise have not come to know. Neither, however, has been inclined to discuss his motives for putting on the sacred robes and joining a monastery, or for taking them off and returning to the world. Terwiel, however, draws more explicitly on his experience as a monk and frequently mentions the monastery to which he belonged, whereas McDaniel does so only rarely. Terwiel's account is concerned mainly with rural Thai society and draws a sharp contrast between the magical Buddhism of the Thai villager and farmer and the more orthodox religion of the educated urban elite. McDaniel's later experiences in Thailand appear to be both broader and more extensive, and, in the present book at least, he is most focused on a cross section of present-day urban society of Bangkok.[17]

The main difference between the two accounts is that while Terwiel's is a more conventional ethnography that makes no mention of named individuals, McDaniel's is organized around two particular named persons—or rather one real, historically known person and one legendary ghost of what may or may not have been a living person. The historically real person is the "magical monk" of the title of McDaniel's book. His name is Somdet To, and he seems to have been one of the most prominent monks in Thai history, one who rose to the peak of Thai Buddhist authority to become an advisor to the Thai monarchy. A public figure of wide renown, he is a person of enduring interest to later Thai scholars, intellectuals, and ordinary people. The main point that McDaniel seeks to make about Somdet To and the reason he is treated at length in the book concerns the nature of his influence and reputation. This rests on his reputed magical powers, both as a living monk and then as a saint or spirit.

The other character, and the one whom most readers of McDaniel's book will find of greater interest, is the Thai ghost Mae Nak. If she and her husband Mak were once real people, they were, unlike Somdet To, not well known, at least in their earthly lives. They would have been ordinary people who became famous only after they died and became ghosts. The other, perhaps more likely possibility, is that they were entirely a legend, a product of folklore and eventually the mass media.

In either case, there are various versions of their story. The basic plot is that Mae Nak and her soldier-husband Mak are living happily in a house on the Phra Khanong Canal in the outskirts of present-day Bangkok during the reign of King Mongkut in the early nineteenth century. Then Mae Nak becomes pregnant, and her husband Mak is sent away to war where he is badly wounded. While he is being cared for in Bangkok, Mae Nak and the child she is carrying both die in childbirth. When Mak returns home, however, Mae Nak and the baby are awaiting him. Neighbors at first try to warn him that his wife and child are now ghosts, but they are attacked and killed in outrage by Mae Nak. Eventually Mak learns the truth when he sees Mae Nak drop a lime from the porch of their house and retrieve it by extending her arm, something that only a supernatural being could do. Mak is torn between his love for his family and his fear of ghosts, but he decides to flee in the night. When he does, Mae Nak pursues him, but he hides behind a kind of tree feared by ghosts. Next he runs to Wat Mahabut, a monastery where he gains sanctuary. Mae Nak then vents her rage at the loss of Mak by terrorizing the neighborhood. Eventually a powerful exorcist captures her and seals her in a jar and throws it in the canal. However, an old couple (or else two fishermen) recovers the jar and opens it, and Mae Nak escapes. Next the monk Somdet To takes on Mae Nak and, through his power, succeeds in taming her ghost. In the more magical version, Somdet To confines the ghost to a piece of bone in her forehead which he then secures to his waistband and which is now reputedly in the possession of the royal family. In the somewhat more orthodox Buddhist version, Somdet To convinces Mae Nak to depart for the afterlife by convincing her that she will eventually be reunited with Mak. This involved holding a Buddhist funeral.

Neither of these two versions seem entirely consistent with what eventually happened to Mae Nak, which is that along with Mak and the baby she became a folk saint or benevolent deity who will grant favors to people. At some point in the mid-twentieth century a shrine was erected next to Phra Khanong on the grounds of Wat Mahabat as the focal point of her cult. The cult includes two kinds of activity. First, there is an annual public Buddhist funeral at which monks chant, as they would at any ordinary onetime funeral, although this would seem to imply that the ghost of Mae Nak is not a regular soul that was being sent on to reincarnation, but rather one that required special periodic Buddhist ritual attention. Second, there are ongoing visits to the shrine by people who make offerings to Mae Nak, Mak, and the baby, for whom there are also nearby, but smaller shrines. The shrine for Mae Nak is surrounded by gifts that include portraits of her as a beautiful young woman, silk scarves, and pretty dresses. The offerings at the shrine for Baby Mak include dolls and toys as well as a TV set that is always on and plays cartoons. The offerings that are made to the shrines are in association with requests for practical help, including an easy and successful childbirth for a woman or the avoidance of military conscription for a man.

The legend of Mae Nak, however much or little based on real persons and events, probably took shape initially as oral tradition or folklore. Eventually it entered the mass media, not only as written literature but also radio (apparently first broadcast in 1928), movies, television, and, more recently, a musical and an opera.[18] On the Internet, in addition to a Wikipedia entry, Mae Nak has many websites. Her story made the front section of the *New York Times* in 2013.[19] There is also a Thai film made by an English director and available in the United States through Netflix. According to McDaniel, Mae Nak is in good standing in elite Thai Buddhism as well as in popular religion. The monks he talked with about old manuscripts, history, or archaeology were as interested in talking about Mae Nak as was everyone else, and they were more interested in discussing magic and animism than textual matters or history.[20] But although Mae Nak is in good standing with local Buddhism and her shrine is located on the grounds of a monastery, there does not seem to be much that is orthodox about her story except for periodically holding a Buddhist funeral for her ghost.

Shrines in general are problematic from the perspective of interpreting Southeast Asia Theravada religious traditions. It is certainly possible to find examples of the apparent mixing of Hindu and Buddhist traditions. The important shrine of Phnom Kulen in Cambodia is an example. It was originally a shrine to the Hindu god Siva that dates to the early Angkor period. The extensive site includes a small river into the rock bottom of which a great many linga have been carved. At the currently most important part of the site on the summit of the hill there is a large stone Shavian lingam and yoni (the male and female genitalia) incorporated into a fountain from which pilgrims draw sacred water. But at some point the shrine was Buddha-ized by the addition of several monuments. These include a large statue of the reclining Buddha carved into the living rock above the lingam fountain. And also, at a

Figure 4.3. Prayers to the reclining Buddha, Phnom Kulen Mountain, Cambodia, 2008.

point not far from the fountain and the statue of the Buddha, a one-meter-long footprint relic of the Buddha appears in concrete—today covered with scattered offerings of paper money left by many of the same pilgrims who also obtain holy water from Shiva's fountain and pray to the reclining Buddha. There is also a statue of the Buddhist river goddess nearby as well. Today supplicants can seek ritual assistance from both obviously Buddhist and "Hindu" (or once Hindu) icons, though how much if at all they make a distinction between the two or care about their close proximity is questionable. Probably they are all simply regarded as icons of religious or magical power and part of Buddhism. The shrine can also be seen as another example of the borderless or boundary-crossing nature of popular religion noted in chapter 1.

Examples of other such apparent efforts at Buddha-ization are not hard to find. However non-Buddhist folk or popular shrines and monuments in Thailand and elsewhere in Theravada regions of Southeast Asia usually seem differentiated from more fully orthodox Buddhist ones. The grounds of Thai Buddhist monasteries typically contain "spir-

Figure 4.4. Footprint of the Buddha, at the major shrine on Phnom Kulen Mountain, Cambodia, 2008, with cash offerings.

it house" shrines, and the interiors of temples sometimes contain altars devoted to Chinese gods (set up at the initiative of local Chinese benefactors of the temple). McDaniel stresses that in terms of art and iconography, Thai Buddhism is exuberantly creative, inclusive, and culturally welcoming rather than doctrinaire and exclusive, but the core elements are clearly Buddhist. These include statues of the Buddha and murals of scenes from the Buddha's life and his spiritual journey. The implication that Buddhist and non-Buddhist elements and themes are equally balanced or mixed in Buddhist temples, for example, is, from my own limited and less expert experience, misleading. It is not that assorted Hindu and apparently localized spirits and divinities are not abundantly represented in public shrines, but such shrines usually appear as mainly non-Buddhist in nature. Buddhist shrines contain many statues of the Buddha, stupas or pagodas, and sometimes modern-style statues of venerated or saintly monks—and much more rarely a footprint relic. It may be true, however, that the purposes for which people visit Buddhist and non-Buddhist shrines are probably not very different.

The non-Buddhist shrines are of various types. Small "spirit houses" are everywhere, both outside of houses and shops, larger versions of which are placed near hotels, apartment buildings, and office blocks. Tree shrines are also very common and range from small platforms set up by or attached to a tree where incense is burned, to larger and more complex ones (usually banyan trees) wrapped in cloth and surrounded by many small spirit houses and other objects that have been erected as offerings. Trees along roadways are also sometimes wrapped in yellow bands of cloth—recently to protect them from being cut down. Large banyan tree shrines may be associated with known named divinities.

Figure 4.5. Cambodian women bathing themselves and obtaining water from the lingam fountain on Phnom Kulen Mountain (Cambodia, 2008). Now Buddha-ized, the shrine was originally devoted to Shiva but now includes major Buddhist icons as well set in close proximity to Hindu ones.

The Mae Nak shrine in Bangkok is built under a large banyan tree on the peripheral grounds of a Buddhist temple. And this, along with the annual laying of her ghost by monks, indicates that she has been Buddha-ized. An interesting question is when this took place—with the very origin of the story or at some later point.

The shrines built on the grounds of hotels, apartment buildings, and office blocks can be large expensive concrete or marble structures dedicated to an Indic divinity, often the four-faced Brahma, though sometimes thought in popular terms to be the "four-faced Buddha." Near where we lived for a while in Chiang Mai there was a large marble Brahma shrine apparently inspired by the Erawan Brahma shrine in Bangkok and set in the corner of a parking lot for an office building. Around the statue of Brahma were crowded offerings including statues of horses and elephants and incense, and at the base in front was a parade of larger model elephants and horses.

Such shrines are not necessarily devoid of Buddhist icons. This shrine in our neighborhood included a small mass-produced statue of the Buddha placed behind Brahma and facing the back of the shrine. Anyone would assume it was not the main feature of the shrine. This Buddha, moreover, was not a "regular" Thai Buddha but rather a Chinese version (actually the God of Happiness), known locally as "the fat Buddha" because of his rotund body and his ability to offer financial help. Some of the largest shrines take the form of buildings that house the deity and surrounding accouterments and offerings, though in the case of the most visited ones, the buildings are also surrounded with gift horses, elephants, zebras, and a great many spirit houses. Some such shrines contain such a prolific and dense collection of objects and images that they could only be sorted out through a detailed examination. One such large and very crowded shrine outside of Chiang Mai was devoted to the deified spirit of a twelfth-century king who had been killed in the battle that occurred at that place. The main building of this shrine contains a statue of the king surrounded by weapons of the period and the usual abundance of offerings. There were no Buddhist icons apparently present in the main part of the shrine, but three large statues had been erected along the other side of the highway, apparently as an orthodox Buddhist counterpoint to the main, apparently not very Buddhist-looking popular shrine. The area was very noisy as the drivers of the many vehicles on the road honked in an effort to capture

Figure 4.6. As iconic structures of Buddhism, urban temples in modern Thailand are often the focus of ornate architectural embellishment (Chiang Mai, 2010).

at least a little of the sacred energy within the field of spiritual power through which they were passing.

The major shrines of Bangkok along with the many more orthodox Buddhist temples and monuments form a major part of the religious architecture of the city. They reveal the rich diversity of the spirits, divinities, interests, and other dimensions of contemporary popular Thai religion. The best-known religious monument in the city and perhaps in Thailand is the Erawan Shrine in downtown Bangkok. The shrine centers on a large statue of Brahma seated in a raised open pavilion. The name Erawan comes from the original Erawan Hotel (today the Grand Hyatt Erawan Bangkok), in front of which the shrine was erected in 1955 when the hotel was under construction. The popular story is that the shrine was built because the workers were being bothered by local spirits angered by the intrusion. Perhaps a small shrine would have sufficed, but the Erawan was a major hotel, deserving, therefore, an edifice on a similar scale. Building the shrine appar-

Figure 4.7. A neighborhood Brahma shrine outside an office complex in Chiang Mai, 2006.

ently more than achieved its intended purpose. Over time its reputation as a site of spiritual power, a popular monument, and a major Bangkok tourist attraction grew and became national in scope.[21] Subsequent events added to its reputation as a shrine. At one point the statue of Brahma was attacked and damaged by an apparently mentally deranged man who was then killed by an angry mob, adding an always spiritually important element of bad death to the mystique of the shrine. More recently it was the scene of a deadly bombing—an indication of its great iconic significance.

In addition to the Erawan Brahma monument, there are other well-known shrines in Bangkok. A 2013 article in the *New York Times* on lottery playing in Thailand lists several popular places where lottery

Figure 4.8. Zebras at a shrine in Chiang Mai. While statues of the more traditional elephants and horses remain the most popular animal offerings, zebras have become common as well (Chiang Mai, 2010).

devotees seek supernatural help with winning numbers in the very popular two-digit illegal lotteries.[22] One of these is the Mae Nak shrine where a jar of numbered balls is available for those who wish to use this method of number search. Another is the Tree of One Hundred Corpses, a roadside tree shrine devoted to the spirits of pedestrians killed in traffic accidents in the area. And yet another lottery-number shrine is on the third floor of a police station in Chinatown devoted to the ghost of a nineteenth-century Chinese lottery pioneer who is given offerings of betel nut, coffee, and cigars. The police are reported not to care that most of the public traffic in and out of the building consists of people visiting the shrine in search of winning lottery numbers.

There are also many online lists of Bangkok shrines recommended to be of interest to tourists. In addition to those of Mae Nak and the Erawan Hotel Brahma, these include several others in particular. Two of these are large, ornate monuments to Indic gods located in downtown Bangkok, evidently built as imitations of the Erawan Shrine, in this case in front of the Bangkok Central shopping complex. One is devoted to Ganesha and patronized especially by persons seeking business or economic success, and the other to Trimurti. The main concern of devotees here is supposed to be success in love and marriage, for which the appropriate offering is red roses (a Western-derived innovation—Valentine's Day has also become popular). A third tourist-recommended shrine is that of the local goddess Tubtim whose main function is fertility and whose patrons are said to be mainly women seeking to become pregnant or to have an easy and successful birth. The shrine is also located in downtown Bangkok on the grounds of a large hotel, but it is a traditional tree shrine rather than a newly created, commercially motivated monument. The website warns (or tantalizes) tourists who may wish to visit this shrine that they should be prepared to blush because the offerings consist of graphically carved and brightly painted anthropomorphic wooden phalluses, ranging in size from small to huge.

The Issue of Syncretism in Thai Religion

In his book, McDaniel takes note of the shrines of Bangkok. And here there is a tension between his descriptions and generalizations (which seem very well informed, skillfully crafted, pertinent, and often intriguing) and some of his more theoretically oriented pronouncements and criticisms of existing scholarly interpretations of Buddhism and its place in the total field of Thai religion. For example, in his opening discussion of the concerns he will address in the book, he objects to the tendency of some recent (though unnamed) students of Southeast Asian religious change to resort to economic explanations and globalization.[23] And later he notes that "often the heterodox aspects of Buddhism in Thailand are seen as a product of modernity, consumerism, globalization, the Internet, economic anxiety."[24] Judging from this and many other statements, however, this would seem to include his own interpretations as well. For example, in his discussion of the shrines of modern Bangkok, he states,

> The Narayana, Indra, Lakshimi, Erawan, and Ganesha shrines are particularly popular with those aspiring to become wealthy, which

> would make them particularly appropriate, since they are in front of Bangkok's most expensive malls and hotels.[25]

Regarding globalization, McDaniel provides examples throughout the book that make his dismissal of the concept somewhat inappropriate. Consider here his description of a modern successful monastery:

> For an individual monastery to grow, it needs to be a "full service" religious center, which means that it has to offer a plethora of different ritual centers that speak to a wide variety of visitors. Visitors to Wat Srapathum, Wat Mahabut, and other places have the opportunity to trade and rent amulets, purchase CDs or posters, prostrate to a variety of images, meditate, consult with astrologers, release fish, eels, and birds, eat ice cream, listen to chanting, obtain corpse oil or holy water, have their wrists bound with sacred string, admire murals, listen to sermons, sit in an (often air-conditioned) library, and even play soccer and innocently flirt with men and women their own age.[26]

Except for the corpse oil, his description sounds rather like a successful temple is a Thai version of an American mega-church in Southern California or Texas. Or consider again the Erawan shrine. At some point in the past the god Brahma, along with the other popular Indic divinities, made his way from India to Southeast Asia. That is perhaps to be considered ancient historical diffusion rather than what is usually considered to be modern globalization. But the Erawan is certainly not just a traditional Thai shrine. It is illuminated at night with sophisticated modern lighting and sits in front of an international five-star hotel. And as McDaniel notes, it has played a part in the global adventures and misadventures of the billionaire Taksin Sinawarat (who made his fortune in modern telecommunications). He supposedly prayed at the shrine and was accused of engaging in black magic there in an effort to save himself before being overthrown as prime minister by the military and beginning an odyssey from Asia to Europe to the Middle East in search of sanctuary and a so-far-failed political comeback. The Erawan Shrine itself has, at least in a limited way, gone global. Replicas of it have been created in China and in Caesar's Palace in Las Vegas.

All of this sounds like globalization on steroids, though perhaps not if the concept is taken to mean simply the flow of modern technical, economic, cultural, and religious influences and goods from the West to the East and their uncritical acceptance there. If the concept is taken to mean two-way or multidirectional movement and creative interaction rather than simply Westernization, it would seem to be a necessary part of the way of understanding many present-day developments throughout the world, including religious ones.

McDaniel's most disliked concept for analyzing Buddhism in Thailand is not globalization but syncretism, though again the validity of his criticism is partly a matter of how the term is used. Or perhaps more importantly whether it is applied narrowly to Buddhism or to the larger field of Thai religion. McDaniel rejects the notion of syncretism and related concepts including hybridity, domestication, vernacularization, and others as inadequate for understanding Thai Buddhism for several reasons. The most plausible is that referring to Thai Buddhism as syncretic implies that there is a non-syncretic or pure form of Buddhism out there somewhere, which he claims there is not. All forms of Buddhism are local in both time and place. Thai Theravada Buddhism is simply different from Theravada Buddhism in Sri Lanka or Burma or Buddhism in its early historic phase in India. None is more or less correct; they are all simply different. This leaves out of the discussion whether, as it might seem, it is useful to distinguish between textual or orthodox Buddhism and popular Buddhism. He makes the strongly relativistic statement that "despite having certain cultural axioms, there is no core of Thai Buddhism."[27]

Buddhism in Thailand Is Whatever Buddhists Believe and Do

The problem of how to conceptualize the cultural and historical complexity of Thai popular religion—of Thai beliefs, practices, and values and the tendency to readily borrow and accept new ones from diverse sources without resorting to the dictionary definition of syncretism (or its various equivalents)—relates to the larger problem of delimiting the overall nature of Thai religion.[28] This is a problem that McDaniel stresses and that no one has yet solved. Thai popular religion clearly involves much more than textual Buddhism, including various Hindu (or Buddha-ized Hindu) divinities, local spirits and ghosts, corpse oil, dead baby spirits, amulets, and many other things, including more recently St. Valentine's Day, red roses, and zebras. Although he is himself a textual scholar, McDaniel takes the more anthropological or relativistic view that Thai Buddhism is what Thai Buddhists seem to identify, believe, care about, and do rather than what is in the canonical texts. But where Thai Buddhism begins and ends remains a problem. In some places in East Asia, more than one religious tradition is culturally recognized. The Japanese, for example, distinguish between the major organized religious traditions of Buddhism and Shinto, while practicing both. In Thailand there is no second, equivalent, recognized, and named religious tradition. There is only one religion of identity for the Thai, and that is Buddhism. Some small number of ethnic Thai may have converted to Christianity and so regard themselves, but adding Christmas or St. Valentine's Day to their repertoire of ritual activities and festivities does not make them Christians.

BUDDHISM IN INDONESIA

So far our treatment of popular Buddhism has mainly concerned its practice in the four major mainland Theravada countries, above all Thailand. Buddhism of course exists beyond these countries in Southeast Asia as well. Theravada Buddhism spills over national boundaries as Thais and members of other Buddhist ethnic communities have in one way or another ended up as ethnic and religious minorities in surrounding countries—for example, as already noted, in Malaysia. Buddhism in Indonesia also differs from other places in that it lacks a strong association with one or another particular ethnic community such as the Thai in Thailand, the Khmer in Cambodia, the Lao in Laos, and the Burmese in Myanmar. The total number of Buddhists is small (usually put at less than 1 percent of the population), but this is out of proportion to the importance of the religion. Indonesian Buddhists are currently divided into three sects, including Theravada, Mahayana, and Buddhayana (roughly, progressive Buddhism), an Indonesian creation. Most Buddhists are reported to dwell in Sumatra, Java, Bali, Kalimantan, Sulawesi, and Lombok.[29]

As with Hinduism (but even more so), Buddhism in Indonesia is at once a very old and a new religion. In terms of history, Buddhism has ancient roots in Indonesia, especially in Java. The great ninth-century Mahayana Buddhist monument of Borobudur in central Java is the largest Buddhist temple in the world (and Indonesia's leading tourist attraction). Buddhism in Indonesia began to decline in the fourteenth century with the general conversion to Islam, though it has been held by some important scholars to have continued as a major influence in the subsequent syncretist (*abangan*) religious variant of Java.

While few living indigenous Buddhists appear to have endured into the modern period, a revival occurred in the twentieth century. This may have been rooted in part in a more general interest in Eastern religions influenced by changing Western views. More specifically, the visit of a missionary monk from Sri Lanka who visited Java in 1934 is credited with reintroducing Buddhism.[30] The present significance of Buddhism is, however, above all a post-colonial development. For whatever exact reason or reasons (though probably including the grandeur and cultural importance of Borobudur and the national significance of Buddhism in Indonesian history and civilization), Buddhism was, along with Hinduism, Islam, and Catholic and Protestant Christianity, chosen as an official *agama*. This recognition gave Buddhism a national prestige it probably would have otherwise lacked. But it also provided a further option for those individuals or groups in need of an approved religion to which to convert. This was of some importance, for example, for the Chinese whose religious practices were eventually added as "Confucian" but then dropped by the New Order regime before being added again following the departure of Suharto. Buddhism also, along with Hinduism, provided an option for other Indonesians seeking an approved *agama* other than Christianity or Islam or Hinduism.

Such an instance of Buddhist conversion occurred on Lombok, a small island with a turbulent religious history among the indigenous Sasak population. While some dimensions of religious complexity were therefore long-standing—most notably the ongoing struggle between syncretism and orthodox factions of Islam (to be discussed in the next chapter), Buddhism entered the picture in the late 1960s. Several anthropologists have studied and reported on what took place. The Finnish anthropologist Leena Avonius, who did field research in north Lombok in the late 1990s, has described religious developments of that time.[31]

In brief, on Lombok as elsewhere, government efforts (supplemented by the military) to enforce the adoption of one or another of the approved *agamas* were intensified by the Suharto New Order regime in the late 1960s. At that time Buddhism was a largely unknown *agama* on Lombok, but it had potential appeal to some of the Sasaks. At the time the Sasak population was divided among three religious sections. These included two Islamic factions plus remaining unconverted Sasaks known as Boda who adhered to their own religious traditions. Here, as in many other regions of Indonesia at this time, religious identities became fused with political ones, which led in some instances to lethal attacks. The orthodox Muslim faction wanted both the syncretic faction and the as yet unconverted Boda to become orthodox. The syncretist Muslims and Boda, on the other hand, both viewed Buddhism as a preferable alternative to orthodox Islam, in part because it seemed more compatible with their indigenous customary practices. When pressed to convert, both some syncretist Muslims and more Boda chose Buddhism. However, when this caused great consternation among some important orthodox Muslim government officials and led to further meetings and harsh criticism of the choice of the syncretist Muslims, most of these recanted in favor of adopting orthodoxy, though how orthodox their actual religious beliefs and practices became is a different matter.[32] The Boda were urged by religious officials to choose Islam (preferably) or else Hinduism on the grounds that there were no Buddhists around to show them how to become Buddhist, while there were many Muslims available to teach them Islam and Hindu Balinese to instruct them in Hinduism. Most of the Boda stuck with Buddhism, in part because they kept pigs as an important part of their farming practices and did not want to give this up, as they would have to if they became Muslims.[33]

In order to pursue conversion to Buddhism, the Boda sent a delegation to meet with the Buddhist authorities in the Department of Religious Affairs in the Indonesian capital of Jakarta (in Java) to plead their case and seek advice about dealing with the problem. The delegation received a sympathetic welcome and was given assurances of support. The delegation returned home and several months later made a second visit to Jakarta to learn more about Buddhism. They returned home with literature about Buddhism and set about introducing and developing Buddhism in the Boda villages. Buddhist prayers were taught, other rituals were learned and practiced, and plans were made and funds began to be collected to build a Buddhist *vihara* (temple). Over time *viharas* were built in most Boda communities, though without resident monks.[34]

Eventually the arrival of Buddhism on Lombok brought further complications because Indonesian Buddhism had become more complex. A schism had developed between adherents of Theravada orthodoxy and a localized Indonesian version that had adopted a new concept of the Buddha. This development had begun in 1965 when a Javanese Buddhist named Dhammaviriya, a follower of an Indian Buddhist leader Bhikku Ashim Jinarakkhita, published a book called *Kutuhanan Dalam Agama Buddha* (God in Buddhism), presenting Buddha as God. His support for the divinity of Buddha was based on old Javanese texts that referred to Sang Hyang Adi Buddha. Following the publication of the book, Dhammaviriya went on to found an organization and a new sect of Buddhism named Buddhayana (roughly, "progressive Buddhism"). This was based both on the central proposition that Buddha was in reality a god and the equivalent of the supreme divinities of Christianity and Islam, and that Buddhism also had books and prophets similar to those of the Western religions.

Government religious authorities welcomed this interpretation of Buddhism as a monotheistic religion because it brought the religion more fully in line with the official model of an *agama* as monotheism. But not all Buddhists accepted the new interpretation. Some regarded the change as an unacceptable alteration to a core notion of Theravada doctrine—the form of Buddhism that had been established or reestablished in modern Indonesia. It appeared to some that, while perhaps politically correct, the notion of Buddha as God was a doctrinal innovation that was unjustified by the accepted canons of Theravadaism. Eventually the dissatisfied Theravada Buddhists broke away from Buddhayana and established their own organization that became the Sangha Theravada Indonesia, a development that was followed by the establishment of an also separate organization of Mahayana Buddhists. In 1979 the three organizations held a conference in order to try to resolve their differences. However, the Buddhayana followers continued to hold to the divinity of Buddha while those of the Sangha Theravada Indonesia continued to object. On Lombok, both Buddhayana and Sangha Theravada Indonesia were established as competing sects by the 1990s. In the Boda Buddhist village of Bentek in northern Lombok, the inhabitants in the 1990s were divided. Half were followers of Buddhayana and half of Theravada. The two groups were living in separate sections of the village. Both were using the same temple but with different priests and services. The split was somewhat reminiscent of the older schism in the Sasak Muslim population. The Theravada people regarded themselves as upholders of international Buddhist orthodoxy and the Buddhayana followers as deviants.[35]

BUDDHISM AND POPULAR RELIGION

The main controversy over the past years in the interpretations of Buddhism in the mainland Theravada countries has been concerned with the overall nature of religion. Most interpretations recognize the obvious fact that there is much more to Thai, Burmese, Lao, and Khmer religion than textual Buddhism. Roughly speaking, the non-Buddhist elements include indigenous, Indic or Hindu, and perhaps Sinitic ones—though it is not always easy to sort these neatly into such boxes. The list includes, for example, the cult of the rice goddess, the dragon or *naga*, and the other supernatural beliefs and practices associated with the cultivation of rice. Given their widespread presence throughout Southeast Asia, the notions and practices involving "bad death" can also be regarded as indigenous. This would also seem to be the case with the animism and magic associated with the construction of houses and other buildings. Spirit possession or shamanism and exorcism may have diffused at some unknowable point from elsewhere but can probably also be assumed to have been present far back in time. The Indic or Hindu-Buddhist elements can be seen not only in archaeological contexts, but also in still used and recently created shrines in Thailand and elsewhere that often feature Hindu or Buddha-ized Hindu divinities.

But these are not the main problem. This is rather the overall nature of religion in Buddhist societies. Is there one integrated religion or several distinct traditions? And if the latter, are these related to different and distinct sectors of society, or does everyone adhere to both the more Buddhist and the less Buddhist traditions? And if so, how aware are people of such differing traditions and how much do they care about them? Here there have been various interpretations. The first is that while Buddhism is the religion of identity, in terms of content it is mixed, blended, or synchronized with local animism and magic and imported Hinduism. The second is that Buddhism and magic/animism are separate and conflicting religions that exist side by side, though with Buddhism dominant. The third is that Buddhism and other traditions are a single religion for most people, except for a small social, religious elite that recognizes a distinction between philosophical, textual, or orthodox Buddhism and non-Buddhist beliefs and practices. The fourth and final interpretation is that indigenous magic, animism, and Hinduism are impossible or very hard to separate from Buddhism, not only for villagers but for everyone. In this view Buddhism includes everything of a religious nature that people who identify themselves as Buddhists believe and do.

Buddhism in Indonesia presents a different problem. Although it has an ancient presence, it is also a new religion, one developed above all for religious and political reasons, and it has been seen by both Indonesians and outside scholars in these terms. Buddhism became a present-day religion in Indonesia largely because it was defined as an acceptable one as a result of the constitutional mandate requiring all citizens of the republic to be adherents of monotheism—a rather flexibly interpreted concept that came to mean in actuality any of the larger world religions. Without the mandate of Pancasila and the shelter Buddhism provided for some people whose religious identity did not gain official approval, the number of Buddhists would be far smaller. Of those who became Buddhists, many did so as the best choice among the limited range of required possibilities. These included Chinese citizens whose religious practices were identified as Confucianism and were added to the approved list but then dropped by the New Order regime before being reinstated three decades later. Of the indigenous peoples facing the necessity of joining an approved religion other than Christianity or Islam, the more common choice was (as noted in the previous chapter) Hinduism. The unconverted Boda Sasaks of Lombok are an exception. Under other circumstances they might have decided that Hinduism would have suited their needs, but this was the religion of the Balinese, the ruling group on Lombok for several centuries before the Dutch took over and with whom they did not wish to be associated.

5

POPULAR ISLAM IN MALAYSIA AND INDONESIA

Islam is the predominant religion of identity in both Malaysia and Indonesia, especially the latter, which has the largest Muslim population in the world. Muslim minorities also occur in several other countries. These include Moro groups in the southern Philippines, especially coastal Mindanao and the Sulu archipelago, who form the eastern extreme of the ethnic Malayan-speaking Muslim world of insular Southeast Asia. There is also a Malayan-speaking Muslim Cham minority in Cambodia and a Malay Muslim community in the far south of Thailand. Islam in all of these places is overwhelmingly Sunni; the small numbers of Shia Muslims in Malaysia derive from immigrants from other parts of the Islamic world.

As with Theravada Buddhism, Islam did not arrive and expand into a religious vacuum. Some of the peoples who either initially or subsequently converted—often presumably following the lead of rulers or chiefs—had been influenced to varying extents by previously existing Southeast Asian Indic religious traditions in addition to indigenous ones. The forms of Islam that developed throughout Southeast Asia have often been described as syncretic, though the extent of this has varied. Occasionally two popular forms of Islam have developed, one more localized and syncretic and one more orthodox or standardized. Indeed, such dual traditions are perhaps the most famous of all dimensions of Islam in Indonesia. As Islam developed in Southeast Asia, it accommodated existing social as well as religious circumstances. The most important social characteristic of Southeast Asia in general is the relatively strong gender equality that contrasts markedly with the male dominance and patriarchy found throughout some of the other parts of the Muslim world and often correctly or not attributed to Islam itself. The spread of Islam into Southeast Asia was also generally peaceful.

THE DEVELOPMENT OF ISLAM IN SOUTHEAST ASIA

The Islamization of Southeast Asia has tended to involve two gradients. First, Islam spread basically from west to east over several centuries. It apparently was first established in northern Sumatra and from there moved southward and eastward into the Malay Peninsula, Borneo, and Java and eventually reached present-day eastern Indonesia and the southern Philippines. As it moved eastward its thrust diminished in some places. When Java, situated to the east of Sumatra, accepted Islam, many Javanese converted in a nominal way, keeping much of their previous Indic and indigenous animistic beliefs and practices and eventually identifying and labeling their own non-orthodox version of the faith. Most of the people of Bali, to the immediate east of Java, never converted at all, and while some peoples further east in the Lesser Sunda Islands did so, it was in pockets, with many retaining their indigenous religious traditions or sooner or later converting to Christianity. To the northeast, Islam reached only the southernmost area of the Philippines, though here its lack of further spread may be attributable to the arrival of Spanish colonial rule that brought large-scale conversion to Christianity.

In addition to the west-to-east movement, the Islamization of insular Southeast Asia also (and perhaps more importantly) often involved a coastal-to-interior gradient. Conversion took place first in the coastal regions and in some instances never reached deeply into the interior. In none of the larger islands from Sumatra to Mindanao or the Malay Peninsula did all of the inhabitants convert. In Borneo, the largest island outside of New Guinea, the penetration of Islam beyond the coast was generally very shallow. In Java most of the inhabitants did eventually convert, but those on the north coast did so more completely than did the people of the interior. In some places there was also a lowland–highland gradient in terms of which Islam developed first and more fully in the lowlands than it did in the more remote mountains. Where Islam did penetrate into the interior of the larger land areas, it was often over waterways, as on the coasts.

The often sharp decline of Islamization beyond the coasts and lower reaches of major rivers, as in Borneo, involved several geographical and cultural differences between the two zones.

Islam could have penetrated landward simply by the expansion of Muslim coastal populations. In some instances this probably occurred, but if so it was often limited. In the pre-colonial era, population densities were generally not great enough to encourage much expansion into the interior. And the interior was not a welcoming environment for people who did not already know how to live there. The coastal populations were generally organized as states designed to control commerce on the major rivers that were the main means of movement and transportation. These people lived by fishing, agriculture, and trade. The peoples of the interior lived by hunting and gathering and shifting cultivation. They were organized on the basis of place, as autonomous bands, villages, or river sections. Many were warlike and often headhunters who would not welcome the expansion of coastal Muslim populations even if such people had wanted to move inland. The interior areas might have been desirable territorial acquisitions for the coastal Muslim states, and if so this might have promoted Islamization. But in general such states were not in a position to go beyond securing the alliance or nominal submission of the nearer interior peoples, and often not even this.

The colonial takeover and eventual pacification of the interior areas changed this, but it was often a long-term process. In British Sarawak the complete pacification of the upriver Iban took a century, and in any case did not lead to much if any inward expansion of coastal Muslim ("Malay") peoples. In Indonesia the Dutch did not favor the further expansion of Islam into interior areas and instead did what they could to encourage conversion to Christianity as an alternative. The republican Indonesian government did more to encourage the further settlement of the outer islands, including their interior areas—their purpose being to relieve overpopulation and landlessness in the crowded inner islands of Java and Bali. The government also sought to encourage or coerce the as yet unconverted or non-*agama* groups to convert to one or another of the approved world religions. The list included Islam, but this was not necessarily the popular choice.

The arrival and spread of Islam in Southeast Asia is generally assumed to have been linked to trade, and the main early and often enduring centers of both were in coastal areas. The coastal areas—at least where trade and towns were centered—were open and pluralistic in nature. For a long period of time the trading towns and cities of Southeast Asia had been ethnically and religiously mixed. Traders included Muslims from India and the Near East as well as non-Muslim Chinese (and eventually Christian Europeans) who lived in different quarters and generally got along, but (as it was famously put by the colonial scholar John Furnival) interacted mainly in the marketplace. For Malays and other local coastal dwellers, who had previously followed mixed indigenous and Hindu traditions, conversion to Islam offered advantages. It helped to bond them to foreign and other local Southeast Asian Muslims and probably helped them compete in business with the non-Muslim Chinese who had their own bonds of family kinship, ethnicity, and religion that made them such formidable traders and successful shopkeepers.

The situation in the interior was again very different. Here trade was also important but limited. The interior peoples were mainly self-sufficient in providing what they needed in terms of food, clothing, housing, tools and weapons, and ritual activities. But they also greatly valued certain luxury goods from the outside, above all ceramic jars and other containers, glass and ceramic beads, and gongs and other brassware. These prestige goods and heirlooms were exchanged through lines and networks of trade with the coast and beyond, whereby interior peoples paid for imported luxuries with a range of forest products they gathered themselves or obtained from yet other interior peoples—especially in Borneo and the Malay Peninsula, the nomadic hunter-gatherers. Such trade was generally individualistic, relatively limited, and small scale. Goods might change hands many times between people who were personally acquainted and could be trusted.

Compared to the peoples of coastal areas, Islam had little in the way of practical benefits to offer such interior tribal peoples. And in addition to lacking the advantages it offered on the coast, there were certain liabilities that related to the ecological adaptation and cultural traditions and preferences of the interior groups. Their eating and drinking practices—especially in the context of hospitality and ritual feasting and celebration—were incompatible with the Muslim taboos on the consumption of pork and alcohol. Of these taboos, the ban on pork was the most important, both from the perspective of Muslims and potential converts. Pigs were both hunted and eaten as a major source of meat and raised for sacrifice and feasting among many groups. Other animals, including chickens and in some areas water buffalo, also served for sacrifice and fasting, but the ritual use of pigs was widespread. In the interior of Borneo, for example, meat from large animals is scarce, and pork is therefore important, especially in places where deer are regarded as sacred and therefore taboo. Pig hunting in Borneo is an avid and exciting practice, but it is also useful to cultivators as a protection for gardens. And here also conversion to orthodox Muslim practices would have cut converts off from indigenous ceremonies and the annual round of festivals.[1]

Having provided this general overview of Islamization in Southeast Asia, we now turn to the nature of popular Islam, first in Malaysia and then in Indonesia, the two major Muslim countries in Southeast Asia. Here many issues have been raised over the years. Most basically there is the question of what Islam is like as a part of the broader totality of popular religion and how this has changed over time, especially in recent decades.

POPULAR ISLAM IN MALAYSIA

My most extensive personal experience with Islam has been in Kelantan, a Malay state in northwestern peninsular Malaysia, where I first went to live in 1966–1967 and to which I returned every several years for shorter periods mainly over the next twenty years. During the periods when I lived in Kelantan I usually stayed in and around the town of Pasir Mas, a district capital and market center. The town itself was situated on a large bend in the wide Kelantan River and was ethnically diverse. The shop houses were mainly the homes and businesses of Chinese, though there were some Malay and immigrant Muslim shopkeepers from India and Pakistan as well. There was also, as usual, a large open-air market crammed with stalls and individual traders who were mainly Malays, including a large portion of women. The surrounding rural areas with a few small exceptions consisted of Malay villages set among rice fields and orchards. The exceptions were communities of Chinese cultivators along the river in places that had been there for a long time. Further away and nearer to Thailand there were a series of Thai villages that had been there since the nineteenth century. Beyond the coastal plain and river delta were the vast forests occupied by the scattered indigenous non-Muslim groups referred to today as Orang Asli.

Malay religion in this area, as elsewhere in the Kelantan rice plain, was dominated by Islam, though it was Islam of a traditional Malay character that existed alongside of less orthodox, customary beliefs and practices. The limited ethnic diversity had little bearing on Malay Islam or popular religion generally. The Thai, about whom more will be said below, did have a wider role, however, in the religious and cultural life of the Kelantanese Malays.

Islam and Colonialism

The development of Islam in Kelantan, as in the other Malay states that came under British control in the late nineteenth and early twentieth centuries, was influenced by colonial policies. Colonialism was established by treaty rather than conquest and took the form of "protection." Colonial rule in such situations was referred to as "indirect," meaning that government was administered through the traditional apparatus of the state (as altered to fit colonial notions of good government) headed by the existing Malay sovereign. The highest British officer in the state was a "resident" or "advisor," the latter term meaning his official role was to provide advice rather than to issue orders or proclamations. British colonial authority was further restricted in that it was not to apply to matters of Malay religion or custom (*adat*). These were deemed to be the exclusive concern of Malay authority. The British in Malaya considered Islam a matter to be handled with care. By the time that control over the Malay states (as opposed to the Straits Settlement of Penang, Malacca, and Singapore) was established, the British had had long and diverse experience in dealing with Muslim peoples in other parts of the empire. They were also aware of the previous and continuing problems that the Dutch had in the strongly Islamic areas of the neighboring Netherlands Indies (present-day Indonesia), especially with the Acehnese of far northern Sumatra.

The generally peaceful handling of Islam under indirect colonial rule in Malaya can probably be attributed to various things. These included the prohibition of missionary efforts to convert Malays or other Muslims to Christianity. The institutionalization of the authority of the Malay rulers over matters of Malay religion and custom took the form of establishment of state councils of religion, custom, and ceremony. Religious courts and law were separate from secular criminal law to which Muslims were also subject. Religious courts were therefore mainly limited to matters of marriage, divorce, and inheritance. The authority held by the councils of Malay religion and custom was otherwise very broad. More or less by definition, religion, Malay culture, or the Malay way of life were combined into linked but mutually exclusive categories, as indicated by the terms *religion* and *adat*, or custom. *Religion* referred specifically to Islam rather than to a broader notion of supernaturally oriented beliefs and practices. *Adat Melayu*, on the other hand, referred to Malay customary beliefs and practices in general, including ones with a supernatural dimension as well as those of a more secular or worldly nature. Insofar as anyone recognized discrepancies between the beliefs, practices, and laws of Islam and those of *adat*, the resolution was a matter for the Malay ruler and the council of religion and custom rather than for some group of ulamas or religious scholars and authorities. After the British departed in 1957, many of the institutions of religious and customary authority they helped to create or shape were kept more or less as they were.

The British appear to have succeeded in avoiding potential conflicts involving Islam by adopting successful practical policies. But they did not show much interest in studying it. This was much the opposite of what occurred in the Netherlands Indies. The Dutch in Indonesia were less successful in creating and implementing practical policies that avoided conflict with Muslims, especially in Sumatra. But unlike the British, they took Islam seriously in scholarly terms and left a legacy of literature (above all the research, writings, and policies of Christiaan Snouck Hurgronje) that is mainly lacking for British Malaya. The British colonial scholars were interested in Malay religion, but their interests were more in what they generally termed "Malay magic." This phrase included popular beliefs in spirits and practices involving spirits, curing, sorcery, charms, spells, omens, divination, and shrines as applied in practical pursuits—curing, personal protection, fishing, cultivation, and other such matters. Colonial officials serving throughout the Malay states came across tidbits of folklore, which they described in notes and articles published in journals and in longer monographs. The main approach was based on the work done by folklorists in Great Britain and Europe. Trained anthropologists did not become involved in Malay studies until very late in the colonial period, or after it had ended.

The colonial scholarship on the Malays includes two types of accounts. There were first the purely descriptive notes and longer collections. Interpretation is perhaps never lacking in any descriptive narrative, but in these accounts it was mainly implicit. The greatest of the longer collections is W. W. Skeat's *Malay Magic*, published in 1900 and still in print.[2] Subtitled "An Introduction to the Folklore and Popular Religion of the Malay Peninsula," *Malay Magic* is seven hundred pages in length. The word "Introduction" in the subtitle was used without apparent irony.

The second type of colonial account was the works of synthesis and interpretation, and here the two main scholars were R. J. Wilkinson and R. O. Winstedt. When these colonial scholars turned to Islam, their interpretations were mainly negative. They commonly made two sorts of points. One was that Malays were often lax in holding to the central tenets of Islam. In an overview of Malay Islam originally published in 1906, Wilkinson began by observing that Malays were more inclined to emphasize animism than Muslim monotheism: "The average Malay may be said to look on God as upon a great King or Governor—mighty, of course, and just, but too remote a power to trouble himself about a villager's petty affairs—whereas the spirits of the district are comparable to the local police, who may be corrupt and prone to error but who take a most absorbing personal interest in their radius of influence and whose ill-will has to be avoided at all costs."[3] Wilkinson, who was fond of extravagant metaphors, went on to say in conclusion that "the Malay has gone on preserving custom after custom and ceremony after ceremony until his whole life is a sort of museum of ancient customs—an ill-kept and ill-designed museum in which no exhibit is dated, labeled or explained."

The general point was that understanding Islam and other aspects of Malay religion required an archaeological perspective. Islam was at the surface, but beneath it were other layers that required excavation if the fuller historical and cultural reality was to be exposed. Winstedt, the most famous of all the colonial Malayanist scholars, again developed this line of interpretation in his book *The Malay Magician*. As a subtitle of the later edition indicated, on top was Islam in the form of Sufism, beneath which was Hinduism, and beneath Hinduism was a base layer of primitive shamanism. It is possible to see in such statements an assertion that the British had done the Malays a favor in colonizing them—or at least that they could use a new layer of Western civilization on top of everything else.[4]

Clothing and Dress

The traditional characteristics of popular Islam in Kelantan could readily be seen in the local dress of women. This reflected several considerations, including economic ones. Common everyday non-religious dress mainly followed Malay customary practice rather than orthodox Muslim rules or preferences. Both in town and in villages, women wore ankle-length, sometimes tightly wrapped and revealing, batik sarongs and waist-length, short-sleeved blouses (*baju*). Shawls were optional and worn in various ways, often draped over the shoulders or over the head or sometimes wound into a loose turban. Veils were never worn, and heads were usually bare. Around their homes and throughout the neighborhood, the common, casual practice was for women to wear only a sarong, tied above the top of the breasts and reaching only to the knees. This was also the bathing costume worn at the river or at the household or neighborhood well, often in sight of the village lane. For dress up (for a wedding, for example), the preference was for a more expensive blouse and sarong, adorned if possible with gold jewelry, and a shawl–head scarf.

Some women, for certain purposes, dressed in a way that was more fully in keeping with Muslim norms. This involved a looser, much more form-concealing long overblouse (*baju kurong*) that reached the knees and covered most of the lower garment. A woman so dressed was covered from her neck to her ankles This costume usually also included a scarf that could be worn in various ways, though it usually was worn in a way that left part of the hair in view. Dress of this sort had both a social and a religious meaning, in that it was religiously correct and denoted higher status. It was, for example, appropriate for women who were schoolteachers or office workers or attending functions with husbands who had such positions.

The fairly flexible dress code for women reflected a more general pattern of behavior. Women were not secluded, though again there were variations that reflected both religious propriety and social status. Poorer women took more liberties than those of higher standing and income, and those without any special claims to religious status were less guarded than those who wished to appear pious. Women in general were separated from men in religious, ceremonial, and festive contexts but not otherwise in public space. The open market was crowded, and male and female shoppers and traders jostled among and past one another. Coffee shops were mainly for men, but women would often work in them and sometimes serve men or stop by to make purchases or chat when out and about. Women rode in trishaws that were always peddled by men and rode in shared taxis driven and partly occupied by men, though usually sitting in the front seat with only the driver. A woman riding behind a man on a two-wheeled vehicle would be assumed to be his wife. Beyond such general practices, a woman's stage of life was important. The conduct of a sexually mature but unmarried woman was of greatest concern, followed by that of a married woman of childbearing years. Post-menopausal women were relatively free to move in public social space and interact with men, and the older the freer, it seemed. Divorced women of childbearing age were in a special category. They were vulnerable to gossip and joking about being on the lookout for a husband. They were a favorite topic of conversation among some men. The economic hardship faced by many such women, who usually had children, meant that they often had to work in very public occupations, such as market traders and sellers, though married women did so as well.

Men were subject to few Muslim restrictions on dress, though religious standing was also communicated through clothing. Everyday dress for ordinary men included either a plaid sarong (worn either full ankle length or knee length) or Western-style trousers. Shorts were generally looked down on and avoided (except in playing sports) as something worn only by laborers and the Chinese. A Western-style coat with lapels added status to either a sarong or trousers, though this came at a cost in comfort in the heat. There were also "safari" suits modeled on those introduced by British colonial officials and favored by men in higher positions of government or authority. The appropriate head covering for a man who wore a safari suit or Western jacket and trousers was a stiff black brimless oblong hat or *songkok*.

While not required, religious dress for men was quite different from such secular costumes in a number of ways. For one thing, the sarong rather than trousers was always worn as part of a religious costume, as was a loose-fitting Malay shirt rather than a Western-style one. Such dress was generally worn by all men when going to the Friday mosque service and on a daily basis by those following religious vocations. The most important part of Islamic religious dress for men involved headgear. This consisted of two items, including a white skullcap (in Kelantan, *kopiah*) and a white turban (*serban*). Except when worn to pray, the skullcap alone was a more common emblem of some special religious status. Its general significance among adult males was that it showed a man was either a religious leader or an ordinary man having made the pilgrimage to Mecca—such a person was also identified and addressed as a hajji. The completed outfit consisted of a turban worn over a skullcap. Such a turban was only worn by a man with some sort of distinct, special religious identity. This included being a traditional religious teacher (*tuan guru*) or a student of such a traditional religious teacher. There were also differences in turbans, namely that those worn by religious teachers were larger and more loosely wound and with a longer tail hanging down behind.

Mosques, Prayer Houses, and Schools

The local organization of Islam in the Kelantan plain focused on the mosque (*mesjid*), prayer house (*surau*), and school—of which there were several types, though the most important was the *pondok*. The prayer house was a neighborhood structure built by a local community or an individual on private property. It was used for various purposes including the required daily prayers, special prayers during the fasting month, and funeral ceremonies for a deceased member of the community, and as a place where children were taught to read the Koran. None of these activities were required to be carried out in the *surau*. All could be and often were done in private houses as well. The mosque, on the other hand, was a required building and institution. All Muslim households belonged to a particular mosque where the men of the family were supposed to participate in the communal Friday noontime prayer and to fulfill other obligations.

As noted above, Malay children are taught to read and chant the Koran. In addition to this elementary instruction, there were several more formal sorts of Muslim schools. First, although all government-run Western-style or national schools taught Islam as a required subject for Muslim students, there were also "Arabic schools" that were modeled on Western- or British-style schools that combined standard subjects with instruction in Arabic and religious classes. The school uniforms consisted of more Islamically oriented dress, especially for girls, and the teachers were referred to as Ustaz rather than Che' Gu', the standard terms of reference and dress for secular schoolteachers.

There were also many *pondok* schools in the area. These are the more traditional Muslim schools, though their history in Kelantan and Pattani in earlier periods is not well known. They have a number of

Figure 5.1. A village *surau*, rural Pasir Mas, Kelantan, Malaysia, 1967.

characteristics. They were organized around a teacher known as a *tuan guru* (literally, "lord teacher") who had developed a reputation for religious knowledge and who himself had usually studied with a famous teacher. Some *tuan guru* also had a reputation for magical powers and, if so, were sought out for blessings and charms. The teacher was surrounded by students who lived in small individual huts known as *pondok*, for which this type of school was known. The students were all male and were responsible for their own food and other expenses and contributed what they could to the support of the teacher. Since secular subjects were not taught and since students were all male, the schools had by the 1960s come to be seen as old fashioned. Some therefore had begun to include the more modern Arabic school organization and curriculum as well.[5] The *pondok* schools in and around Pasir Mas were more than schools in a narrow sense, but rather religious communities. They consisted of the house of the *tuan guru* (or houses if he had several wives, as some did), a prayer house, and a teaching center. The small houses or huts of the students and those of families that considered themselves to be followers and members of the community surrounded these. As schools in a strict sense, the significance of the *pondoks* was declining. But as communities or neighborhoods, they remained important as centers of strong Islamic identity. In the Pasir Mas area they were one of the bases of the political power of the PMIP (or PAS), the Pan-Malaysian Islamic Party, which had controlled the state government since independence in 1957.

Malay Magic

As a historical or ethnological record, the British colonial accounts of Malay religion left much to be desired. But they emphasized (probably overemphasized) Malay religion at that time as including a wide array of supernatural beliefs and practices. Some of these clearly had something to do with Islam, but others had little. By the late 1960s some of both the Muslim and the non-Muslim folk religious beliefs and activities were still around but were becoming less acceptable. In the realm of folk Islam, there were, for example, several living saints around who were referred to as *tok wali*. These were usually recluses who were believed to have certain magical powers. Such powers included the ability to predict the future, a skill known locally as *mulut masin*, or "salty mouth," and that could be applied to winning the lottery. There were also shrines and holy or magical places known as *tempat keramat*. The most important of these shrines in the area was near the neighboring town of Tumpat. This was a tomb known as Kubor Datuk (the grave of the honored one). It was covered by a shelter and attended by a caretaker who accepted offerings for the upkeep of the shrine on behalf of the saint. People came and made requests for help (by reputation, the grave was especially efficacious with problems involving children). If the request was satisfied, the vow was fulfilled by a further visit to do whatever had been promised, such as sacrificing a goat and holding a feast by the grave. Such practices have more recently been condemned as unacceptable by Islamic reformers.

Tempat keramat also included certain trees in which spirits were believed to live, caves connected to myths that were said to contain sacred objects that would sometimes appear, ponds believed to hold magical cannons that would fire when danger threatened, and graves

Figure 5.2. In the late 1960s, rice field spirit-propitiation ceremonies (*puja padang*) were still occasionally held in rural Pasir Mas but were in decline and attracted little interest. The one shown here (in 1967) was attended by only a few curious children.

where people could meditate, be healed, dream of a winning lottery number, or fulfill vows. Many people, however, said they no longer believed in such things or that Islam forbade them. Some notions of magic and supernatural power were still very much present, however, as I learned early on in my first stay in Kelantan.

Gossip and concerns about sorcery or *ilmu jahat* were common. Such concerns had much to do with the commonness of divorce and the fact that men had the right under Islamic law to divorce wives, even without their agreement, by using the *talak*. There was also the further fact that men could take additional wives, again without the permission of their existing ones—even though only a small percentage of men actually did practice polygamy. A woman was thus vulnerable in several ways, to being divorced against her will or to becoming an unwilling co-wife. To make it worse, a man who had no desire to do so might be lured away from his wife or into a polygamous union by another woman who was using love magic. There were, it was said, many divorced women around on the lookout for a new husband, if only for economic reasons. A man with resources who married a woman who appeared to lack equivalent ones or evident physical charms, like youth and beauty, was a likely candidate for gossip about love magic. One such form of magic people knew about was *nasi kukus* or "steamed rice." This was made by a woman squatting over a plate of cooked rice while reciting a spell willing the man to be consumed with desire for her. Another form of love magic included binding a photo of the desired person to one of the person seeking to attract him or her and again reciting a spell. Beyond sorcery, men were also believed to be inclined to want to *berbini muda*, or marry younger wives. Magical medicines to enhance male sexual potency were also readily available for the older man who succeeded.

I learned of an incident of alleged sorcery and counter-sorcery in a polygamous marriage shortly after moving into Pasir Mas. Mat, a teenage Malay boy, befriended us and, upon learning of my interest in religion, told me that he was very interested in magic. Mat went on to explain that he was learning about such things because of what was going on in his own family. What he told me was that his mother was being attacked by sorcery (*ilmu jahat*). She was the second and younger wife of his father, an older man who worked as a clerk in a government office in Kota Bharu where he lived part of the time with his older, first wife. According to Mat, the senior wife had never accepted his own mother who was frequently ill and believed this was because magic was being directed against her. His mother therefore was taking steps to counter the occult attacks.

What Mat told me about these counter-sorcery efforts introduced me to an important dimension of sorcery and counter-sorcery in Kelantan. This was that it crossed ethnic and religious boundaries. Mat's mother had by then turned to Thai supernatural assistance. There were Malay *bomoh* (curers or magicians) around. But the Thai were considered to be the heavy artillery of the occult in Kelantan. Throughout Malaysia generally there is considerable ethnic and religious diversity. But the Thai are one of only a few groups that are known as specialists in magic. The Javanese also have such a reputation in some areas. But there were few Javanese immigrants in Kelantan.[6] Some of the Thai practitioners were monks, and others were former monks. Part of the Thai reputation for occult powers seemed to be that as non-Muslims the Thai were freer to engage in matters of sorcery than were Malays. Mat himself went along on the trips that his mother took to consult the Thai monk from whom she was obtaining magical aid. When he told me about the latest trip, he showed me a piece of yellow cloth covered with Thai signs and figures. The monk had made it for him as protection, and he greatly valued it though he did not know what any of the symbols on it meant. He let me look at it but did not think I should touch it because I was not a Muslim.

The Thai lived mainly in a series of villages located near the border that had been established in the nineteenth century at a time when Siam claimed control over Kelantan. The local Thai are fluent in the Kelantanese dialect of Malay, are in some ways indistinguishable from rural Malays, and get along well with them. Their villages were generally far enough away from those of the Malays that Thai pig raising did not usually present a problem. Some local Malays visited the Thai villages occasionally to watch festivals held at the Buddhist temples, but the Thai reputation for magical skills was probably the most important draw.

The Thai villages in Kelantan were in a good position to attract clients and provide occult services. For one thing there was the border itself, which had a strong and multifaceted attraction. While the southernmost provinces of Thailand remain mainly Malay in ethnic composition, the towns are an ethnic mixture of Malay, Thais, and Chinese. The Thai border town of Golok is easily accessible from the Kelantan plain. People frequently travel there for a day of shopping or sin. Consumer goods that were either not available or more expensive in Kelantan were for sale and could be carried back easily without paying import duties. Smuggling flourished because rice was transported openly in bundles by train in the 1960s and later more clandestinely by fast cars in the 1980s. There were bullfights in Golok and Thai boxing and gambling. Prostitution was also practiced openly. The appeal of occult services provided by the Thai in Kelantan thus drew upon the more general appeal of Thailand and the Thai villages in Kelantan as exotic places of otherwise locally forbidden activities. The Thai villages on the Kelantan side of the border could be reached within several hours or less from most of the towns of the Kelantan delta, though people seeking occult help came from elsewhere in Malaysia as well. At the same time, the Thai practitioners were not members of the communities in which their clients lived and therefore were less apt to be sources of gossip about who had come to see them.[7]

Cultural Performances, Spirit Mediumship, and Exorcism

While there was already criticism and opposition in earlier periods, the Kelantan plain in the late 1960s remained open to traditional activities and performances that subsequently came under increasing attack by Muslim reformers. The traditional performances included Malay *wayang kulit*, or shadow play; *mak yong*, a costume drama; and *main puteri*. All three included animistic ritual activities involving the invocation and propitiation of spirits along with Islam. In the case of the theatrical performances, apart from what took place in the stories enacted in the plays, the rituals were peripheral from the perspective of the audience who would usually not see them. With *wayang* there were rituals involving invocations and offerings before the beginning of the show intended to enhance it. In addition, there were also much more elaborate periodic performances involving trance and spirit medium ceremonies.

Main puteri spirit medium performances were also very common. The sound of the drums and gongs carried long distances across the rice fields at night. These differed in several ways from *wayang* shows. *Main puteri* was entertaining, and the séances attracted a local audience of

Figure 5.3. The Malay *wayang* or shadow play (shown here from the back of the screen) flourished throughout the Kelantan plain in the 1960s before declining as a result of Islamist objections—and perhaps competition from newly arrived television (Pasir Mas, Kelantan, 1967).

neighbors and family. But they had a serious supernatural purpose, usually that of curing through exorcism. The spirit medium group was usually hired specifically for the purpose of curing an ailing person. This involved exorcising the spirit or spirits that might be attacking her (most commonly) or him and rejuvenating the ill person's own spirit. A *main puteri* group consisted of one or more spirit mediums and three or four musicians who might also act as mediums.

ISLAM IN KELANTAN

As should be clear by now, popular religion in Kelantan in the 1960s involved a mixture of Islamic fundamentals, quasi-orthodox Islamic beliefs and practices, and more distinctly non-Islamic traditions. However phrased and explained, the mixture was not spread evenly throughout the Malay population. Here I will offer some generalizations made by

Figure 5.4. A Malay woman *mak yong* actor in costume performs at the *puja pantai* (beach propitiation) festival in Tumpat, Kelantan, in 1967.

Amin Sweeney, a British Malay studies scholar who in the 1960s did extensive research on the Malay shadow play in Kelantan for a doctoral dissertation at the University of London in 1970 that was published as a book several years later. He discussed Islam in relation to Malay attitudes and involvement with the shadow play and other popular cultural performances, including *mak yong* theater and *main puteri* spirit medium activities. He writes that

> we see that it is possible to speak of two extremes in Kelantan: at one end of the scale are those, who, although acknowledging themselves Muslims, are inclined to be lax in their observations, and are able to hold a large number of beliefs, manifestly non-Islamic, but which they feel can be compatible with their belief in Islam; who indulge in various ritual practices, which, again, are non-Islamic, and more likely to make vows to perform such a ritual on fulfillment of a wish rather than to have performed some Islamic practice such as *sembahyang hajat* (prayers for an intention). At the other end of the scale are those who eschew any belief which they believe is tainted

Figure 5.5. A well-known and talented Malay woman spirit medium dancing during a *main puteri* performance in 1967.

> with unorthodoxy. These are the two extremes. The great majority of Kelantanese, however, have views regarding belief and practice which place them at various points between the two poles.[8]

These generalizations are in accord with my own knowledge and understanding. Sweeney does not, however, attempt to estimate the relative size of the groups at each of the poles or the distribution of those in the middle—whether, for example, it formed a classic bell-shaped curve. His more specific information concerns the less orthodox end of the spectrum. This included the *dalangs* and others involved in shadow play groups he studied as well as those in *mak yong* and *main puteri* spirit medium groups, all of whom dealt in animistic rituals as a normal part of their activities. The middle range included persons who considered themselves proper Muslims but also liked the shadow play and *mak yong* theater. They were little concerned with the animistic rituals involved with these activities and had a live-and-let-live view of things or saw them as a hallowed part of Malay *adat*. They were also, in

Figure 5.6. A prominent Pasir Mas *tuan guru* (Pasir Mas, Kelantan, Malaysia 1967).

my experience, either apt to be tolerant of spirit medium practices or had recourse to them when the need arose.

At the other end of the religious spectrum were those who identified themselves with strict Muslim orthodoxy and disapproved of traditional theater and spirit medium performances. Such objections were based on several grounds. One was that the performers were apt to be immoral people since performers and spirit mediums were occasionally women who mixed with men. Another was that *wayang*, *mak yong*, and *main puteri* all involved the invocation and propitiation of spirits, something that was forbidden in orthodox Islam. Yet a further objection was that the music that was a fundamental part of *wayang* had an unacceptable effect on people even if they were not exposed to the animistic rituals.[9] Other than noting their objections, Sweeney does not say much about who the stricter Muslims were. In my experience in the Pasir Mas area, such people were apt to be those who lived in neighborhoods surrounding traditional *pondok* religious schools and looked to the *tuan guru* as an important spiritual (and later political) leader. They also included mosque personnel and other religious teachers. In the rural areas they were often villagers who had been able to make the hajj, which had sharpened their identity as pious adherents of Islam and who tended to come from the higher, landowning ranks of society.

Finally, he notes that the opposite poles of relaxed and tolerant versus strict orthodoxy were associated with contrasting political loyalties. The stricter Muslims were aligned with the Pan-Malaysian Islamic Party (PAS or PMIP), which controlled the state government and which saw part of its purpose to be advocating a purer or reformed version of Islam and therefore purging it of improprieties. Those at the opposite extreme of popular Islam disliked the PMIP and favored the United Malays National Organization, or UMNO, which controlled the national government and which has generally supported a more moderate version of Islam and sided with efforts to preserve Malay traditions that strict Muslims oppose.[10]

Muslim Politics and Religious Change

By the mid-1960s, religion in Kelantan had begun to change as efforts were made to follow a purer or reformed version of Islam, though again these developments were not equally acceptable across the Malay popular religious spectrum. This was a result of a number of developments, one involving education.

Religious study was traditionally valued but limited. Throughout the Malay world, children learned to read the Koran as a prerequisite for the initiation of boys at the age of puberty. Such learning emphasized memorization of the sounds of the words rather than cognitive understanding. Such learning therefore had the characteristics of partial literacy, noted in many places in the world.[11] The number of men who cognitively learned to read and write was small but increasing. Scripture in such circumstances is a form of magical power that can be used in the preparation of charms and amulets. In Kelantan in the late 1960s, the characteristics of partial literacy were still evident, especially in the realm of magic. However, there were also other, more advanced forms of religious education which helped set the stage for the Islamic reform and the synthesis of religion and Malay nationalism then manifest in Malay politics. Over time, the Malay community had become less isolated from and more integrated into the larger Muslim community of Southeast Asia and beyond. Colonial control made travel within and

Figure 5.7. A rural hajji, Pasir Mas, Kelantan, Malaysia, 1975.

beyond Malaya easier and safer. The participation in the pilgrimage, one of the five obligations of Islam for those who could afford it and were physically able, had increased with the arrival of steam-powered ships. Some pilgrims also studied at centers of Islamic learning, especially in India or Pakistan.

In addition, the religious reform that was taking hold at the level of popular religion during the mid- and late 1960s was strongly interrelated with the political struggles that had begun especially with national independence. The appeal of PAS was based on its commitment to Islam and to Malay rights. How politically Islamic the country or a state should be was a matter of primary importance for some Malays but secondary for others. Throughout much of the country the progress and economic success of the large Chinese community loomed over other political concerns. Kelantan, however, with its very large if poor Malay Muslim population, had more leeway to emphasize Islam than did most other states with their large non-Muslim ethnic communities.

UMNO also represented itself as a Malay nationalist but also pro-Islamic party—though one that had to also cooperate with the large non-Muslim minority ethnic groups, above all the Chinese, which had formed mainly during the colonial period. And as the party that ran the national government, UMNO had access to considerable resources. UMNO's strategy for capturing the Kelantan state government and its national parliamentary seats was therefore a matter of carrots and sticks. The sticks were the absence of development and infrastructure projects that would not appear as long as the state remained in PAS hands. The main carrots were mosques. Hence there was a flurry of mosque building. The thinking here was that, as devout and traditionally oriented Muslims, the Kelantanese voters would be most favorably impressed by grants for new mosques. Although the mosques were accepted, the Kelantanese continued to favor PAS in larger numbers, though UMNO was fairly able to contain the success of PAS in other states.

In the Pasir Mas area and throughout the Kelantan plain generally, the success of PAS was partly linked to the traditional religious schools. As schools in a strict sense, the significance of the *pondok* was declin-

Figure 5.8. A federally funded mosque dedicated by the UMNO deputy national prime minister (seated) was intended to show support by the federal government for Islam (rural Pasir Mas, 1967).

ing. But as communities or neighborhoods, they were important as centers of religious activity and strong Islamic identity. In the Pasir Mas area in the late 1960s they were one of the main bases of the political power of PAS.

Later Developments

With the first election in Malaysia following independence, PAS won control of Kelantan and remained in power for the next seventeen years. Then after a short interlude, the party returned in 1990 and has remained in power through the recent elections of 2013. The struggle has continued to be primarily fought out in symbolic and ideological terms, though also based on economic conditions. During the first period of state control, PAS presented itself as an Islamic party but did relatively little to create changes in local Malay culture or lifeways in specific terms. Perhaps the major innovation was to change the weekly holiday from Sunday to Friday, in keeping with the Muslim calendar. The PAS state government did little to change female dress practices or to attack unorthodox Malay ceremonies and performances that involved animism or Hindu elements. Such changes were perhaps avoided out of concern for offending Malays who continued to value these things and who were sensitive to being criticized as inadequate Muslims.

UMNO and the national government sought to demonstrate its commitment to Islam by providing funds to renovate or build mosques. For its part, the PAS state government was able to do little to promote development beyond building a bridge on the lower Kelantan River linking the western half of the delta and plain with the capital of Kota Bharu and the eastern half. Over two decades during which I returned every few years to Kelantan, there was little obvious development. This was a time of rapid economic growth in the west coast of the peninsula involving especially the establishment of Western electronics factories and other light industry that made the country one of the success stories in the developing world. In Kelantan there was not much in the way of manufacturing or industrialization. Many Kelantanese families relocated to federal land development schemes outside the state, and many men from villages migrated to work in the west coast urban centers.

In terms of religious change, however, traditional Malay performances declined. This may have been due in part to intensification of religious objections to the syncretic, animistic practices of spirit mediums, the shadow play, and traditional forms of theater such as *mak yong*. It may have also had something to do with the arrival of television, which offered popular alternative entertainment.

Islamization after 1990

The efforts by PAS to control Malay religion and culture—and above all to promote a stricter and what it regarded as a purer version of Islam—increased after the party returned to power in 1990, a period covered well by Gerhard Hoffstaedter in his recent book, *Modern Muslim Identities*.[12] This effort has involved several new initiatives, some substantive and some mainly symbolic.

Sharia Law

Since the colonial period or before, some parts of sharia law have been applied to Malays and other Muslims. These have, however, been limited mainly to matters of marriage, divorce, inheritance, and morality. Criminal acts, such as robbery and homicide, have been dealt with through laws and courts that apply to everyone. After 1990, PAS sought to implement the full range of sharia law, and the state government passed an enactment doing so in 1992. This included the serious category of *hudud* crimes, including robbery, theft, fornication and adultery, the consumption of alcohol or other intoxicants, and apostasy. The *hudud* crimes carry traditional penalties ranging from flogging to amputation and execution. Although the implementation of the laws was to be applied only to Muslims in Kelantan, the national Malaysian government blocked their application on constitutional grounds. The passage of the laws never having been rescinded by the Kelantan government, the question of *hudud* law has remained a major symbolic issue in the ongoing political struggle between PAS (and the larger opposition coalition of which it is a part) and UMNO and its coalition partners. The issue is kept alive because it appears to have benefits for both sides. The benefit for PAS is that it can satisfy its Islamist Malay supporters in Kelantan and elsewhere by seeking to implement full sharia law without having to actually do so. The benefit for UMNO and the governing National Front coalition is in showing that PAS is a backward and dangerous party, both to the non-Muslim half of the country and to the progressive civilized Malays (referred to as Islam Hadhari), especially those of the more developed west coast regions of the country. In other words, the *hudud* controversy (like most of the other ideological differences between the two parties) has tended to support the political status quo—PAS strength in Kelantan (and occasionally and briefly in strongly Malay regions elsewhere) and UMNO and its allies everywhere else in Malaysia.

The state government also attempted to implement other policies that did not fall within the provisions of *hudud* offenses and punishment. One of these has involved a stricter separation of unrelated men and women in public places, for example, by requiring separate lines for the two sexes at supermarket checkout counters. This has been combined with an attempt to encourage women to do better at wearing head scarves in public. The enforcement of such proper behavior and dress has been in the hands of the religious police (the JAWI). However this enforcement has been uneven—that is, more successful in concentrated urban areas than in rural ones—where in some instances the inhabitants have been unsympathetic to the religious police and unwilling to inform on rule breakers.[13]

The Purge of Malay Culture

Another initiative was a more emphatic effort to purge Malay popular culture of pre- (and non-) Islamic elements. This has focused especially on "Hinduism." One such practice that was extremely popular in the early phases of my fieldwork is the *bersanding*. This is the wedding ceremony centering on the bride and groom dressing as royalty (the bride in a non-Muslim gown, head uncovered, wearing a crown) and sitting on thrones on a dais while being approached by male and female well-wishers and then served a feast. The *bersanding* was not considered to be a legal part of the marriage—which was the Muslim *nikah*, the signing of the contract of marriage between the groom and the male guardian of the bride that took place separately—but it was the social wedding and the main ceremony. There were several possible objections to the *bersanding*, including the non-Malay dress and uncovered hair of the bride. These, however, could be overcome by implementing a proper Muslim dress code for the bride and other women involved. But the problem of the traditional Malay wedding was also simply that

Figure 5.9. Traditional Malay wedding ceremonies centering on the *bersanding* ritual remained common and popular in Pasir Mas in the 1960s and beyond, though they subsequently came under Islamist criticism because of their Indic-Hindu origin and the bride's revealing costume (Pasir Mas, Kelantan, Malaysia, 1967).

it was "Hindu," for no distinction was made between the religious and non-religious dimensions of Indic traditions.

Islam, Tourism, Development, and National Culture

As in many other places in Southeast Asia with few other economic avenues open to development and increased prosperity, tourism has a strong appeal. Kelantan is the poorest state in West Malaysia. Malays comprise 95 percent of the population, and most of the Malays in the state are small farmers and fishermen concentrated in the delta and along the coast where rice land is insufficient. As noted earlier, there has been, for various reasons, little industrial development or other opportunities for wage labor.

Tourism has been implicated in the reformist Islam-inspired political controversy over traditional Malay theatrical performances—now termed "the arts."[14] The PAS effort to purge Malay religion and culture in Kelantan of unacceptable practices after its return to power in 1990 included an assault on the main forms of Malay theater in Kelantan—spirit medium performances having already been mainly or entirely eliminated. These forms included *mak yong* (the acting out of stories on stage by costumed actors) and *wayang kulit* (the shadow play, involving puppets behind a backlit screen). There were several objections: *mak yong* involved men and women performing together on stage, both *mak yong* and the shadow play were animistic, and both were based on stories involving Indic mythology—the Ramayana and Mahaberata in the case of the shadow play. The performances could be enjoyed simply as entertainment and valued as secularized forms of Malay tradition and for nationalistic or ethnic reasons. *Mak yong* was also recognized by UNESCO as a World Heritage cultural performance, the only such recognition accorded to anything or any place in peninsular Malaysia.

Such considerations notwithstanding, the PAS government banned and sought to prevent the performance of both *mak yong* and *wayang kulit* plays. It went so far as to remove the material objects of both forms (shadow play puppets, *mak yong* costumes, and gamelan instruments) along with other items of traditional Malay culture, to gather dust on the upper floor of the state museum. This all, however, brought pushback from Malays and others who valued the performances as part of Malay culture, which was being eroded rapidly by modernization and globalization. The pushback then became politicized as UMNO and the national government made it an issue and accused PAS of needlessly destroying Malay traditions. The federal government offered to fund the building of a new cultural center in Kelantan to support the effort to revive the dying arts since this was something with tourist potential. The PAS state government agreed to lift the ban on *mak yong* and *wayang kulit*. They did so, however, with the provision that the Hindu stories be suitably Islamized, whether performed in Kelantan or elsewhere by Kelantanese theatrical troupes. The provision was met by fairly superficial face-saving changes. Most notably the names of the main characters in the Ramayana were changed from the Hindu Rama to the Muslim Rahman and similarly from Siti to Sita. One famous *dalang* (puppeteer), however, was willing to use the Muslim names only during the first few minutes of a performance before switching back to the original Hindu ones.[15]

Beyond tourism, Kelantanese performances and traditions are important in terms of the politics of national culture. British colonial rule created a plural society in Malaysia in which Muslim Malays form only a small majority of the population. Since independence the main political struggle among Malaysians has been over the rights and opportunities of the Malays and other *bumiputera* (indigenous peoples) versus those of the very large Chinese minority and the smaller Indian one. But national political issues go beyond such legal rights. One of these issues has been the use of Malay as the official national language, although this was settled long ago. Another is the role of Malay royalty as official rulers of most of the states, and of the country as a whole. Whatever negative views some Malaysians (including some Malays) have about the Malay rulers and the royal system, these issues are forbidden as topics of open political discussion. The role of Islam and the place of Malay culture in the national culture remain matters of political dispute. Non-Malays and perhaps some Malays favor multiculturalism in terms of which the national culture would be based upon the diverse cultural traditions of the Malays and the Chinese and Indians (and here the indigenous non-Malays tend to be left out). This means that for the Malays and their non-Malay allies, fundamentalist Islam presents a problem insofar as it means the destruction of Malay traditions, above all those that remain in the heavily Malay regions of the country, particularly Kelantan.

POPULAR ISLAM IN INDONESIA

We should perhaps begin the discussion here by noting that any competent treatment of popular Islam in Indonesia is a daunting task, one that is far more complicated than in the case of Malaysia. In Malaysia, Islam is almost entirely the religion of the Malays, a single ethnic community. As noted above, there are significant differences between Malays in different areas of Malaysia, but today these are very secondary in comparison to the commonalities. Indonesia is an entirely different situation. The Muslim population is ethnically and geographically diverse. Outsiders who write about Islam are fond of saying that Islam in Indonesia (or sometimes Malaysia as well) is "moderate." It shows that the conflicts, intolerance, militancy, extremism, and suppression of women's rights now widely associated in the West with Islam are disproved as inherent or general characteristics of Islam, because they are not characteristic of the country with the largest Muslim population in the world. This is certainly a valuable point to make and one that should be a more important part of Western and world opinion than it is. But while true in a general way, it can be misleading in that it overlooks the range of cultural and religious and ethnic variation, including variation in popular Indonesian Islam.

Even specialist scholars of Indonesian Islam would be hard pressed to fully document this diversity at the level of popular religion. Several groups stand out in this regard. One is the Acehnese, located at the northern tip of Sumatra, who became famous for their long anti-colonial war with the Dutch and more recently for their rebellion against the Indonesian government, their fervent Islamism, and their desire to be ruled according to sharia law. A second are the Minangkabau (or Minangkabau Malays) of the west coast of Sumatra, who are known for combining patriarchal Islam with matrilineal (tracing descent and reckoning inheritance through the female line) *adat* kinship. A third and most famous of all are the Javanese of central and west Java who are famous for traditionally recognizing and practicing two versions of Islam, including an orthodox one and a non-standard or syncretic one. Beyond such well-known groups, most accounts of Indonesian Islam as popularly practiced paint a picture that is similar to that of the Malays of Kelantan and elsewhere provided earlier. This includes a strong identity with Islam and an adherence to basic Muslim practices (the "Five Pillars"), combined, however, with various syncretic traditions, though with these increasingly challenged by reformist political Islam.

Because of its great expanse and diversity, it is to be expected that popular Islam in Indonesia will vary from one place and ethnic community to another. This variation has long been a central interest to outsiders and to Indonesians themselves. In the scholarly literature it is generally discussed both in accounts of particular Muslim groups and in more comparative studies.

Students of Islam in Indonesia have long taken special interest in those religious traditions that depart in one way or another from orthodox beliefs and practices. Although schism and deviation occur in all of the world religions, these are probably more evident in Islam because the basic principles and required beliefs and practices are simpler and clearer than in most other world religions. A proper Muslim is a person who follows the five fundamental requirements—though matters become more complicated when such a person belongs to a community that has other supernatural beliefs and practices as well. Non-standard forms of Islam are not limited to Indonesia. Depending on what is meant by non-standard, syncretist, or heterodox Islam, it could be applied to Malay religion as practiced for a long period in Kelantan and probably many other places throughout Muslim Southeast Asia as well.

The Sasak of Lombok

Let us now consider two examples of poplar Islamic religion in Indonesia that have received the greatest attention as involving an important distinction and struggle between different versions of Islam. The first of these groups are the indigenous Sasaks of the island of Lombok, where Islamic identities have long been divided between the *wetu tiga* and *waktu lima*.[16] The second are the Javanese who have (by most interpretations) been long divided between more syncretic *abangan* and more orthodox *santri* orientations. Both the Sasak and the Javanese popular religious traditions raise the question of how differing forms of Islam came into existence to begin with. Why would people who did not want to practice orthodox Islam and did not even want to be identified as regular Muslims at all convert in the first place? Here it should be noted that the original circumstances that led some of both the Sasaks and the Javanese to become nominal Muslims are somewhat obscured by the mists of time.

In the case of the Sasaks there are or were actually three different religious sectors. These include the *waktu lima* Muslims who, while keeping some syncretic traditions, identify themselves as ordinary Muslims and over the years have become more so. Then there are the *wetu tiga* who see themselves as a special sort of Muslims who uphold the traditions and admonitions of their ancestors. Then finally there are the Boda (or "original") Sasaks who follow many of the same practices as the *waktu tiga* people but never converted at all and who, when later required to convert to an officially recognized religion, did not choose Islam but rather (as discussed earlier) Buddhism.

The Sasaks form the indigenous population of the island of Lombok, which is located just east of Bali. As is common in Indonesia, there are both mythical or legendary and modern historical efforts to explain conversion. The former, as recorded on palm leaf manuscripts, tend to involve cultural heroes referred to as Muslim saints (*wali*) who arrived and convinced people to convert to Islam through the force of their personalities and the performance of miracles. The legendary hero in this instance was the son of a Muslim Javanese ruler who was sent with an expedition to convert the people of Lombok. The modern accounts indicate that the initial conversion began in the first half of the sixteenth century and seek to understand subsequent developments. According to the Swedish Lombok specialist Sven Cederroth, the early converts were highly syncretic Muslims who retained much of their indigenous religion as well as that of the Hindu-Buddhist traditions to which they had long been exposed as a part of the last great pre-Muslim Javanese empire and civilization of Majapahit. Here there is also a legend that the two oldest Sasak villages on Lombok were founded by a prince of Majapahit who, for some reason, fled from Java to Lombok (as other Majapahit refugees had to Bali).[17]

The more complicated issue is how the Sasaks became divided into two separate, named groups of Muslims, in addition to the unconverted Boda. There is to begin with the old idea that the names *wetu tiga* (or *waktu tiga*) and *waktu lima* derive from differing practices. Both names are numerical—specifically, *wetu tiga* means "three times," while *waktu lima* means "five times." This was interpreted to mean that the syncretist *wetu tiga* prayed only three times a day while the more orthodox *waktu lima* prayed the required five times. This possibility seems to remain unconfirmed insofar as the number three has other meanings in *wetu telu* (or *wetu tiga*) tradition, but beyond that the question remains of how the schism developed. Here also there had been an older and broader context of social and religious turmoil. Sasak society was divided into commoners and nobles and had a long history of conflict over the rights and obligations of the two sectors. There were also ethnic animosities between the Sasaks and the Balinese and a long history of messianic movements on the island.

Whatever the name signified, until the end of the nineteenth century the *waktu tiga* sect dominated most of Lombok. The situation began to change after the Dutch, using violent force, conquered and took control of the island, which had been ruled for the previous two centuries by Balinese kings. Both the Dutch and the Balinese had been harsh overlords. As a result, Islam gained appeal as a contrasting identity to both the Hindu Balinese and the Christian Dutch. During the first part of the twentieth century, *waktu lima* orthodoxy spread to most of the Sasak communities in the middle of the island while the mountainous north and south remained almost entirely *wetu tiga*. Against expectations, *wetu tiga* traditions continued to flourish, in part at least because of the physical separation of the two sects.

The situation changed again as *waktu lima* Sasaks began to move into the highlands and live in much closer proximity to *wetu telu* villages. Once there they began to criticize what they regarded as the improper syncretist practices of the *wetu telu* and pushed the acceptance of their view of proper Islam. The main change came in the wake of the Suharto coup and takeover in 1965 and the massive purge of communists and others accused of communism. Here as elsewhere the New Order regime made a much greater effort to force *agama*-ization—compliance with the constitutional requirement that all Indonesians be adherents of a monotheistic religion. It also ceased to recognize any form of Islam except what it regarded as orthodoxy. And here also non-adherence to an approved religion was linked to atheism, which in turn was associated with communism. This meant further that religious non-conformity posed a mortal risk in areas where people, for whatever exact motive, were being executed by the military, police, or vigilante mobs.

The development of Islam on Lombok in New Order Indonesia therefore involved the three religious sectors of Sasaks in different ways. Here as in many other regions of Indonesia at this time religious identities became further politicized. The *waktu lima* already regarded themselves as devout, proper, and orthodox Muslims. They not surprisingly saw *agama*-ization as an opportunity to strengthen their effort to force the *wetu telu* people along with the remaining pagan Boda to abandon their older traditions and accept orthodoxy. As word of murders spread, the *wetu telu* living in some villages felt threatened, withdrew from contact with *wetu lima* people, and remained as much as possible at home for the duration of the turbulence. When government officials held meetings outlining the choices of approved religions facing the *wetu telu* for required *agama*-ization, many, including some five hundred in one village, initially chose Buddhism and were officially recorded as doing so. This, however, caused great consternation among some important Muslim government officials and led to further meetings in which the neo-Buddhists were harangued about their decision. As a result, most of the *wetu telu* who had chosen Buddhism recanted and officially became orthodox Muslims, though how orthodox their actual religious beliefs and practices became is a different matter. As noted earlier, some or all of the Boda, who had also chosen to become Buddhists, continued to adhere to this choice rather than switch to Islam.[18]

The *Abangan* of Java

The *abangan* Muslims of Java are the best known and by far the most important of the Indonesian people who identified themselves as adhering to a non-standard form of Islam. Unlike the *wetu telu* Muslims of Lombok, the *abangan* were not a remote people living on a small and somewhat remote island. By the 1950s, when their numbers were probably at their peak, *abangan* or Kejawan (Javanist) Muslims included two-thirds of all Javanese, who currently number about ninety million and form the largest ethnic population of Indonesia.

Dutch colonial scholars had noted the nature of the *abangan* religion as a non-orthodox form of Islam. But it became a major topic of concern in the 1950s as a result of the research and publications of Robert Jay, Hildred Geertz, and above all Clifford Geertz, especially as he dealt with it in his well-known book *The Religion of Java*. These and several other young scholars were part of a research team in which each worked on a different topic but also collaborated. They were mainly anthropologists but were doing something that was relatively new in anthropology, which was to go beyond the earlier focus on "primitive" cultures and instead focus on complex, civilized societies associated with towns rather than only villages. This also meant that they found much religious complexity rather than the typically more uniform religious beliefs and practices of tribal societies. Statements of the sort that could be made about the culturally more uniform Nuer or the Trobriand Islanders—that they believed this or practiced that—were less appropriate and more in need of qualification.

Geertz's topic in the Modjokuto (the fictitious name of the town of Pare in the interior of central Java where the study was done) Project was religion. He organized *The Religion of Java* on the basis of the complexity of Javanese religion and interpreted it (though not very explicitly) via Max Weber's sociological approach to religion, which emphasizes that different classes, economic groups, or status groups have different religious orientations. The basic mode of interpretation was ideal-typical analysis that stressed commonalities rather than detailed variation. In accord with this approach he found three main variants in Javanese religion, each linked to three different socioeconomic groups. By the 1950s religion in Java had become very politicized, with the different variants and subvariants having their own national organizations or political parties.[19]

There was first the peasantry that surrounded the town. Their religious orientation was syncretist Islam, mainly animism, magic, and ritual feasts. Like the *wetu telu* of Lombok they considered themselves to be Muslims, but Muslims of a special sort, that is, Javanese Muslims or *abangan*. Their religion in his view was a non-orthodox form of Islam both in terms of content and in terms of identity. As peasants, *abangan* concerns focused on making the crops grow and other practicalities of rural life. Monotheism, while perhaps acknowledged in the abstract took second place to animism. *Abangan* beliefs centered on spirits, just as ritual activities deemphasized or omitted the requirements of Islam and ritual and included curing, sorcery, and magic.[20]

The second variant was associated with the market, that is, the traders and shopkeepers of the town. This was orthodox Islam whose adherents were known as *santri* or "students." The main religious institutions of the *santri* were the prayer house, mosque, and school, and the main practices were the Five Pillars of the faith plus household feasts that featured Islamic prayers and chanting, held especially during Muslim holidays, though also for other specific purposes including healing and the life crises. While the *santri*, as orthodox Muslims, would have much in common with orthodox Muslims elsewhere, it was more complicated than this. For one thing, as a cultural relativist as well as a follower of Weber, Geertz was inclined to stress that the *santri* were also Javanese. And, for another, he also stressed that there were two subvariants of the *santri*. These were the old-fashioned traditionalists on the one hand, and the reformists or modernists on the other. Though they emphasized a different identity, the old-fashioned *santri* shared a lot of syncretic beliefs and practices in animism and magic with the *abangan*, whereas the modernists wanted to purge Islam of syncretism and to incorporate progress, modern knowledge, and education in it.[21]

The third variant of Javanese religion was associated with the government elite and bureaucrats and therefore also with the traditional aristocracy—the Dutch, like other colonial governments, having followed the practice of incorporating the traditional elite into the apparatus of the state. This was the *prijaji* variant whose adherents, like the *abangan* and the old-fashioned *santri*, were religious syncretists, though in a somewhat different way. *Prijaji* syncretism was above all based on "Hindu-Buddhism" more than indigenous animism. But here matters become somewhat vague, for Geertz does not claim that the *prijaji* openly or surreptitiously worshipped the Buddha or any of the Hindu divinities once present in Java. He means rather that their religious values derive from Hindu-Buddhism. And here he also tends to mix broader social and cultural (and especially aesthetic) values and interests with more purely religious ones—for example, he constructs an elaborate model of the elite Javanese personality and spends a lot of time on the importance of the shadow play and other forms of theater and art as a focus of *prijaji* interest and a paradigm of religious-cultural values. From the perspective of religion in a more narrow sense, the central *prijaji* activity was the practice of mysticism, especially the cultivation of inner strength and quietness that will enable a person to overcome external adversity through meditation.[22]

Geertz's account made the variations in Javanese religion widely known and seem very important. Most or all scholars of Java and religion in Indonesia have probably accepted some form of the general differences among the popular syncretist religious traditions of some Javanese and those of others, specifically between more and less orthodox adherents of Islam—differences that the Javanese themselves recognize and name. But there are questions as well as criticism and rejection of some parts of his interpretation.

To begin with, there is the question of why many Javanese converted to Islam in name only or with only minimal acceptance of even the most basic or core provisions. And why were the Javanese different from the many other Indonesian peoples for whom the process of popular conversion was more complete, even if not entirely so in that much was not uncommonly retained of pre-Islamic religious beliefs and practices? Geertz makes comparisons, but these mainly refer to the Middle Eastern heartland (or in a later book—*Islam Observed*—between Java and Morocco) rather than to different places in Indonesia.

A further objection was that he overemphasized the difference between Islam in Indonesia and elsewhere in the lands of Islam. Throughout the Muslim world, popular religion included spirit beliefs, magic, mystical practices, and local saint worship, as well as more fully non-standard sects. A related counter-claim was that Javanese mysticism derived from Muslim Sufism rather than Hindu-Buddhism on which he placed so much importance. This is significant in that little else is offered in support of the general assertions of the centrality of Hindu-Buddhism beyond the popularity of the Hindu epics (the Ramayana and the Mahaberata) in Javanese theater. There appear to be no assertions about non-*santri* Javanese worshipping Hindu (or Buddha-ized Hindu) divinities as done by Thai Buddhists, for example. Here there is also the question of whether the non-orthodox Javanese were simply keeping a lot of non-standard beliefs and practices in addition to those of textual Islam, as did various other Indonesian peoples, or whether they were also skipping or skimping on the orthodox requirements as well.[23]

A somewhat different claim—and one that is now probably generally accepted—is that Geertz wrongly emphasized the existence of three variants of Javanese religion when there were really only two. These included more orthodox-oriented *santri* Muslims and the less or non-orthodox Javanist or *abangan* Muslims—the *prijaji* being relegated to a class or status group and not a distinct, culturally identified or emic form of religion. Today the *prijaji* are often not mentioned in discussions of Javanese popular religion.[24]

The Collapse of Non-standard Forms of Islam

The most important issue raised concerning Islam in Indonesia in recent years has been that recognized, syncretic, or "non-standard" traditions have collapsed or are in the process of doing so. The anthropologist and religious specialist Robert Hefner makes the case that Indonesian Muslims have either accepted adherence to orthodox Islam or, to a much lesser extent, converted to another governmentally approved religion.[25] Hefner asserts that similar changes are also taking place in the popular practice of other world religions in Indonesia (but provides no examples, although Balinese Hinduism would seem to fit), though what is occurring in Islam is especially important by virtue of the size and widespread nature of Muslim populations. His particular concern is with what he calls the collapse of the *abangan* religion of Java. But he also argues that there are or have been many other versions of non-standard Islam in Indonesia and mentions the Gumai of South Sumatra, the Bugis and Makassar peoples of South Sulawesi, and the Sasak of Lombok as examples.

Here there may be a need for further clarity in the meaning of "non-standard Islam." Among Indonesians, such notions are, as noted, apt to be politicized. What seems to matter most is what the people in question—and their local critics—think, say, and do in the way of making and applying such distinctions and how they interpret and label identities. In his account of the Sasak schism, the Swedish anthropologist Sven Cederroth describes the severe and sometimes violent history of conflict between the syncretist *wetu tiga* and orthodox *waktu lima*.[26] But he also asserts that the struggle has involved various things, including a lot of symbolism, and that the underlying popular religious worldview of the two groups is not all that different, at least not as different as the extent of the hostility between them would suggest.

Here again we see the necessity of keeping in mind the distinction between religious content and religious identity. Are non-standard traditions of Islam to be considered only those that the adherents and others actually identify and name as non-standard, as is true in the case of the *abangan* Javanese and the *wetu tiga* Muslim Sasaks of Lombok? Or do people who conform to most of the textual requirements of Islam and label themselves as orthodox Muslims while also adhering to many syncretist non-Muslim religious beliefs and practices also follow non-standard Islam? For example, Hefner identifies the popular religion of the Bugis and Makassar of Sulawesi as including some non-standard Muslims and cites the French anthropologist Christian Pelras as a source of this inference. Pelras, in his book on the Bugis, does not use "non-standard Islam" or any equivalent phrase to describe Bugis religion. He does consider Bugis religious beliefs and practices remarkable, in that the Bugis see themselves as being very strong Muslims and have such a reputation among other Indonesians. He also sees their religious beliefs and practices as including a lot of syncretism—pre-Islamic animistic traditions, including those of transvestite spirit mediums (*bisu*) and elaborate spirit shrines.[27] But including the Bugis in the category of non-standard Islam would seem to set the non-standard bar fairly low. The traditional practices of many—perhaps most—other Indonesian Muslim peoples could be included as non-standard Islam as well. So, for example, could the Malays of Kelantan in the 1960s and 1970s, as described earlier. This does not negate the basic point that popular non-Islamic syncretism is in decline or has collapsed throughout modern Indonesia.

Why then are non-standard forms of Islam (at least as a matter of religious identity) gone or in a state of collapse? To begin with, the collapse appears to be recent. In his book *Varieties of Javanese Religion* (published in 1999 and based on fieldwork evidently done in the early 1990s), the British anthropologist Andrew Beatty does not discuss such a collapse, at least in the stark terms used by Hefner, which he likely would have noted if it had been apparent at the time.[28] His treatment of *santri* and *abangan* in rural Java suggests that at that time the two variants of Islam were still enduring traditions. In the case of the *wetu telu*, observers have noted a long decline (greatly accelerated after the onset of the Suharto rule), although there may have been a revival following the collapse of the New Order regime.

The decline of religious Javanism has roots in earlier developments, including the increasing politicization of religion that was in full swing in the middle of the twentieth century. In addition, there was the constitutional (Pancasila) policy requirement that all Indonesians be adherents of a monotheistic religion (an *agama*). As applied, the indigenous religious traditions of tribal peoples (who were regarded as backward and isolated peoples in general need of development and modernization) were seen as not making the grade and were defined as "not yet having a religion"—unless or until the peoples involved succeeded in convincing the religious authorities they were already following a version of an approved *agama* (in apparently all instances Hinduism) and were willing to further develop it along textually oriented orthodox lines. Examples of non-approved religious beliefs and practices also included the many and varied Javanese mystical cults.[29]

Following the takeover of Suharto and the onset of the New Order in the late 1960s, efforts to increase the religious provisions of the

Pancasila increased. Religious loyalties and identities were sharpened and became even more politicized, especially as a result of the imposition of military rule and the ensuing mob violence and the annihilation of large numbers of communists, suspected communists, and others. In some places at least, not having an approved religious identity came to have or to seem to have dire consequences. People with an ambiguous or non-approved religious status (if they were aware of it) were apt to feel threatened. Communism was equated with atheism, and atheism was outside the boundary of the government-sanctioned religions. However this situation was viewed by non-orthodox Muslims as well as adherents of indigenous religious traditions, it was a time of extensive and turbulent conversion.

Some Indonesians chose to become Hindus, some Buddhist, and some two million *abangan* Javanese converted to Christianity, presumably to avoid having to accept a stricter form of Islam. On the face of it these developments would seem to have further increased religious diversity and pluralism (meaning legitimate and accepted diversity). But they were also and more importantly a step in the direction of a more self-conscious, nationalized, and politicized popular Islamism, and away from the traditional acceptability of syncretist Javanist Islam as a nationalistic alternative.

Eventually the conflict, bloodshed, and efforts to coerce conversion of the early Suharto years subsided. The effect of the religious policies of the New Order regime was to promote or enforce stricter popular adherence of a more orthodox or textual version of all of the officially accepted *agama* religions, though most importantly Islam. Although it might have been expected to bring a return to liberal religious pluralism, the end of Suharto's rule—initially at least—brought a further sharpening of popular Islamic identity. This was associated with widespread violent conflict between Muslim and generally more vulnerable Christian communities involving mob killing and the burning of houses, churches, and mosques. In the Moluccan islands where the worst violence occurred, more than ten thousand people died.[30] On Java several hundred people were lynched by mobs as witches.[31]

While such conflict eventually subsided, other long-term developments served to diminish religious syncretism and the legitimacy of Kejawan (Javanese) nationalism. Practices that were not in accord with Islam but were kept came to be put into a separate category of *adat*. In very general terms, *abanganism* simply did not replicate itself. Older generations of *abangan* practitioners were replaced by new ones who have been taught basic textual Islam by neighborhood Koranic teachers and in government schools. Mass media brought more awareness of Islam and Islamism elsewhere in Indonesia and the world, and more communication and the Internet increased contact with other Muslims.

Islam and the Decline of Syncretic Traditions in Malaysia and Indonesia

In both of the modern countries of Malaysia and Indonesia, the most important issues in studies of Islam have been the existence of popular religious traditions that either depart from or include much more than standard, orthodox, or textually specified Muslim beliefs and practices—the so-called Five Pillars. In Malaysia the departures have often been approached in the language of colonial scholarship—that is, in terms of generalizations about Malay beliefs and practices as a whole or "on average," or of what "the real Malay" believed and did. In more recent decades and in response to changing political and other developments, much more attention has been paid to variations between urban and rural or regional sectors of Malay society. In the distinctive Malay state of Kelantan, which is historically rich in both Islamic and non-Islamic popular religious traditions, the most sophisticated interpretations are those that note a range of individual variation between poles of Islam and non-Islam—and how locations in this range relate to other social and political differences. In Indonesia the focus has also been on the synthesis of Islamic and indigenous and pre-Islamic traditions in popular religion, especially on ethnic instances in which greater and lesser commitments to orthodox Islam and syncretist Islam are not only present but emically labeled as such. Here the clearest and best-known instances of culturally identified dual religions have involved the Sasaks of Lombok and the vastly larger population of Java.

In Malaysia and Indonesia there are many differences in the modern context of popular Islam and religion in general. But in both countries, increasing Islamization has involved the tendency to see the world in terms of global competition and struggle between Muslims and non-Muslims, above all the Christian (or secular) West, as endless international news stories report. But locally—and of more concern here—it has also involved an effort to purify Islamic belief and practice and to purge these of syncretist or non-Muslim traditions that have been traditionally present throughout much of Southeast Asian popular religion. In Kelantan this has brought a political struggle over whether to preserve or forbid any of the syncretic Malay traditions, even ones from which the traditional animistic and magical parts have been eliminated. In Indonesia "non-standard" forms of Islam are reported to be in a state of decline or collapse. In both countries there has been a common trend in increasing Islamization through the efforts of government, political parties, religious officials, and courts and as influenced by developments in Islam elsewhere in the world brought by the modern mass media and the Internet.

6

CONVERSION AND POPULAR CHRISTIANITY

The most important and widespread form of recent religious change in Southeast Asia has been the spread of the world religions into regions and among peoples where they had not formerly existed. While this expansion has involved Buddhism, Islam, and Hinduism, Christianity probably accounts for the bulk of the change. From a larger perspective, what is occurring in Southeast Asia is part of a global shift in Christianity: its expansion in the developing world coupled with its decline in its once core area of Western Europe. The global spread of Christianity is hardly new of course, having begun in a major way when Europeans first crossed the Atlantic Ocean and Christianized the New World, and it continued elsewhere in relation to subsequent European expansion. Christianity arrived for certain in Southeast Asia early in the sixteenth century. It was introduced first in the Philippines and to a much more limited extent by the Portuguese in the Malay Peninsula and in present-day eastern Indonesia and East Timor, followed by French Jesuits in Vietnam, and eventually further developed by the British and Americans.

THE HISTORY OF CHRISTIAN CONVERSION IN SOUTHEAST ASIA

The expansion of Christianity in Southeast Asia entered a new phase in the nineteenth century, one that has continued into the present. Some of this has involved people converting from one of the other world religions. Much of it, however, has occurred on the ethnic margins of Southeast Asia, among peoples who formerly adhered only to their own local traditions of belief and practice. In continental Southeast Asia, such peoples tend to live in the mountainous areas of Thailand (where they are referred to as "hill tribes"), Cambodia, Laos, Vietnam (where they are called ethnic minorities), Burma/Myanmar, and peninsular Malaysia among the Orang Asli.[1] The Hmong are the best known to Westerners, but there are Yao, Akha, and Karen as well as many others. In the islands of Southeast Asia, conversion has been a somewhat more complex matter than on the continent in terms of who has converted to what and why. But again the most extensive recent Christianization has also been among the indigenous minority peoples who dwell in the often mountainous interior regions of islands outside Java and Bali. These include the Toraja peoples of Sulawesi, the various Dayak groups of Borneo, and the Batak (this name is going or has gone out of use) peoples of Sumatra, to again name only a few of a great many such groups.

Why has this pattern of conversion occurred? One answer to such a question would be that it reflects the larger expansion of Western civilization and political, military, and economic power, the efforts to contest or inhibit these by socialist and more recently Islamist movements in some regions notwithstanding. Another such answer might be that recently converted peoples of Southeast Asia have been overtaken by the outside world, modernity, and its universalistic religions, especially Christianity.

A more specific answer would be that the spread of Christianity in Southeast Asia was mainly based on missionization, which in turn had much to do with colonialism.[2] Though early missionization sometimes came before it (as in Vietnam), colonial rule did many things that fostered the introduction and spread of Christianity. It involved pacification and the creation of a structure of European government that made countries safer and easier for missionary penetration. It also exposed the native peoples to the power and wealth of white Christian peoples and suggested to some that these were linked to religion. In some instances at least colonial authorities saw Christianity as a useful way of promoting civilization, development, and progress, in part as an expression of their own religious views. Missionaries could be a further extension of colonial authority and provide more eyes and ears where colonial officials were either not there at all or thin on the ground.

Yet the imposition of European colonial rule was a varied rather than a uniform development. It did not simply favor the introduction and spread of Christianity at all times and places. Outside of the Philippines and perhaps a few Christian Portuguese enclaves, early colonialism was mercantilist and aimed at making profits and creating commercial empires rather than spreading Christianity or administering large territories. The early introduction of Christianity in Vietnam by Jesuit missionaries came long before the beginning of French colonial rule. The broader development of Christian missionization was mainly linked to the later, more territorially oriented phase of colonial rule that developed in the middle and later part of the nineteenth century. Missionaries were encouraged and aided in some places but not everywhere or in all circumstances. Colonial governments often followed the practice of directing the efforts of missionaries to particular places, so that native people in some instances became Baptists and in others Lutherans, Methodists, Catholics, or Seventh-Day Adventists—the theological differences between the various denominations being regarded as secondary considerations. Such direction was given both to avoid replication of effort and also to avoid political problems—for example, those likely to arise where Christian missions were established in or near Muslim areas. And in some places at least, while the foundations of Christianization were created under colonial rule, the greatest expansion in conversion has been in the post-colonial period. And while Thailand was never colonized (though it was certainly influenced), the conversion of its indigenous ethnic minorities has been as extensive (or more so) as anywhere else in the mainland.

THE STUDY OF CONVERSION

Religious conversion refers to the deliberate, sometimes formal, acceptance of a new religious tradition, one that usually exists as an organized entity and has a named identity. In conventional Western thought conversion is commonly seen as an individual decision based on the belief that the new religion is truer, more suitable, or more satisfying than the previous one (if there was one). And Westerners take for granted that they (at least as adults) can similarly abandon a religion anytime they choose. While social scientists recognize distinctly personal motives for conversion, they are usually more inclined to emphasize collective or more general reasons. These can include a range of historical, political, economic, or ecological considerations, some of which will be brought out in the examples to be discussed below. Conversions may occur at the individual level (and this can be very important in the case of an influential leader who begins a more general process), but they often involve households, communities, or parts of communities.

Closely related is the matter of free choice. Westerners also tend to see—at least today—decisions about conversion as being up to the individual, with no restrictions or interference from government or religious bodies. The largest world religions (Buddhism, Christianity, Islam, and Hinduism) are almost by definition "universalistic," both open and welcoming to converts. They are in Max Weber's phrase "religions of ethical prophecy," although within these major types there may be differences. While usually guaranteeing "freedom of religion" in their national constitutions, governments tend to limit freedom of religious choice in various ways. In a few countries of Southeast Asia conversion is a matter of free choice while in others it is subject to legal or political restrictions. A few countries have religious pluralism that approximates modern secularism or Western notions and practices of religious liberty, but others do not. The varied instances of the socialist or neosocialist countries and of Malaysia and Indonesia have already been noted.

Conversion to Christianity has been studied and written about by missionaries, historians, and anthropologists, among others. For their part, anthropologists tend to concentrate on living peoples and their immediate past and deal with earlier history mainly to the extent that it is necessary to do so as background. The anthropological study of conversion and its consequences in Southeast Asia (as elsewhere) is a fairly recent topic of interest. Previously anthropologists had tended to be more concerned with the religious traditions of unconverted (or generally less changed) groups. This preference was based partly on the assumption that it was best to study indigenous religious beliefs and practices before they were wiped out or fundamentally altered by Christianization or conversion to another world religion, or by modernization generally. Formerly anthropologists tended to follow missionaries and colonial administrators in referring to the non-converted or traditionalists as "pagan" (used as an adjective as well as a noun). Like *primitive*, this term has now been dropped, usually in favor of *animist* or *animism*. But while perhaps an improvement on *pagan*, *animism* can be misleading insofar as it suggests that animistic beliefs are all there were to pre-Christian religion, or that Christian converts no longer believe in spirits, neither of which is the case. Anthropologists today try to be as accurate as possible in referring to indigenous terms for supernaturally based beliefs and practices and therefore often stress that there was no single word for "religion" or supernaturally based beliefs and practices because they were lumped together with other customs and traditions.

In the recent period there has not been much choice. Finding a people to study who have not yet become Christian or converted to another world religion has become much more difficult than it was several decades or more ago. Today in Southeast Asia the number of non-converted peoples has diminished enormously, at least outside of the socialist or post-socialist countries that have restricted missionary activities and prevented or discouraged conversion. But for whatever reason religious conversion and its consequences have become a major interest, and there are now high-quality studies for both continental and island Southeast Asia.

The anthropological study of conversion in Southeast Asia has mainly focused on conversion to Christianity by peoples who had previously had their own culturally specific religious traditions. But accounts tend to vary according to the point at which the research was done in relation to when conversion occurred. Some studies have concerned people who have become Christian in the past, often several or more generations previously, perhaps even in the nineteenth century or at least under colonial rule when quite different conditions prevailed. Such accounts are historical in nature, based on oral tradition, written records, the published stories of missionaries, or the narratives of still-living informants, or some combination of these. While there have been some excellent, detailed studies along this line, the crucial matters of why people converted and what happened as a result seem liable to shifting interpretation. Committed Christians may be inclined to look back on conversion in more spiritual terms of revelation or salvation than in economic or political ones. Similarly, the consequences of conversion (such as the fission of villages between converts and non-converts, which was common in Borneo, at least) may be glossed over.

There have also been studies based on field research done while the events of conversion were ongoing or recent. In Southeast Asia a number of such studies have concerned the Hmong, Karen, and other peoples of the northern mainland as well as ones in Borneo and elsewhere in the island region. Such studies seem clearer and fuller about the motives, circumstances, and consequences of conversion than do the more historically oriented or retrospective ones.[3]

THE REASONS FOR CONVERSION

When social scientists study and interpret conversion, they attempt to answer various questions. These include why people are led to change their religion and the consequences of doing so. The first question concerns both the general circumstances in which conversion occurs as well as the more specific reasons or motives involved. Anthropologists and others have studied and discussed a range of motives that extend from the mythical to the practical. In northern continental Southeast Asia, for example, mythical explanations are based on reported stories involving mysterious books. These foretell the arrival of strangers from far away bringing magical books that will enable oppressed tribal peoples to overcome their inferiority to dominant lowland groups. The stories are seen as anticipating the appearance of Western missionaries, though which came first is hard to know.

Practical explanations hold that people who convert are led to do so in part at least because accepting a new religion is seen as a way of improving the circumstances of their lives. Here there have been two very different (though not necessarily mutually exclusive) sorts of interpretations. The first focuses on the role of incentives provided by missionaries and other advocates of conversion that encourage people to become Christians. The popular pejorative term sometimes used for people who have been said to convert to Christianity because of such economic incentives is "rice Christian." In the most literal use of the phrase it refers to hungry people who convert in order to obtain rice and other food. Both Western missionaries and critics or opponents of Christianity have used this term as a derogatory label for what is deemed to be inauthentic or non-spiritually based conversion. Some anthropologists have also used the phrase "rice bowl" conversions for those appearing to be based on practical calculation and getting ahead.

For their part, anthropologists and other scholars who have studied conversion in Southeast Asia have sometimes favored a different sort of economic motive. Put simply, this interpretation holds that one of the attractions of Christianity over the old indigenous religion is that it is less costly in time and resources than indigenous practices. Discussions of this sort of consideration can be found in accounts of conversion in both Borneo and northern mainland Southeast Asia, and probably elsewhere as well. And while such an economic explanation might seem to be offensive from the perspective of advocates of Christianity, practical appeals appear to have been popular with both missionaries and Christian converts as well as anthropologists.[4]

Here there are numerous examples. The Japanese anthropologist Hayami Yoko reports that when she asked Karen Christians in Thailand why they had converted, they told her almost invariably that they did so because they couldn't afford to keep feeding the spirits—though she goes on to say that such considerations couldn't be all that was involved because the more recent upsurge in conversion had taken place in a period of economic improvement. In central Borneo, according to the American anthropologist Herbert Whittier, partly at the missionaries' urging the Dayaks also came to see Christianity as much less costly than the old religion, which had a great many time-consuming omens, bothersome taboos, and expensive sacrifices.[5] In the old *adat* religion, if a taboo had been broken an animal would have to be sacrificed, while in Christianity a sin could be forgiven through prayer and without other costs. In her more detailed account of the Christianization of the Akha of northern Thailand, Cornelia Kammerer, another American anthropologist, explains conversion as something like ritual bankruptcy without the stigma, an acceptable way out of the cost of expensive ceremonies in difficult economic circumstances. She reports that during her first period of fieldwork in the 1980s there was little interest in Christianity and few if any conversions. But when she returned later, conversion was in full swing. The difference, she thinks, was that the Akha had become poorer because the Thai government had imposed more stringent restrictions on their traditional practice of migratory shifting cultivation.[6] Robert Cooper similarly notes that the six Hmong families who had converted in the village he studied in Thailand were the poorest.[7] And Nicholas Tapp reports that Hmong converts he knew were primarily motivated by the desire to achieve some economic advantage.[8]

Over time as Christian missions were established and developed they offered further attractions that encouraged further conversion—schools, clinics and hospitals, influence with government authorities, and access to development agencies. The importance of the role of missions in providing medical services and education may have been greater in the past than it has been in the recent period. Previously, Christian mission schools and hospitals were all that existed in some regions. This is no longer the case in many places, but it probably continues to be so in some. In Borneo, some Dayaks who had been politically or economically successful told me their achievements were due to mission schools. And in West Kalimantan, Baptists ran (at least at the time I was there) the reputedly best hospital in the province. There is a strong mission presence in some areas such as northern Thailand, but here and throughout many regions, government hospitals, clinics, and especially schools are now also widespread. Conversion often also had an important ethnic dimension. It enabled people to belong to a world religion while retaining their own ethnic identity. There is also the view that Christians are progressive while people who have not converted are backward.

In sum, the motives and circumstances that led to the conversion to Christianity have been multiple. But for whatever reason or reasons people choose to convert, there is also the question of what kind of Christian to become. In many cases this was a simple matter of which missionaries got there first—Methodists on one river, Seventh-Day Adventists on another, Catholics on yet another, and so on—though over time alternative choices became available.[9] Some church missions were not dependent on colonial control by their own national government. While the U.S. colonial presence in Southeast Asia was limited to the

Philippines (and then only after 1898), American Baptists were among the most active and dynamic missionaries in many places from the early nineteenth century onward.

CONVERSION IN BORNEO

In what follows we shall consider conversion in three instances. We begin with Borneo, where there have been significant differences in the post-colonial period between developments among Dayak peoples in the Malaysian and Indonesian sections of this very large island. From there we will shift to the north in mainland Southeast Asia and consider specifically the Karen of both Thailand and Burma/Myanmar. And finally we shall note the latest development in the Christianization of Southeast Asian peoples. This is what has occurred in the wake of the wars in Vietnam, Laos, and Cambodia among refugees that have resettled in the United States and in other Western countries. Much of the conversion that has occurred has taken place after the refugees were resettled, but it began in some instances before they left Southeast Asia.

In Borneo, as elsewhere in Southeast Asia, colonialism helped pave the way for missionization and conversion. The imposition of colonial rule made missionizing easier and safer. Missionaries could travel in the interior and establish mission stations under the auspices of the government authority, such as it was throughout the interior. In British Sarawak, forts were established at river junctions as administrative centers and as a means of monitoring native movement. Towns and markets were developed and churches were built whence Christianity could be spread, though some more intrepid missionaries went far beyond these.

The establishment of colonial rule supported conversion in less obvious ways as well. One of these involved the elimination of headhunting and the decline of the cult of skulls. Like conversion, the circumstances and motives of headhunting were not singular. It was a military tactic used by stronger groups to frighten weaker ones—used to great effect by the Iban, today the largest, most widespread, and most politically powerful Dayak group in Sarawak. It was the way young men gained manhood and authority and attracted female attention and adoration. It was based on feuding and revenge. But headhunting was fundamentally an important religious activity, surrounded by ritual in all phases and having important mystical purposes, including the promotion of the general spiritual well-being of the village and the enhancement of agricultural fertility, especially of the rice crop. New skulls (*antu pala* or "ghost head" in Iban) represented or contained spirits and were ceremonially welcomed into a longhouse and displayed in an honorable high place. Eventually their spiritual potency would diminish, however, and they would need to be supplemented by fresh heads.[10]

The eventual elimination of headhunting, welcome as it probably was by weaker and more vulnerable native groups, left a gap. It did not, however, bring an automatic end to the cult of skulls. While the basic and widespread idea was that over time old heads needed to be supplemented by new ones, traditionally acquired through headhunting, an adaptation in thinking seems to have occurred—perhaps as a result of suggestion by colonial authorities looking for ways to promote pacification. This was that new skulls in a village did not have to be from newly killed victims, but simply new to the village that acquired them. An exchange in "used" skulls developed that took several forms. The villagers in one Bidayuh Dayak village told me that they had previously been part of an alliance group of villages that passed existing skulls among its member communities. Old skulls were also simply purchased. This I inadvertently learned when I was making inquiries about some rare carved half skulls that I had found out about in another Bidayuh village and was told they had been bought in Indonesian Borneo.[11] In some areas of Sarawak, colonial officials themselves became involved in the exchange of skulls as a means of diminishing the temptation to take new heads. Old skulls were collected and kept at the forts and loaned out like library books for use in pagan ceremonies and then returned.

However, because of these various adaptations that prolonged the viability of the cult of skulls, the eventual elimination of headhunting was not itself decisive. But it did serve to weaken one of the pillars of the traditional religion, as did other vulnerabilities to be discussed below.

East Kalimantan

The conversion to Christianity in the deep interior of Borneo began in some areas before World War II but gathered momentum thereafter. One somewhat surprising early center of conversion developed in the

Figure 6.1. Religious architectural syncretism: the entrance door to Santo Stefanus Catholic Church (Datahbilang, East Kalimantan, Indonesian Borneo, 1996) is decorated with painted traditional Kenyah-Kayan dragons.

Apo Kayan highlands of eastern Borneo, which during colonial rule was Dutch territory and after independence became part of Indonesian Kalimantan. The Apo Kayan is a very remote area, traditionally accessible from the coast only by foot and sturdy longboats on white-water rivers and requiring many days of travel to get into or out of. In addition to a small number of Punan hunter-gatherers, indigenous peoples are Kenyah and Kayan Dayaks. These are stratified longhouse dwellers that live by shifting cultivation of rice and hunting and gathering, supple-

Figure 6.2. The entrance gate to the Kayan Catholic Church of Saint Anthony at Padua (Mendalam River, West Kalimantan, 1994) is embellished with Dayak dragons and hornbill birds.

mented in more recent times by other economic activities including cash crops, logging work, and migratory wage labor. Though pacified (meaning the cessation of headhunting) by the Dutch, they were otherwise left mainly to themselves before the war and Indonesian independence a few years later.

As described by the American anthropologist Herbert Whittier on the basis of fieldwork in the Apo Kayan circa 1970, several things are notable about the spread of Christianity in this region.[12] One is that an area so far from the coast should have been a place where conversion began earlier than it did in some regions closer to the coast. This contradicts the reasonable generalization that Christianity would move inward and upriver and arrive last in the deep interior. However, the process took a long time, progressing over decades. Another is that a number of different missions competed for converts, thus giving inhabitants a choice among several different versions of Christianity, even if they generally had only limited understanding of such differences beyond what each forbade or permitted people to do—in terms of eating, drinking, and divorce. A final anomaly is that the first Christian converts in the Apo Kayan were not the result of missionary efforts in the area. They were rather Dayaks who traveled regularly from the upriver areas to the coast to trade and came under the influence of missionaries who had arrived in 1929 and established missions in the lower river areas.

By 1938 the large Kenyah village of Naha Kramo, located downriver from the Apo Kayan, had become more than half Christian, though what this meant beyond identity is not known. At this time the man who was to eventually become the paramount chief of the entire Apo Kayan visited Naha Kramo. As a result he became convinced that Christianity was more powerful than the *adat lama* (the "old customs," the closest term for traditional religion at the time). He converted and returned to the main Kenyah village of Long Nawang in the Apo Kayan, where he attracted a small group of followers. The existing chief of Long Nawang and most of the villagers were not impressed. But the chief was tolerant and permitted the Christians to build their own longhouse, the assumption being that the two religions could exist separately side by side. This worked initially but not for long. The first Western missionary arrived by small seaplane in 1940 but did not remain. By the early 1940s Christianity had gained a foothold, but resident missionary activity did not begin until several years after the war.

Other developments associated with conversion seem more typical of the development of Christianity in the interior of Borneo. The first missionaries took up residence in Long Nawang in 1950 and remained for four years. They were from the Christian Missionary Alliance, based in the United States. Many new converts were made during this period, but tensions also grew between the Christians and the adherents of the *adat lama*. The problem was probably rooted in part in the general strategy followed in seeking converts. The missionaries based their appeal in practical considerations they assumed would be easily understood by the natives, namely the claim that if they converted they would be relieved of the need to bear the burdens imposed by the old religion. The *adat lama* required them to follow many taboos, to pay fines for breaking them, and to heed the omen birds that frequently kept them from leaving the village to work in the fields or for other purposes because of the threat of danger. More generally the missionaries, at least at first, did not attempt to convince the natives that their old religion was based on the belief in non-existent spirits, gods, and supernatural or magical processes. They argued rather that Christianity was more powerful than such things—as with the popular Western folk (or Hollywood) notion that holding up a cross will repel a vampire. One problem was that the old religion was based on the cultural premise that *everyone* in the village would observe the taboos and participate in the communal ceremonies. Not doing so threatened the well-being of the entire community, not just the converts, according to traditional reckoning.

As of 1950, when the first permanent missionary arrived to take up residence in Long Nawang, the religious loyalties of the village were divided three ways. Some were Christian, some had continued to follow the old religion (or had reverted to it), and some had become adherents of a reform movement known as Bungan, to be discussed in a later chapter.[13] By 1952 the resident missionary saw that the village was in danger of splitting apart along religious lines. In order to prevent this, he decided to try a trick. He had a rattan fence set up that divided the different religious sections of the village, consecrated it with a ritual, and told the villagers that the spirits from one side could not cross it to the other. The point was that the religious practices of each section could be carried out without hindrance from the other.

Problem solved—but not for long. The villagers were willing to give the magical rattan barrier a chance, but after several months they became convinced it was not working. They did believe that the right sort of barrier could block the movement of spirits, but this was not a piece of rattan cane. What was required was a water barrier. This was why cemeteries, from which the spirits of the dead were not welcome to return, were always located on the opposite side of a river from the village. The only solution was therefore for one religious group to leave and form a new village across the Kayan River. The followers of *adat lama* did so, founding the village of Nawang Baru (New Nawang) on the other side of the Kayan and up a ways on the Nawang River. In another instance a large longhouse that had also included Christians, *adat lama* people, and Bungan followers divided three ways after its high chief died and each established separate new communities.[14]

The Stigma of Communism and Further Conversion

As with Islamization, conversion to Christianity in the Kalimantan entered a new phase in the early 1960s. Although far from centers of governmental power, the effects of the religious policies of postcolonial Indonesia eventually reached the Apo Kayan. European missionaries returned to Long Nawang in 1960 but left in 1962 with the beginning of Konfrontasi (Confrontation). This was a political and military effort by Indonesia aimed at the prevention of the addition of the British Borneo colonies of Sabah and Sarawak to Malaya to form Malaysia. The main military activity took the form of attacks and counterattacks along the border between Malaysian Sabah and Sarawak and Indonesian Kalimantan. This included the Apo Kayan, which was occupied by Indonesian army units. Although not their primary mission, the army took it upon themselves to effect the conversion of the remaining *adat lama* and Bungan Dayaks into an approved *agama* religion. The soldiers put aside whatever persuasive subtleties the missionaries and previously converted Dayaks had used to promote further conversion in favor of forceful assertions. The military position was that all Indonesians were now required to have a religion, and that those who did not were in danger of being taken as communists. The soldiers might have preferred conversion to Islam rather than Christianity, but they realized that this was discouraged by the local reliance on pigs for meat.[15] In addition to forcing conversion, the soldiers destroyed much of the material culture of both the *adat lama* and the Bungan religions.

By the early 1970s, when Whittier carried out his fieldwork, conversion to Christianity in Long Nawang was nearly complete. There were a few older men who had publically reverted to Adat Bungan after the army left. At first government officials living in the village reacted against their adherence to paganism but then agreed to let them alone if they could produce a "book" showing that Bungan was comparable to Christianity. The men had limited abilities to read and write Indonesian but after considerable effort were able to produce fifteen pages that satisfied the officials.[16] In the splinter village of Nawang Baru, which had been formed two decades earlier by adherents of *adat lama*, most of the inhabitants had also converted to Christianity. Here, however, there were more holdouts or reconverts. Seventeen older men claimed to be adherents of *adat lama*, although others in the village said they were actually following the reformist religion of Bungan Malan. The matter was unclear because the religious activities they practiced were mainly limited to small curing rituals rather than the major ceremonies, for the performance of which they also lacked both the wherewithal and sufficient participants.

Christianity had also become more complicated as it had grown. In the Apo Kayan generally it included three churches (two Protestant and one Catholic). There was the original Protestant Christian community that had developed in Long Nawang under the influence of the American-based Christian and Missionary Alliance. This was a conservative or evangelically oriented group that had become an Indonesian church, renamed the Kemah Indjil Garedja Masehi Indonesia, generally known by the acronym (as are Christian churches throughout Borneo, often without knowledge of the meaning of the acronym) KINGMI, which is widespread throughout Indonesia. The second and somewhat less conservative Protestant church was the Geredja Protestant Bagian Indonesia, or GPBI. The last Christian church was Roman Catholic, or RK, though this was then found in only one village in the region.

In Long Nawang the two Protestant communities to some extent replicated the earlier schisms that had formed between Christians, *adat lama* adherents, and Bungan followers. Although there were exceptions, the village was geographically divided along religious lines, with KINGMI families living in one section and GPBI ones in the other. This was not an uncommon development.[17]

In Long Nawang the differences between KINGMI and GPBI were less a matter of theology or belief than of morality and society. The locals themselves did not see much difference in the religious beliefs and practices of the two churches. The sermons and lessons came from the same books, and they sang the same songs. On the other hand, KINGMI people tended to think that they were somewhat better than GPBI because their church was there first. KINGMI had more political power in the village, and the elite saw this as a validation of their position.[18]

Given this combination of similarities and the advantages held by KINGMI, it would seem that GPBI would not have been able to compete at all. But it did have a significant advantage of its own that partially offset its weaknesses. KINGMI was socially more conservative, and while this was a matter of pride, it was also somewhat of a problem, and this was part of the reason that GPBI had been able to become established in the shadow of the earlier church. In local terms KINGMI was criticized as having "too many sins." The sins that were particularly important in this case were ones that came into conflict with traditional Dayak norms and practices involving marriage and divorce, which in general tended to be liberal, a matter of nature taking its course. Divorce in particular was an important issue. It was, among other things, a customary response to a marriage that did not produce children, for it gave both partners the opportunity to try again with someone else. Divorce was forbidden by KINGMI, a sin that brought expulsion from the church, but tolerated by GPBI and thus a major reason for joining it in a community that valued belonging. The fact that KINGMI was said to have too many sins was not out of line with the emphasis that the early missionaries had placed on the burdens of the taboos of the *adat lama* as a good reason for giving it up in favor of Christianity.

THE KAREN OF THAILAND AND BURMA

From the interior of Borneo we now move to the middle and northern reaches of continental Southeast Asia. The Karen today are recognized as a large indigenous ethnic minority group living on both sides of the mountainous border of eastern Myanmar/Burma and western Thailand. In Myanmar, where the largest number of Karen dwell, they amount to several million or more (the last census was in 1931), while in Thailand there are about a half a million, making them the largest of the indigenous "hill tribe" peoples in the country. Mostly they live contiguously over a large area and all speak Tibeto-Burmese languages (though even this is a matter of some doubt). The Karen are more carefully referred to as a collection of ethno-linguistic groups now identified by a common term. Most Karen are divided into two main linguistic groups, the Pwo and the Sgaw, the former found more in the lowlands or plains, the latter in the uplands. Though in both Burma and Thailand the Christians are in the minority, the existence of "Karen" as an ethnic identity is a consequence of conversion.

Karen peoples are conventionally divided into several religious categories, including animist (or "customary ritualist,") Buddhist, and Christian—though, again, while such labels are simple, the content of the traditions involved is not. The "animists" are those who identify themselves as followers of customary beliefs and practices rather than with either Buddhism or Christianity. The Buddhists are simply those who identify as such, including those who mix Buddhism with animist traditions. The Christians are those who tend to most strongly emphasize a separate religious identity involving one of the usual mission-oriented churches, originally above all American Baptists but also various other Protestants, Seventh-Day Adventists, and Roman Catholics. There are (or have also been) Christian sectarian, syncretist millenarian groups. Most Christians in general are Sgaw. Buddhists include both Sgaw and Pwo, though with the difference that orthodox Theravada adherents are concentrated among the lowland Pwo while the sectarian Buddhists tend to be highland Sgaw. Assigning numbers or percentages to the various religious types is difficult, especially in Burma, but Buddhist Karen exceed Christians, probably by a large margin in both countries. However, while the Christian Karen are a clear minority, the Christianization of some, along with related colonial policies and practices, created a Karen identity that did not formerly exist.

Christianity and the Karen in Thailand

In Thailand as in continental Southeast Asia in general, Christianity has been and is mainly a religion of the ethnic minorities. The Thai majority identifies itself overwhelmingly with Theravada Buddhism, even though the scope of Thai popular religious practices is much wider. The Portuguese established Roman Catholicism in the sixteenth century. A French mission arrived a century later, but its concerns were limited to the existing Christian community consisting of Portuguese, Eurasians, and other foreigners from various Catholic outposts in other places in Southeast Asia. This remained the case throughout the next two centuries, though the ethnic range of the non-Thai Catholic population increased. The existing restrictions on proselytizing were removed by edict in 1879, though with little apparent immediate effect.

The Karen are something of an anomaly in terms of Christian conversion among the indigenous ethnic minorities in Thailand. The mission to convert the Karen began as an extension of the one in Burma and therefore started long before efforts among the upland peoples elsewhere in Thailand. Since Siam/Thailand was not colonized by a European power, the advantages enjoyed by missionaries and then by those natives who had converted to Christianity in some places were not present. Conversions did occur and churches were founded and endured. The early successes, however, were followed by a drop-off in activity by the latter part of the nineteenth century whereby only a few churches endured.

Buddhism forms another difference between the Karen and the other indigenous upland peoples of Thailand. While relatively few of the hill tribe peoples in Thailand have become Buddhists, many of the Karen have either long been so or have more recently converted. Since Buddhism is the predominant religion of Thailand, it is strongly associated with the dominant Thai. It tends, therefore, to have correspondingly less appeal to the ethnic minorities. This ethnic link has sometimes been pointed out by anthropologists who have studied the minority hill tribe groups as a part of the reason for their preference for conversion to Christianity rather than Buddhism.[19] In both Thailand and Burma, the Karen attraction to Buddhism is long-standing and appears to pre-date the arrival of Christianity. Further, "Buddhism" in both places is not a unitary religious tradition. There have been various types of Buddhism in both countries. Some of these are commonly described as Buddhist sects or Buddhist millenarian movements that are quite different from orthodox Theravadaism. And it is these sects that seem to have had a special attraction for the Karen.

Protestant mission efforts in Thailand began in the nineteenth century but without the spectacular early effects or subsequent consequences of those in Burma. After the very early period, little occurred at all until the 1950s and then as a result of several developments. There was the arrival of a new wave of American missionaries with an abundance of both resources and enthusiasm. Thailand had become a target of opportunity in a region where missionizing opportunities had disappeared or diminished or were rapidly doing so in several adjacent areas that had formerly received much attention. In Burma, Protestant missionaries seeking to take up stations were hindered in entering the country (because of the turmoil that had developed following independence and the ensuing Karen and other ethnic rebellions) and were diverted to Thailand where they were welcome. The closing of China and of the many missions there brought a much larger relocation to the available Southeast Asia countries, with Thailand again providing a prominent opportunity. By this time, moreover, Christian mission efforts in Thailand had come to be based on the realization that the minority hill tribe peoples were better prospects than the ethnic Thai Buddhists. The tribal minorities were also probably more in need of what the missionaries had to offer in the way of practical help.

Renewed mission interest in Thailand in turn coincided with a shift in the attitude of the Thai government toward the hill tribes. Previous to that time the highland minorities had been mainly left to themselves to practice shifting cultivation in the forested mountains in the northern and northeastern parts of the country. The Thai government did not much like them. They saw them as non-Buddhist, migratory, opium-growing, backward, wandering migrants who had, they thought, often arrived in Thailand from China or somewhere else only recently and therefore did not have much right to be there. But living as they did mainly in remote areas away from the Thai, they were not a great problem, at least not great enough to do much about.

The threat of communism did much to change this. China had become communist in 1949, and nearby communist-nationalist civil wars were being waged in Vietnam and Laos. The Christian missionaries, especially perhaps the American ones, came to be seen as allies. They could be expected to be loyal to the Thai government because they required its permission and needed its support, and by being close to the peoples near their mission stations they would know what was happening. Moreover, it was becoming time to gain more control over the hill tribes, to reduce or stop their migratory practices, to civilize them, and perhaps to assimilate them. In terms of religious conversion, the Thai government's first choice would undoubtedly be to have them become Buddhists, and efforts were made to bring Buddhism to the hill tribes both for reasons of religion and security. At one point in the late 1960s the government and Buddhist officials created a missionary program aimed at converting hill tribe populations to Buddhism. The purpose was both to spread Buddhism and to further the integration of the highlanders into national society. But such efforts had little success. The Buddhist monks that were sent among the hill tribes were generally not able to communicate well with the various peoples they had targeted or therefore persuade them to convert. Most of the hill tribe peoples did not want to become Buddhists. Christianity for the government was a compromise but not a bad one. It was a step toward civilization and extending state control over the highlands.

From the perspective of the hill tribes, conversion to Christianity had both practical and ideological attractions as well as whatever the appeal of the missionary's message of salvation, redemption, and revitalization had. The ideological attractions of conversion were that in becoming Christian they were joining a religion of civilization, one, moreover, that was followed by the rich, powerful, and technologically advanced Western world. Conversion to Christianity also enabled the converts to retain their own separate ethnic identity from the lowland Buddhist majority.

Before the arrival of Christianity, the Karen of northwestern Thailand were something of an exception among the highland minorities in having embraced Buddhism in some places. Here they had been drawn to the worship of saintly or magical monks who introduced Buddhism into many villages. Such Buddhism was focused especially on power, protection, and fertility. The famous saintly monks organized the building of temples in newly settled areas where older relics and temple ruins were discovered and assumed to be endowed with magical power.[20] A new temple would cool the area and bring fertility and prosperity. The magical monks also provided amulets for protection and scrolls for use in traditional Karen rituals. They fitted in well with existing Karen religion.

Though hardly differing much from ordinary popular Thai religious beliefs and practices, this sort of Buddhism was not approved of by the national, government-regulated official Theravada organizations; they sought to convert its Karen adherents to a more politically correct orthodoxy as part of their mission efforts among the hill tribes. For the Karen, on the other hand, non-orthodox Buddhism, aside from its spiritual attractions and ritual uses, had some of the same ethnic political appeal as did Christianity—something that distinguished them from the more orthodox Theravada Thai Buddhist majority. Some of the famous saintly Karen monks were associated with Karen nationalism. The Karen Buddhist temples did not always welcome Thai Buddhists.

As elsewhere, in the region studied by the Japanese anthropologist Yoko Hayami in the 1980s and 1990s, Karen popular religion (as sometimes happened in the interior of Borneo) included three orientations, although the lines between them were not always clear. Some were adherents of traditional beliefs and customary practices. These involved animism, agricultural rituals, protection magic, supernatural healing, and spirit medium practices—in other words much the same range of traditional beliefs and activities as elsewhere in Southeast Asia. The Karen had no named identity for this complex and did not refer to it as "religion," as they would Christianity or Buddhism. They saw it instead (and again this is common) as part of a larger realm of customary practices, lifeways, and even language that therefore included supernatural as well as non-supernatural notions and activities. In Borneo, for example, and in many other places in insular Southeast Asia, such adherents would be identified as *adat* people.

At the other extreme was Christianity, which is identified as such, or with the belief in Ywe, their term for God taken from the creator spirit in the Karen version of the story of the lost book. Conversion to Christianity in the area was fairly recent, extending back only to the early middle of the twentieth century. Most of the conversion has been a result of steady growth since the 1960s, in which Karen converts have themselves played a major role. It had been a response to the resources and the educational and other opportunities provided by the Christian missions, and the association of Christianity with progress and modernity—in other words again much the same mix of influences as noted in other places.

The Christian Karen are more clearly differentiated from the non-Christians than are the Buddhists.[21] Since the non-Christians tend to participate in important Buddhist rituals as well as the traditional Karen ones, and since the Buddhists appear to believe in spirits and engage in some traditional activities along with Buddhist ones, the line between the two is somewhat blurry. The Christians, on the other hand, do not participate in the Buddhist ceremonies. They also tend to live separately, since again as elsewhere many Karen ritual activities are community based.

And although not necessarily a matter of ritual or dogma, the Christians also tended to be architecturally set off from the non-Christians, or became leaders in innovations later accepted by others. Before around 1960, all of the Karen tended to live in the same type of house, one built lightly, largely of bamboo, raised above the ground, and with a thatched roof. Such houses cost little in terms of cash expenditure, use readily available materials, and can be erected quickly once the wooden and bamboo poles have been obtained and the grass or palm thatch has been prepared. The new wave of Christianization included a commitment to physical as well as spiritual progress. Launched in the general spirit of "cleanliness is next to godliness," the Christian converts inaugurated a village improvement program in 1965, which included order and neatness as well as improvements in sanitation and hygiene.[22] Over the course of a five-year program, wells were dug and sanitary toilets installed, animals were fenced in, house yards were enclosed, and streets were built. The non-Christians were not necessarily oblivious to such improvements, which were also being promoted in other development efforts. This was also true of the changes in house-building practices, specifically the trend toward much heavier (and much more costly) building with sawn lumber, glass windows, and the use of corrugated metal roofing, which though much more expensive and much hotter than thatch, is longer lasting, and in any case more prestigious. The extent to which such changes were entirely a direct consequence of the ethos of Christianization or in part also the result of Christian economic improvement is more difficult to resolve, for in the long run the desire for material progress in housing is common throughout Southeast Asia.

Karen Conversion in Burma

The Karen of Burma have an especially prominent place in the annals of Christian conversion in Southeast Asia. The conversion of the Karen began early in the history of Protestant mission efforts in the region. The first American Baptist missionary arrived in Burma in 1813, and the first Karen baptism is recorded as having occurred in 1828. The American Baptist mission, which continued to be particularly important, developed especially in the 1830s, shortly after the first Anglo-Burmese War (1824–1826) and the British colonial takeover of part of lower (or southern) Burma.[23]

The early efforts also seemed to be particularly successful. The history of missionizing efforts in Southeast Asia includes many instances in which decades or more of work brought rejection or only the most meager harvest of souls. The Bidayuh in Borneo once told me about a nineteenth-century missionary who spent his entire life at work in the area without making a single convert, though this may have been an overstatement. In Burma the early missionaries found the lowland,

Buddhist Mon and Burman (or ethnic Burmese) peoples generally unreceptive to Christianity. The Karen and other ethnic minorities offered much better prospects. The Karen seemed extraordinarily eager to convert, and the first conversion was followed quickly by many others. Missionaries arrived in some villages to find people waiting for them because they had heard news that marvels involving strangers were taking place. The attraction of the missionaries to the Karen and the Karen to Christianity appeared to be mutual. As potential converts, the Karen seemed to have nearly everything a missionary could want, including a need for earthly help as well as spiritual salvation.

Most importantly, Karen conversion appeared to have a miraculous dimension. The early missionaries came to believe that they were welcomed because they were fulfilling a Karen prophecy, one that meshed with nineteenth-century Protestant (especially Baptist) messianic notions that the world could end at any time, perhaps very soon. They also found that Karen religious beliefs had certain stunning parallels to those of the Old Testament.[24] Here there were two Karen myths that the missionaries presumed to have been in existence since before their first exposure to Christianity. Both involved the creator god Ywe.

All Karen know the first story in one version or another. In it Ywe creates the world and the first man and women. The couple lived among the trees where there were seven kinds of fruit. Ywe told them that of these they could eat six while the seventh was forbidden. One day, however, a large serpent came along and persuaded them to try the seventh fruit and they did. The result was that they became liable to suffering, aging, and death. The serpent was an incarnation of the female deity Mü kaw li, who then taught the couple the elements of their culture and religion, including how to grow rice, the names of the various spirits that also inhabit the world in which they lived, and the name of the ancestor spirit, Bgha. She also taught them how to propitiate the spirits that cause illness, and the method for securing the life principle *k'la* or soul that must not wander from the body because this will bring illness.

This myth, or the first part of it at least, is much the same as the Old Testament story of the creation of world, the temptation of Adam and Eve, and the fall of man. The name of the creator god, *Ywe*, was also strikingly close to *Yahweh*, the Hebrew name for God. As for the divinity who tempts the couple to eat the forbidden fruit, the missionaries assumed that this had to be Satan, though this overlooked the fact that Mü kaw li was a female deity who, after causing their fall, taught the Karen the useful things they would need to survive. From these parallels the missionaries surmised that the Karen could well be one of the ten Lost Tribes of Israel. They had obviously changed their culture in many ways over the course of their travels and with the passage of time, but they had preserved the central story of the Old Testament. If so, the Karen were a people of the Old Testament waiting to hear the story of the Son of God as revealed in the New Testament.[25]

Although it had no parallel in the Old Testament, the second myth was perhaps even more important. For the Karen the story explains the troubles they have had in the world but also foretells their redemption. The basic story is that Ywe gave a precious book to each of his several children. The children were the ancestors of the Karen and the various other peoples known to them. The book was the gift of literacy that became the basis of the wealth, power, and civilization of the lowland peoples who came to look down upon the Karen and oppress them—a notion that certainly has some basis in sociological truth. The Karen missed out because they were foolish and did not realize the great value of the book. They neglected it, with the result that it was destroyed—in some versions by carelessly burning it up in a swidden fire. In any case the loss of the book was how the Karen became inferior to the lowland people. Their fate however was not forever inevitable. Ywe also tells them that at some future time the Karen will get a second chance. The book will be returned to the Karen by someone and this will enable their redemption. The implication is clear: this time they must make proper use of the book.

In some versions of the myth the lost text is a Golden Book and in others there is a gold book, a silver book, and a paper one—the latter the easily destroyed one given to the Karen. Similarly there are both two foreign brothers and a single White Brother (the younger brother of Ywe) who will return with the book or books. Such variation is not surprising in that the Karen are a large conglomeration of different peoples spread over a wide area, and in that the stories were a matter of oral tradition before being committed to writing in the nineteenth century. The details notwithstanding, the early missionaries (or some of them, and at least for a while) took the story of the book as a matter of divine intent. Here was God's plan unfolding in a remote corner of the world. The lost book was of course the Bible brought by the missionaries who were the brothers from far away.

The missionaries did not always interpret the stories in the same way.[26] The Baptists favored an Old Testament view of Ywe along the lines noted above. A Catholic missionary, on the other hand, tended to a more New Testament interpretation that suggests similarities with Jesus Christ. In this version Ywe has a wife and son, becomes a savior who dies but comes back to life, and travels in a boat to somewhere in the west from whence he will eventually return.

Another problem is a lack of information about the origin and spread of the stories. The early missionaries, who interpreted the stories, had also collected them. If the Karen were one of the Lost Tribes of Israel, they had always had the stories, but there were other possibilities. Even the assumption that the missionaries obtained the stories from the Karen may be an oversimplification. Some Karen may have learned either or both of the myths as well as the name *Ywe* from the missionaries (or other Karen) and incorporated them into their stories and passed them on as part of their explanation of how they became Christian.[27] It is also very possible that the Karen in the past learned some version of the story of the lost book from some non-Karen indigenous group. Prophecies about strangers bringing lost books have turned out to be common myths across northern continental Southeast Asia.[28]

The early appeal of Christianity was clearly messianic, based on the older beliefs in the arrival of a prophet bringing a lost book and with it political power and well-being. The occurrence of stories of the return of lost books across a wide area in the nineteenth century makes it difficult to know if they might have originated with the Karen or some other group, or were introduced from the outside.

The early missionaries thought that the Karen stories of Ywe, the lost book, and the brother revealed a connection to the Old Testament and a prophecy that foretold their arrival and the revitalization of the Karen. It has also been pointed out that the stories themselves may have had a Buddhist millenarian origin. The widespread occurrence of stories of lost-books-to-be-returned-by-a-stranger in northern Southeast Asia is consistent with the widespread occurrence of both orthodox and sectarian forms of Buddhism throughout the region. News and rumors of the arrival of white strangers bringing a sacred book appear to be built upon this older foundation of millenarianism. The defeat of the Burmese state by the British in the First and Second Anglo-Burmese Wars further encouraged the Karen to suppose that miraculous developments were occurring with the colonial takeover.[29]

In spite of its seemingly miraculous beginning, the conversion of the Karen did not always go smoothly. The processes of Christianization and revitalization moved beyond the control of missionaries. New sects formed that combined the cult of Ywe, Buddhism, and Christianity. The author of a missionary account published in 1828 noted arriving in a Karen village to find a cult centered on the worship of what turned out to be an English prayer book brought by an ascetic who also preached abstention from eating pork and fowl.[30] The missionary assured them that the book had no value for the purpose for which they were using it. Another missionary found a village in which the people had a real Bible that they were worshipping as a fetish. Not all Karen were willing to convert and, as elsewhere, missionaries encouraged the creation of new villages to separate those who did convert from those who did not. Some churches withdrew from the official Karen Baptist Convention and formed an independent, self-supporting Baptist denomination. There were also frequent declines in Christian faith that were probably due to disappointed millenarian expectations.

The Consequences of Conversion

Such setbacks notwithstanding, however, the Christian villages that were established and held together brought progress and a life that was better than the inhabitants had previously known. This was partly a matter of millenarian hope, but it was also a consequence of the practical benefits of missionization. One village was described as something from a missionary's dream, consisting of well-built houses placed in neat rows, the ground beneath and around them free of rubbish. The street through the village was wide and straight and lined with fruit trees and flowers. The gardens were also neatly laid out and the crops were well cultivated. The missionaries also provided schools, help with business dealings and extraction from indebtedness to moneylenders, and access to the British colonial administration. They also taught the Christians defensive skills and encouraged them to form militias by which to defend themselves in times of trouble.

Thus in a way the prophecy of the white brother, the return of the lost book, and the social redemption of the Karen came true—though only for a time. For whatever exact set of reasons, within a few generations the efforts of the missions brought the Christian Karen into the forefront of Burmese life and political power. As a result of missionary efforts to educate the Karen to teach them practical and defensive skills, the Karen converts came to distinguish themselves in education, nursing, and the military. The education and skills they acquired made them very useful to the colonial regime. A powerful Karen police force was raised to help dispel disorder during the Third Anglo-Burmese War in 1885. By this time the Christian Karen had come to play a similar role as did some other Western-educated or militarily oriented ethnic minorities in the British Empire, that of colonial favorites whose loyalty could be counted on and whose usefulness was rewarded accordingly.

The development of the Christian Karen also encouraged ethnic nationalism. They founded the Karen National Association in 1881, intended to advance their interests in the country. This was the first such ethnic association to be created in Burma.[31] By 1931 only about 17 percent of the Karen had become Christian, but they amounted to two-thirds of all the Christians in Burma. Their Christian leaders realized, however, that a successful national movement would require the support of Karen in general, not only the Christians. When they formed the Karen National Association, they moved quickly to draw in the non-Christian Karen as well.

Eventually, however, the conversion, modernization, and nationalism of the Karen also brought problems, and for some, devastation. The emergence of the Christian Karen as a successful religious-ethnic group in colonial Burma included a special relationship with the British. But this did not endear them to the Buddhist Burman majority. The latter had fought three wars with the British and had lost their state and monarchy as a result. The resentment of the Burman majority toward the Karen was all the worse because they had traditionally looked down on them as a lowly and backward minority.

Karen ethnic nationalism eventually turned into conflict. This took the form of a war of rebellion between Karen separatists—among whom the Christians had a prominent role—and the post-colonial Burmese state. Incorporated as it had been into the British Empire as a part of India, Burma gained early independence in 1948, with (as was also the case in India) inadequate provision for the ethnic complexities and religious animosities that existed within its borders. The Karen nationalists had wanted and expected their own state in independent Burma but were let down by the British in the negotiations leading to independence and then left out of the further discussions that were supposed to consider their status afterward. The Karen nationalists revolted and became separatists—a path also followed sooner or later by other ethnic minorities that occupy the peripheral regions of the country surrounding the Burman ethnic core, including the Kachin and the Shan. Joined as it was by Karen units of the military and police, the insurrection had some early success before becoming more distinctly defensive, but was never settled.

The rebellion was to some extent an expression of long-standing Karen millenarian tendencies. Notwithstanding the partial Christianization of the Karen, including many of the nationalists, and their success in various secular activities, the old millenarian myths and prophecies continued to have some meaning, though in specific terms they changed. Some leaders in the resistance reinterpreted the story of Ywe and the White Brother whereby the Golden Book became aid to the Karen in the form of arms shipments. Other Karen interpreted the insurrection as linked to the coming of the Christian Messiah.

After taking over the government, the military made a more stringent effort to suppress the rebellion, bombing and burning suspected insurrectionist villages and forcing the displacement of large numbers of inhabitants. The military and the government have been accused by Karen and outside international organizations of human rights violations and atrocities, including the subjugation of women and children to forced labor and the persecution of Karen Christians in general. By 2005 more than 150,000 Karen had fled Burma/Myanmar and were living in fifteen UN-supervised refugee camps located across and spread along the border in Thailand—from which many have by now been relocated to the United States, Australia, and European countries to form yet another diaspora created by war and oppression rooted in religious, ethnic, and political conflict.[32]

Figure 6.3. The fate of many Karen: the UN refugee camp at Mae La, Tak Province, Thailand, on the Thailand-Myanmar border, in 2006. The camp has held up to fifty thousand refugees from Myanmar. A fire in 2012 destroyed some five hundred of the closely packed wood, thatch, and bamboo houses.

THE CONVERSION OF REFUGEES

Throughout this discussion of conversion it has been stressed that those who became Christian in the last two centuries belong mainly to the ranks of the non-Muslim and non-Buddhist ethnic (and overseas) minorities of the interior and highland regions, and that the majority Muslims and Buddhists have generally avoided conversion. There have been some exceptions, one of which will be briefly discussed as the final case study of this chapter.

The conversion of mainland Southeast Asian peoples took a new turn in the wake of the wars that ended in 1975 in Vietnam, Laos, and Cambodia. The establishment of communist regimes in these mainland countries brought the migration of many inhabitants as refugees seeking to escape from retribution or the disruption, impoverishment, or displacement that followed to find sanctuary and a new life in the United States and other Western countries. More than one million Lao, Hmong, Cambodians, and Vietnamese refugees and their later relatives and their descendants are now living in the United States.

The pattern of conversion among the refugees was in some ways similar to that followed by other and previous ethnic minorities, but there was a difference. The conversion to Christianity that began in the nineteenth century was based in part on two influences. One was the view that Christianity was a religion associated with the power, wealth, and progress of the Western world that appealed to minority peoples in the process of being more fully incorporated into the developing states in Southeast Asia. The other was that, outside of the Philippines and Vietnam, the religions of identity of the dominant groups of the Southeast countries was either Islam or Theravada Buddhism. This meant that conversion to Islam in Indonesia and Malaysia, or to Buddhism in Thailand, Cambodia, Laos, and (perhaps to a lesser extent) Burma, was associated with becoming a part of the dominant lowland or coastal ethnic population, as in the Malay phrase *masuk Melayu*, or "entering Malay," for converting to Islam—a development that many of the ethnic minorities did not favor. In Southeast Asia the ethnic minorities who converted to Christianity were therefore avoiding the religion of the dominant majority, while refugees seeking sanctuary in Western countries who became Christian were joining the dominant religion.

The conversion to Christianity among the various refugee communities was a newer development in some instances than others. The Laotian Hmong, who converted in large numbers, had no existing ties to a world religion other than Christianity. The Vietnamese who converted as refugees came from a religiously pluralistic society in which Christianity had long been present—and especially so among those who had sided with the South Vietnamese government against the communist South Vietnamese Viet Cong and North Vietnamese. For the Khmer and the Lao, on the other hand, conversion to Christianity involved a radical break with long-standing identity with Theravada Buddhism.[33]

The exposure of Khmer and Lao Buddhists to Christian influence and their conversion began in the refugee camps in Thailand. Here many Khmer had found sanctuary from the Khmer Rouge and the Lao from the consequences of war and the establishment of a socialist government. Here several things favored conversion.[34] One was that missionaries and Christian workers were present and able to provide access to desired goods and services including advice and help with arranging resettlement. The camp provided an unprecedented opportunity to spread Christianity that had hardly existed among lowland Theravada Buddhist Lao and Khmer populations. Conversion came to be seen as opening doors and providing opportunities. Women in particular spent time and energy developing relationships with Christian religious workers. Some conversions were therefore of the "rice bowl" sort, and here the process involved efforts on both sides. The attraction of Christianity was also a response to other influences. There was not much to do in the camps, so Christian sermons and singing sessions became a wide attraction. Also, the Khmer refugees in particular had been brutalized by the Khmer Rouge in a way that had no parallel in Laos or Vietnam, devastating as the war had been in these places. Cambodian refugees often had serious psychological problems involving despair, depression, hatred, and a desire for revenge. As the converts reported later, the Christian messages of hope, forgiveness, and salvation resonated, and they acted accordingly.[35]

Another influence was the damage that had been done to the prestige of Buddhism among the Khmer. The Khmer Rouge had destroyed institutional Buddhism in Cambodia, forcing all monks to defrock and join the ranks of the ordinary population, and closing the monasteries or turning them into barracks, warehouses, prisons, and places of torture.[36] The refugees had been cut off from most or all Buddhist ritual interaction for several years. The Christian missionaries and religious workers asserted that Buddhism could not help them and that Christianity could. After all that had happened to them, some Khmer refugees found such assertions plausible and came to accept that Christianity was therefore a more powerful and satisfying alternative.[37]

The incentives that first led some Khmer and Lao to become Christian in the refugee camps continued to exist after resettlement, in which churches were often involved. In Canada as also in the United States, the Christian churches urged more than just religious conversion, learning, and participation. They also stressed social values including integration into the dominant society and culture, getting off welfare, and avoiding gambling and drinking. Conversion helped the Christian Khmer to reinvent themselves and to take on the values of individualism and self-interest of American and other Western societies, though over time the differences between the converts and the Buddhists in these respects appear to have diminished. The institutions of Buddhism were difficult to reestablish in the places where the Khmer were resettled, but as an identity their traditional religion had advantages. The majority of Khmer continued to associate holidays, celebrations, and classical culture with Buddhism. This left the Christians with the appearance of having abandoned not just Buddhism but also Cambodianness. The Christians sought to counter such criticism by stressing their own efforts to help perpetuate Cambodian culture. In the earlier period Christian pastors denounced Buddhism and Buddhist activities but eventually gave this up in favor of tolerance and the value of mutual good will.[38]

Over time Buddhism as a matter of identity and symbolism therefore proved stronger, at least among the refugees themselves, though not necessarily among their children. The early spiritual (or psychological) and practical reasons for conversion in the refugee camps and among the first arrivals diminished over time. In Canada church attendance dropped, and some Khmer reverted to Buddhism or attempted to combine both religions by stressing the similarities in moral values, whatever this may have meant in terms of ritual practices. A smaller core of devout, active, and socially integrated Christians remained. This included some who became evangelical workers and returned to their home villages in Cambodia to proselytize, though whether this has created a new trend to conversion among the Khmer there is not evident. The second generation of Khmer Canadians (and Americans) are less attracted to and more confused about either Christianity or Buddhism than their parents.[39] They are drawn more fully into the powerful currents of Westernization that more established Americans themselves often tend to greatly underestimate. The continued importance and longevity of Buddhism among Cambodian Americans and Canadians remains a matter of doubt.

THE NATURE OF CONVERSION

The several instances of conversion to Christianity that have been considered here show something of the range of what has taken place over the past two centuries in Southeast Asia. They show that conversion is probably always a destabilizing process, but not necessarily a revolutionary one. In both the interior of Borneo and the uplands of western Thailand, conversion has been one dimension of a broader sequence of modernizing changes rather than one that was revolutionary in itself—as also was the case among the Christian Toraja in Sulawesi discussed in the chapter on Hinduism. There certainly were consequences. In Borneo at least conversion was not uncommonly associated with the splitting of villages into adherents of traditional or *adat* beliefs and practices, on the one hand, and Christianity, on the other. In addition, here also individuals were aided in gaining an education in schools that at first would not have otherwise been available. Such change in turn has enabled the emergence of new types of leaders in Dayak societies, ones different from those of traditional or pre-colonial and colonial society. But such changes never appear to have had the radical consequences as did conversion among the Karen of Burma. In Borneo the most radical development in conversion involved Kalimantan or Indonesian Borneo and throughout Indonesia generally as the government strongly, and sometimes threateningly, sanctioned conversion to one or another of the world religions, of which Christianity was but one.

The conversion of the Karen in Burma took on the characteristics of some religious movements rather than just conversion. What happened here, at least for a time, is an example of the notion of *revitalization* as developed by the American psychological anthropologist Anthony Wallace (discussed in chapter 8). Conversion here led to developments that were almost certainly unseen by the American missionaries who, for a while believing they were involved in a miracle, urged them to become Christian and helped them gain the knowledge and skills that put them in a favorable position under colonial rule, though eventually in a troubled, rebellious one in independent Burma/Myanmar. The conversion to Christianity that began among the Khmer in refugee camps in Thailand and continued in the resettled communities in the United States and Canada was certainly a radical departure from their long-standing loyalty to and identity with Buddhism. But since the refugees who converted were going to leave for a new life elsewhere, their conversion has probably had only limited effect in Cambodia itself.

7

THE MAGIC OF THE MARKET

Studies of popular religion in recent years in Southeast Asia have focused in particular on matters involving social, political, and economic change. Here the notion of "occult economies" is important. It contradicts the expectations of an earlier generation of social theorists that as societies underwent modernization, religion would decline. While this has occurred in parts of the West, it has not so far in many other areas, including Southeast Asia.

As formulated by the anthropologists Jean and John Comaroff, the notion of occult economies refers to the tendency of people, especially in developing societies (though not only there), to seek improvement of their material well-being and status through magic, sorcery, and animism.[1] A further characteristic of occult economies is the tendency of people to see in magic and sorcery explanations for why some people gain success while most do not. They are concerned with the characteristics of occult economies with specific regard to South Africa, but consider its wider applicability to other parts of Africa and elsewhere as well. In the African version, occult activities include conjuring zombies, obtaining human body parts for use in rituals for personal gain, and making accusations of witchcraft and black magic.

In their effort to apply the notion of occult economies to various areas of the world, the Comaroffs broaden the concept beyond those activities that they noted as especially characteristic of Africa. Occult economies are closely related to religious movements, especially to classic cargo cults of the Pacific Islands (which promise the return of wealth to the natives from whom it was confiscated under colonial circumstances). They are also linked in the United States and elsewhere to current prosperity gospel movements. The latter began in the American Sunbelt as part of Protestant Pentecostal churches associated with faith healing and later with televangelism and mega-churches. The basic theological proposition is that God intends people to be prosperous as well as healthy and will make them so in return for Christian adherence to the Bible (and financial support for the right ministry). They appeal to poor and lower-middle-class Whites, Latinos, and Blacks who are seeking prosperity and happiness through religion in an economic system in which it is difficult to get ahead through ordinary, rational means and hard work.

The association of religious beliefs and practices of an occult nature with economic activities and thought in developing societies is not new to anthropologists. In his 1967 account of economic attitudes among Mexican villagers, George Foster offered a general thesis of the popularity of lotteries among the poor in developing countries.[2] Because of the long odds against winning, he said that lottery playing is regarded as foolish according to middle-class North American values (this was written before lotteries and other forms of legal gambling became widespread and very popular in the United States). Foster argued that this was not really so insofar as it assumed that the poor had better ways of gaining wealth, which in fact they generally did not. The odds against improving their economic status through other sorts of investment or hard work were about as long as those involved in playing the lottery. The tendency therefore was to see economic improvement as a matter of luck or fate or the favor of deities, and the best strategy was therefore to concentrate on these. Other studies followed, including several in Latin America that focused on beliefs in the role of the devil in creating wealth. In her research on miners in highland Colombia, June Nash found that beliefs in the devil and in pacts with the devil were common.[3] The devil, it was believed, controlled the wealth of the mines, which therefore could be gained only with his assistance.[4]

In present-day Mexico, the occult economy is strongly linked to the narco-culture of cartels; the cult of the skeleton saint of death, Santa Muerte; and the search for protection from killing, disappearances, and kidnapping.[5] In the highlands of central Guatemala the main occult figure is Maximon, an apparently ancient Mayan divinity linked to fertility who has evolved, become urbanized, wears a cowboy hat, chain-smokes, drinks heavily, and heals people and helps with other problems.

The differences between such earlier examples and explanations and the recent characteristics of occult economies concern especially communication and technology as well as the spread of modern, urban capitalism. The traditional forms of communication are predominately oral and face to face and include conversation, gossip, folklore, and urban legend. These remain, of course, but a fundamental characteristic of the occult economy is the extent to which oral tradition has been supplemented by modern mass media, including newspapers and television, which thrive on popular interest in religion, religious scandals, and the occult. And while modern technology including the Internet might seem at first to contradict mystical interpretations and activities, in some ways it may encourage them. The Comaroffs note the popularity of "dial-up divination" among middle-class South Africans and the appearance of seers and fortune-tellers in Bangkok who now communicate by e-mail with clients (who tend to ask frequently about economic matters).[6]

Although it is difficult to quantify the occult and therefore occult economies, the Comaroffs contend that they are on the increase, both in Africa and elsewhere, including Southeast Asia. Such an increase, if real, can be attributed to several possible considerations. One of these of course is the development of capitalism during the past several decades, which has brought new wealth but also greater inequality due to its unequal distribution and therefore perhaps an increase in relative, if not also absolute, poverty. Closely related to this is the difficulty of grasping the complexities of economic change and the operation of market forces—a problem enough in developed societies. This further encourages an emphasis on luck or mystical explanations of success and failure. Television has also increased awareness of how other people live and has increased the desire for material possessions, a constant in advertisements. Other people appear to many inhabitants in developing countries to have far more wealth than they do. In Southeast Asia the issue of increase in the occult economy has been raised especially for Vietnam. One interpretation of what happened after the government began to relax its prohibitions on popular religious activity has been that people returned to ritual practices characteristic of the pre-communist era. It has also been argued, however, that the recent religious activity has reached new levels in accord with new levels of capitalist development and economic turbulence.[7]

In China the present-day occult economy involves magical activities that have been revived as the government and Communist Party have relaxed but not fully abandoned prohibitions on religion and superstition. Feng shui (the art of arranging buildings and other objects to direct the flow of good and bad forms of mystical energy) has become a special concern of government officers and workers seeking to protect themselves and to move up in the bureaucracy. A recent front-page story in the *New York Times* reports that the former railways minister in charge of building the world's largest high-speed railway network consulted a feng shui master on auspicious dates for groundbreaking ceremonies. For whatever exact reasons, he was officially dismissed for not only taking huge bribes and maintaining a harem of eighteen mistresses but also for "belief in medieval superstition."[8]

In Southeast Asia, to which we now turn, the main features in the occult economy include visits and pilgrimages to shrines; recourse to spirit mediums, astrologers, and magic monks; and lottery playing and the search for magical winning numbers. I also, without looking, became aware on a later return visit to Kelantan of a looming business failure in which sorcery was suspected and consultation with Thai specialists was underway.

THE OCCULT ECONOMY IN SOUTHEAST ASIA

An article in the Malaysian newspaper *The Star* published in 2012 provides an example of the synthesis of the high-tech and the mystical. When the committee of the Chinese temple of the God of Wealth in Penang installed a new statue, it was provided with an innovative and rapid means of providing lottery numbers. Rather than using the traditional and time-consuming practices of mechanical divination by shaking sticks out of a container and then interpreting what they showed, all seekers need to do is to press a button in the god's stomach and a number is electronically generated and instantly dispensed (though whether people were happy with the results and continued to use the technique was not reported).[9] Similarly, in Malaysia modern buildings are erected using advanced rational knowledge, but mystical considerations have not been eliminated. The Petronas Towers, which at the time of completion in 1998 were the tallest buildings in the world and therefore a marvel of up-to-date, scientific engineering, were also built to have the lucky number of eighty-eight floors.

THE OCCULT ECONOMY IN VIETNAM AND THAILAND

Occult economic beliefs and behavior have attracted particular attention in both Vietnam and Thailand. There have been some commonalities in the two countries as well as important differences. Both spirit mediums and visits to shrines have been described as being particularly important links between religion and the economy in both places—though the specific kinds of shrines have been somewhat different. One difference is that while Buddhism has figured prominently in case studies and discussions of occult economic activity in Thailand, it has received little or no such attention in Vietnam—a difference that is perhaps above all a simple reflection of the far greater presence and importance of Buddhism in Thailand.

In both countries the reliance on practical religion and magic for healing, protection, and material prosperity is ancient. In the past the main economic concerns were those of rural farmers concerned with growing rice, coping with floods and other threats, and the opportunities of village life. As increasing numbers of villagers have moved into or become absorbed by towns and cities, many have retained their orientation to practical religion and magic. Here concerns changed to surviving or prospering in business pursuits; protection from traffic accidents, crime, and other hazards of urban life; and passing school exams—not that all of these are missing from rural life, of course. In Thailand the growth of the modern occult economy was by no means sudden. Development (involving tourism, urbanization, industrialization, political change, and other things) has been going on over many decades. The recession that began in 1997 and hit Thailand hard may have brought an increase in efforts to seek supernatural help deriving from economic anxiety.

Neo-socialist Vietnam

In Vietnam the revival of ritual activity was initially resisted by the government and given a sinister interpretation. Practitioners who peddled "superstition," such as spirit mediums, palm readers, and astrologers, were presented in a bad light as lazy fakes engaging in disreputable, exploitative activities. They were also said to be mainly an urban problem associated with black marketing, smuggling, and other unsavory economic practices, and with ports and border crossings. In contrast to those of virtuous villagers, urban lifestyles and ritual activities were held to be culturally alien and in need of being watched because they formed an avenue for U.S. or Chinese subversion.[10] Nonetheless the policies and attitudes of the party and government softened, and what had been condemned as backward and harmful superstition came to be seen in a more favorable light as "national folklore." The higher level of popular religious behavior was probably also a result not only of the lessening of government objections to it but also a consequence of newer developments as well.[11]

There were also differences between the south and the north, with the greatest development of new occult activity reported to have taken place in the south centering (like the economy) on Saigon (officially renamed Ho Chi Minh City). The history and culture of the south had been somewhat different from that of the north. The north had experienced a longer period of socialism than the south, to which many Catholics and anti-communist dissidents had fled upon partition. The south had an ethnic population of Malay-language-related Chams and ties to Cambodia, while the north was closer to China and had once been part of the Chinese Empire. Philip Taylor brings these differences out in his discussion of the rise of one particularly important southern goddess known as the Lady of the Realm. Her shrine, which is located in the Mekong Delta in a trading town on the border with Cambodia, is a major pilgrimage center.[12]

Obscure in origin, the goddess was probably originally the focus of a rural cult emphasizing fertility. But after her statue was discovered by accident, it quickly came to be believed to be endowed with spiritual power and was set in a new shrine. Here she became a patron of urbanites, especially small traders and businesspeople, some involved in illegal transborder economic dealings. Her devotees, many of whom are women, come especially from Saigon, which became the main urban center of *doi moi* capitalism. Her followers came to believe she could help them become rich and successful. Like the goddess herself, many of these devotees come from rural areas but had moved into the city in search of a better life.[13]

The Goddess of the Realm is important as a type of divinity in southern Vietnam. While there are many divinities in Vietnamese popular religion, most are assumed to have once been living persons who had special characteristics. In life they were well-known warriors, scholars, and officials—sometimes all three—who were famous for defending the country against outsiders. It helped their deification if they died in the process. These male gods are the national type and were brought to the south by settlers from the north in the seventeenth century. In the south, however, there was already a tradition of female deities that the Vietnamese may have gotten from the ethnic Chams, whom they displaced as the dominant ethnic group in the region. Beyond gender, the goddesses differ from the warrior-scholar-official type in various ways. While the male gods derive from historically well-known persons, the female ones do not, or usually not. Whether they actually existed as real persons is usually in doubt; the grave sites of the male deities are well known, while those of the goddesses are not. The Goddess of the Realm appears to have come into existence in her present spiritual state only because her statue was found. No grave or recorded personality exists. The male gods were deified because of their accomplishments in life, while the female gods are known for their suffering. The male gods often died violently but after important achievements. The stories told about the goddesses tell of unfulfilled lives, of dying young, unmarried, and without children. When the statue of the Goddess of the Realm was found abandoned, probably having been stolen by thieves, she was missing an arm, which may have increased her appeal.[14]

This is in part at least because of the widespread belief in Southeast Asia (and not only there of course) that suffering in life can be linked to supernatural power after death. Also, the goddesses have kept their female wants and needs for the nice things and attention they did not have in life, and have the power to help those who provide offerings and devotion. The Goddess of the Realm is believed to uphold morality, but her shrine is located in a border town where smuggling, corruption, and human trafficking flourish (and in this respect she is somewhat reminiscent of Santa Muerte in Mexico). Her cult thrives in relation to the economic context of urban, post–*doi moi* Vietnam. But while the male gods also remain popular or have been revived, the female deities currently have a political edge. While the sometimes deified version of Ho Chi Minh might also now fit the type, the traditional male gods are somewhat out of political favor because they are associated with the feudal past, although they defended the country from external enemies. From the perspective of the orthodox socialist rejection of all religion, both the gods and goddesses are simply superstition. But if people have to believe in something, non-feudalistic female deities are a better choice.

In a comparative perspective, the Goddess of the Realm in Vietnam is somewhat reminiscent of other deities of the occult economies. One is the spirit Mai Nak in Thailand, who may or may not have been a real person, who died a bad death at a young age, and who is now thought to be able and willing to help those who approach her with devotion and respect and offer her things that women like. Another is the recently deified Thai pop star Phumphuang Duangchan to be considered below.

Capitalist Thailand

The modern occult economy in Thailand and elsewhere in Southeast Asia represents a synthesis of religion, capitalism, and the modern mass media and the Internet. And while the earlier differentiation between the quiet serenity of temple compounds and the hustle and bustle of the surrounding commercial city environment can still be found in many places, the two have been merging. Stalls and shops have moved into temples, and temple activities have spread into markets and shopping centers. The occult economy is one of both services and goods and can be divided into four main areas of popular religious activity. One of these is the transactions that take place between spirit mediums, magic monks, fortune-tellers, and other providers of occult services and their clients—to which could be added the expenditures on bus, taxi, and pedicab fares that are involved in transporting them. The second is the vast market for the material commodities of popular religion. The third is the mass media that publicizes the modern occult economy. And the fourth is the lottery, including the exchanges that take place in the search for magical help with winning numbers.

The Thai version of the occult economy is basically similar to that of Vietnam, although there are important differences as well. It is based upon the following:

1. heavy rural to urban migration;
2. the transition from traditional agriculture with limited business, trade, and markets concentrated in urban areas (above all greater Bangkok, the equivalent of greater Ho Chi Minh City) to a much more thorough, large-scale capitalism based on tourism, manufacturing, and export and import sectors;
3. uneven development, the emergence of a poor underclass in both rural and urban areas in the context of growing gross prosperity and highly visible wealth and materialism, and vulnerability to economic shifts;
4. political turbulence involving a less than satisfactory or full transition to democracy and the dissatisfaction of large segments of both urban and rural populations;
5. increasing dissatisfaction with, and the declining influence of, the royal family, which, along with Buddhism, for a long period formed the main symbolic basis of the unity and sovereignty of the state; and
6. the development of the mass or popular media, consisting of newspapers and magazines and above all television, all of which thrive on stories involving the occult.

One major difference between Thailand and Vietnam is that there was no dramatic *doi moi*–like about-face in Thailand, for there had been no communist government that decided to reverse course and accept market reforms. There was rather a pattern that had been developing over decades as Thailand underwent economic and other forms of modernization. The economic collapse of 1997 may have brought a climax, however. The changes came mainly in urban areas. Heavy rural-to-urban migration (as in Vietnam) meant that rural people brought with them their existing beliefs in spirits, magic, and Buddhism but applied them to different problems.[15]

Magic Monks and Spirit Mediums

According to Kitiarsa, Thai popular religion involves two main types of professional practitioners: magic monks and spirit mediums.[16] Magic monks are those who are believed to be charismatic, to have supernatural powers of the usual sort—to heal, provide protection, exorcize spirits, provide winning lottery numbers, and so forth. They are also, however, not merely passive, reluctant, or secret providers of supernatural assistance but active agents who openly engage in occult practices and identify themselves as having the ability to do so. The magic they are reputed to practice is good rather than harmful. One famous virtuoso magic monk was said to be able to provide many kinds of help including setting up spirit altars, lengthening life spans, providing protection against automobile and motorcycle accidents, and blessing businesses, as well as providing tips on lottery numbers.

Though other types of supernatural practitioners also attempt to provide such help, magic monks do so as authentic monks who wear the saffron robes and otherwise do the things that ordinary monks do as well. Their status is based on the prestige of Buddhism as well as on their reputed magical skills and knowledge. Generally accepted by other monks as legitimate monks, they live in monasteries and often have backgrounds in forest monasteries, which are regarded as places of special spiritual power. Some monks, officials, and Buddhist scholars criticize the belief in and practice of magic as fundamentally opposed to the basic doctrines of Buddhism, which is that karma is the determining cause of everything important and cannot, therefore, be negated by magical practices. But monks get into serious trouble only for the most flagrant violations of monastic rules, such as engaging in sexual intercourse. Magic monks engage in practices that might appear to be violations of codes such as the handling of money and the accumulation of wealth, but these are overlooked or accepted. They may be given gifts by persons they have helped gain prestige and influence by passing on donations to their monastery and through other forms of charity. For those to whom they provide magical assistance, they meet needs for psychological help and spiritual assurance.[17]

There are both similarities and differences in the characteristics of magic monks and spirit mediums. Both deal in the occult and must therefore be believed in to have supernatural powers. Both highly regarded magical monks and mediums come from modest rural backgrounds and have risen by gaining reputations for occult powers. But the differences outweigh the similarities. Magic monks, of course, must be men who have been ordained and are based in monasteries. They can rise to great heights of fame, influence, and financial success as advisors to the rich and powerful.

A spirit medium is mainly a healer and problem solver who must be believed in (at least by their clients) to be able to contact spirits, speak with their voices, and persuade them to leave a client in peace or to help them do whatever else needs to be done. While the efforts of a medium focus on dealing with spirits, she or he also may provide other counseling about dealing with life's problems, especially as these often involve marital and other interpersonal matters. Mediums also advertise other services including fortune-telling, soul-calling rituals, business advice, help with school exams, and help avoiding military conscription.

Thai mediums may be men or women, but more typically women, whose clients are often women as well. Some become successful, but most live, like many of their clients, on the social and economic margins of society. As is often the case with both shamans and spirit mediums throughout Southeast Asia, spirit mediums believe themselves to be called by the spirits. The call usually takes the form of prolonged bouts of physical or mental illness that do not respond to other forms of curing; changes in appetite are also a sign that a divinity wishes to make use of a person's body—a wish that is usually said to be only reluctantly accepted of necessity. All mediums traditionally undergo instruction and initiation under the supervision of a senior medium or teacher, though some are now circumventing this under the direction from the deity involved. Once established, mediums receive clients and perform their rituals in their own homes before private shrines. The private shrines illustrate the difference in status between monks and mediums. A medium's shrine will contain statues or other images of a variety of deities, but will always be surmounted by the figure of the Buddha, even though a medium cannot represent or speak with the voice of the Buddha. Unlike the donations made to monks, contributions to a medium for services do not earn merit. The commonness of female spirit mediums may be related in part to the inability of women to become monks or otherwise to ritually perform with the authority of Buddhism.

The lower status and career prospects of spirit mediums in comparison with those of magic monks notwithstanding, their numbers are on the increase, especially in rapidly expanding urban areas, above all Bangkok. While some are positioned higher up on the food chain, most of the clients of urban mediums are urban laborers, factory workers, pedicab drivers, domestic servants, and market sellers, whose numbers represent a large part of the rural-to-urban expansion underway in Thailand and other countries of Southeast Asia.[18] The economic size of the spirit medium sector of the occult economy in Thailand cannot be easily, let alone precisely, tabulated.[19]

Commodification and the Amulet Trade

The range of commodities associated with the occult economy and popular religion in Southeast Asia is very large. Among adherents of Chinese and Vietnamese religious traditions, these include "ghost money" and the various paper models of automobiles, motorcycles, appliances, and other goods that are conveyed to deceased family members by burning in special ovens located at temples and shrines. In urban areas, shops specialize in such goods, which are said to be increasing in variety and lavishness as the desire for comfort and status symbols is believed to be growing in the afterlife as it is in the present one.

Spirit houses and offerings for shrines are major commodities. A visitor to the cities and towns of Thailand will be struck by what seem to be bright-colored Asian dollhouses on stilts sitting along the road in large numbers. These are the smaller, ready-made spirit houses, designed along the lines of open temples and palaces, to be bought and installed on the grounds of houses, shops, and restaurants, and also around some sacred trees and larger shrines. Upscale apartment buildings, office complexes, and hotels have much larger and more lavish, architect-designed shrines. The offerings made to shrines range from the traditional incense and candles to fresh fruits, plastic horses and zebras, pretty dresses and jewelry (for female spirits), and toys and even TV sets for child spirits. Many such goods are sold at nearby stalls and stores. Some of the goods that serve as offerings have other, non-ritual uses, but many others—such as paper ghost money and automobiles—do not.

In the recent period, scholars and researchers have paid particular attention to the commodification of amulets—small, flat, metal or ceramic objects usually showing an image of the Buddha or another deity or well-known religious figure.[20] Amulets have been around for a long time but have greatly increased as collectables or exchange goods in the more recent period. As valued collectables they are sold newly minted and subsequently exchanged between individuals and in stores and markets. Their value is somewhat like that of stamps or coins, based to some extent perhaps on aesthetic considerations and condition, but above all on rarity. They attract collectors who become experts on valuable versions and look for bargains among hawker stalls and sidewalk sellers. The difference between amulets and coins or stamps is that amulets are valued also, in some cases primarily, because of their reputed magical power to enhance luck or provide protection.

The amulet trade has attracted particular attention in recent decades among scholars, though not only as an economic activity or popular cultural pastime, but as one associated with the stature and activities of famous magic monks. While amulets have a long history as a part of Thai spirit beliefs and magic, their Buddha-ization seems to be recent.[21] Though made by Buddhist monks before the nineteenth century, earlier amulets did not carry images of the Buddha or Buddhist saints (famous magic monks). Their full incorporation into Buddhist material culture and growth as a major religious commodity has been attributed to the increase of national Thai anxieties. These first concerned European imperial expansion and the political centralization of the Thai state around the turn of the twentieth century, followed by further stress brought by the effects of World War II and then by the threat of Southeast Asian communism, and after that the insecurities and dislocations brought by urbanization and the threats posed by urban life. The striking and blessing of amulets by or on behalf of famous, revered monks has become a major way for magic monks and their monasteries and charitable projects to turn material charisma into a major occult industry in contemporary Thailand.

The full, modern emergence of the amulet cult and industry came, along with the increase in numbers of spirit mediums and other magical practitioners, with the economic boom of the 1980s and 1990s—followed by the bust of the late 1990s. By this time the amulet trade had clearly developed an economic-collecting dimension in a way that other sorts of good luck and protection charms and fetishes generally have not. In the early 2000s the amulet industry had reached new heights as Thai Buddhism turned more fully into a prosperity religion. By 2006–2007 more than eighty million units of the best-selling amulet series had been sold, a larger number than the population of Thailand. This was in part because a marketing and advertising campaign of historic proportions had been launched, the main theme of which was to link the amulets to the acquisition of wealth. By this time the amulet cult and industry had also become entwined with national politics, ideology, and the monarchy.[22]

The Mass Media and the Occult Economy

As in the development of the amulet industry, the mass media has played a major role in the modern development of the occult economy in Thailand. Newspapers relish sensational stories involving the occult because they attract readers. But because not all Thai can read, television—which is ubiquitous—may be even more important than print. The activities and personalities of spirit mediums, astrologers, magic monks, and others involved in one way or another in Buddhism or the occult are popular (and this is perhaps the more so since critical or unfavorable accounts of the monarchy are prohibited, thus increasing the space available for the public discussion of other cultural matters of national interest). Here two recent case studies are of particular interest, one by Erick White and the other by Kitiarsa.[23] The first concerns a Thai cable TV exposé of spirit mediums, the second the deification of a pop star.

Spirit Mediums Exposed and Publicized on TV

Efforts by religious and political elites to eliminate or control popular religious practices taken to be backward or harmful superstition have a long history. In Siam/Thailand attempts by the monarch and state officials to enforce religious propriety and orthodoxy and reduce misconduct by deviant monks extend back to the Ayutthaya period.[24] Such concerns increased in the nineteenth century as efforts were made by several monarchs to suppress or control practitioners of popular religion thought to pose a hindrance or threat to public well-being. These included an attempt—ably recounted by Erick White—that took place in 1891 when King Chulalongkorn enacted into law a ban on all spirit medium practices.[25]

The ban by King Chulalongkorn, which covered practices by both Thai and Chinese mediums, was aimed at protecting the public. It was enacted following a great fire in Bangkok that had burned a large area and killed many people. The king called for an investigation and was told that a spirit medium had been predicting such a fire. He was also told of further predictions by other mediums and of more fires in different areas of the city. People became worried, assembled, and sought supernatural protection. The law directed police and government officials to prohibit spirit possession, though of course this was easier said than done. Other fires started and other predictions were made. The enactment of the law included the explanation that gangs of spirit mediums were starting fires after predicting them in order to persuade frightened people to pay for their help with deities the mediums could invoke.[26] Whether those behind the ban believed in the supernatural powers of spirit mediums or only in the consequences of such beliefs does not appear to have been established, but it may have involved some of both.

In any case, the furor died down. Spirit mediums either more discretely continued their practices or reemerged, though evidently without causing the sort of trouble that had inspired the ban in the first place. Eventually, however, the problem of spirit mediums returned as a topic for popular journalism, especially television journalism. What took place reflected the conversion of several conflicting trends in popular religion and its political context in modern Thailand.

By the 1980s, "the Thai state was retreating from its historic, self-appointed role to monitor, constrain, and, if necessary, suppress those non-establishment forms of popular religiosity that conflicted with modernist reform Buddhism."[27] And by the 1990s the government had largely abandoned its concerns with both state-regulated Buddhism and the amorphous realm of popular religious practices, including those of spirit mediums, unless clear violations of ordinary criminal law were concerned (for example if a spirit medium had been accused of cheating or robbing a client). In other words, the state attitude had become that people were free to be as superstitious and backward as they wanted to be so long as they were not breaking other laws, much the same attitude as with prostitution.

But at the same time that official tolerance was increasing, popular recourse to occult activities had not diminished. This recourse was directed especially to attaining or maintaining material prosperity, a goal that had been brought on by the previous decade of economic boom and bust. The problems for which people sought help included both more modern economic ones as well as traditional personal difficulties.

Nor had the view of spirit mediums as a public problem been totally forgotten. The attention that came to be focused on mediums and their activities reflected this importance, especially in the politically and economically volatile modern period. With the rise of the modern mass media and its appetite for material, there was a related increase in people seeking publicity for a cause, or themselves, or both. Stories that involved the controversial exploits of occult practitioners, like those of the financial or sexual transgressions of monks, were always attractive. As recounted by White, several such television programs concerning mediums and their practices took place in the late 1990s, one featuring a well-known monk, the other a medium. The first of these occurred from mid-September on into October and represented one of the periodic emergences of spirit mediumship from the background of public awareness into central television attention:

> While the contemporary Thai print and electronic media frequently, if sporadically, cast a critical spotlight on the apparently self-evident irrationalities, dangers and deceptions of spirit mediumship, during these few weeks . . . the coverage was more widespread and sustained than usual. In part this was because it was instigated by Phra Payon, an outspoken Buddhist monk and public intellectual who is well-known for successfully using media to simultaneously further his own modernist, reform-oriented religious projects and advance his reputation as a virtuous monk. The sustained attention, however, also reflected the fact that this time there was more to the story than the usual anguished assertions that spirit mediums were a sign of Thailand's increasing moral chaos, intellectual bankruptcy or spiritual degeneration. The novel addition to this almost stereotypic set of criticisms was that Phra Payon was . . . calling for a legal crackdown on spirit mediums and pushing for the revival and/or rewriting of Chulalongkorn's 1891 law designed to prohibit spirit mediumship.[28]

Beyond entertainment and publicity, however, not much came of the series. At first it appeared that the state would act. There were reports of committee deliberations and plans in parliament, but these finally came to nothing. The government's intent to actually crack down and prohibit (or re-prohibit) spirit mediums may never have been there to begin with. For one thing, there were no fires and apparent acts of arson or comparable threats to life and property as there had been when the first law against spirit mediums was promulgated. Except for the king and royal family who are legally protected, political leaders are fair media game in modern Thailand. More generally, both the public and the Thai state had come increasingly to see spirit mediums and other occult activities in the same way it had come to view prostitution, drug addiction, and the frequently reported scandals involving Buddhist monks—as mainly private problems or ones the state should avoid worrying about unless things got seriously out of hand. Real legal repression was not really wanted. Rather, crimes should be punished by the existing laws.[29]

As theater, however, scandals involving spirit mediums had staying power, especially if a new angle could be found, which it was the following year. This time an independent cable TV channel broadcast a series of programs on spirit mediums as a feature of a weekly show specializing in investigation and exposé. The new angle was the appearance on the first program of a famous medium who had been practicing for twenty-six years. The medium proceeded to confess that what he had been doing was based on deception, and then explained and demonstrated how it was done. Subsequent programs involved investigative reporters who visited other mediums and hinted that what they were doing was also fraudulent, but it was the first program that attracted great attention and follow-up news reports. The program was recorded on location at the medium's shrine, with the medium in costume and performing as he usually did while interrupting periodically to explain what he was doing and how he was doing it. The program was shown before a live audience consisting of the medium's assistants, clients and followers, as well as strangers. The impact of the program was greater than it would have been if done as a newspaper article or series.

The confession that his possession by spirits was contrived included an explanation of how he convinced his clients and others that he was really in a state of trance and protected from harm. This focused especially on acts of physical mutilation that included cutting his tongue and writing in blood, pushing a sharpened skewer through his facial cheeks, and sitting on nails driven through the seat of a chair. The program presented these as though they were faked, the same thing a modern magician does when he cuts a woman in a box in half. In fact, the acts of self-mutilation were only partially faked. The nails in the chair were real but set too close together and the material in the medium's pants too thick for the nails to penetrate his flesh when he bounced up and down on them. The penetration of the skewer through the cheeks was genuine, though its diameter was small enough to minimize damage and pain (I have heard elsewhere that mediums who do this often use the same holes over and over, so the effect is not much different from that of putting on a thick earring). The tongue cutting and writing on paper in blood is fully genuine (I have seen Chinese mediums in Malaysia do it up close on various occasions, bleeding enough and long enough to inscribe a fair number of characters on paper during a ritual, and recutting periodically to keep the blood flowing). The only "fake" thing done here was for the medium to drink alcohol during the process to prevent infection in the wound rather than relying only on magical protection. Nor are the acts of mutilation a routine part of the trance performances done for clients, including new ones. They are reserved for special occasions.[30]

While the television exposé made spirit possession into a sensational and popular scandal, the longer-term effects were, again, a different matter. The scandal may have further undermined the credibility of spirit mediums but probably not that much. The culture of spirit mediumship in modern Thailand is already one of skepticism rather than absolute faith. There is some willful suspension of disbelief, but it is far from complete. Followers and clients say genuineness is "fifty-fifty." Spirit mediums and their followers routinely accuse other mediums of being fakes. Clients do not assume the best in seeking a reliable medium but look for what they take to be positive evidence, such as accurate knowledge and the absence of mistakes in an interview. An experienced medium may provide what is in effect good advice concerning the personal problems brought by a client, and in any case will probably put on a good show, which is certainly worth something. In spite of his confession of fakery and deception, some of his own clients told interviewers on camera that they were still not sure that all mediums were fakes. Some believed that the medium himself was authentic at least some of the time.

LOTTERY PLAY AND THE LOGIC OF OCCULT ECONOMIC THOUGHT

In some (probably most) places in Southeast Asia the lottery has been around a long time. Guillaume Rozenberg, a French scholar of Buddhism, points out that the lottery has a long history in Burma and seems to have had a small place in the colonial myth of British salvation of the downtrodden.[31] According to the late nineteenth-century British colonial writer James George Scott (who wrote as Shway Yoe), an official lottery was introduced into the country by the last monarch, King Thibaw, who ruled from 1878 to 1885. At that time the British overthrew him and annexed what remained of independent Burma into British India. The Burmese government was in dire economic straits, and the king saw the lottery as a way out. He sold licenses to sell lottery tickets for cash, mainly to government ministers and other court officials, who organized and ran their own lotteries. Fierce competition ensued among the owners of the various lotteries who resorted to various ways of attracting players. Perhaps making a good Victorian colonial story even better (and one that, from the British perspective, further justified the ensuing colonial takeover), it showed that the Burmese were incapable of governing themselves effectively. Scott described the results of the introduction of the lottery as a social and moral disaster. People ceased to do the necessary things they had been doing in order to gamble. Fathers sold their daughters, and husbands sold their wives to get money. Even the feckless young king realized the lottery was a road to ruin and tried yet other ways to raise revenue. But it was already too late, and the end of the monarchy and the British takeover of the last independent part of Burma came quickly. All of this now sounds overstated as an assertion of Victorian imperial morality.

The motives for present-day lottery playing in Southeast Asia are multiple. For one thing it can be a matter of amusement based on the thrill of risk taking that is probably a human universal. It can also be a focus of pleasurable social activity, beginning with the often-cooperative search for a winning number, continuing with a gathering to wait for the announcement of the winners and the postmortem discussions of the result, with special interest in near misses as well as the rarer wins. Of course, the social dimension of lottery play can have its downside. The winnings, if any, may have to be divided, and there can

Figure 7.1. A lottery ticket seller at Wat Phra That, a prominent Buddhist shrine and temple on Doi Suthep Mountain (Chiang Mai, Thailand, 2010). Note the Disneyesque lion statue in the background.

be requests for loans or gifts from friends, relatives, and neighbors. If the winning number is believed to be the result of a request made to a spirit or god, a vow has usually been made that will need to be redeemed.

Lotteries in Southeast Asia vary but in general can be divided along two lines. There is first the distinction between those that are legal versus those that are illegal. Those that are legal are ones that are either operated or sanctioned by the government, while those that are illegal are not ("illegal" does not necessarily mean strong negative concern by either the public or the government). The other line of differentiation is based on the size of the numbers involved. The small-number lotteries are those that consist of a few digits. Of these, three digits is probably the most common, while the large-number ones consist of three or four times this number of digits. To some extent, these two lines of differentiation run together. The legal lotteries usually have large numbers,

Figure 7.2. A popular tree spirit shrine on the outskirts of Chiang Mai, 2005. Note the Chinese Lion Dance mask among the offerings before the tree and the helpful ladder.

while the illegal ones have small numbers. Other differences are logical and fairly obvious. Supernatural considerations aside, the odds of winning of course vary according to the number of digits. Assuming that all the numbers are sold and each only once, the chance of winning a single two-digit number are one in a hundred, while those for a three-digit lottery are one in a thousand; a four-digit number can have only one winner in ten thousand if all numbers are sold and each only once. The reality may be complicated since a number may be sold more than once, and not all numbers may sell, or multiple winning numbers may be drawn—all of which makes the rational calculation of odds harder and probably makes the lottery more popular everywhere. In any case, small-number lotteries are much easier to win than large-number ones, but the prizes are correspondingly smaller. A further difference is that small-number lotteries may not be based on the drawing of their own winning numbers, but rather use numbers provided by some larger

Figure 7.3. The family of a woman who successfully sought a better job sets up a spirit house offering at a prominent roadside shrine outside Chiang Mai, in payment of the vow, 2006.

public lottery or some other regularly held form of gambling (such as horse racing) in which the results can be quickly and reliably known. The most common procedure in Southeast Asia seems to be to bet on the last several digits of a larger legal lottery number. In Malay, the general term for small-number lottery playing is thus *tikam ekor*, or "stabbing the tail."

This kind of play falls into the general category of "pariah gambling." As elsewhere the popularity of small-number lottery play seems to reflect a preference for a better chance of winning a smaller amount to a much poorer chance of winning a much larger prize. But there are other attractions as well. Although the main thing is of course winning, lottery play also attracts interest as a social activity. The interest is greater if one knows the identity of the winner and what mystical strategy he or she may have employed to win. The latter information is all the more valuable in the case of someone who is known to have won more than once. In any case, the smaller the size of the pool from which the winner is drawn the larger the portion of the local community who will know her or his identity. A final advantage of small-number play is that finding a small number through a mystical search would be easier than finding or correctly interpreting a larger one from the source that has been chosen or come upon by chance. Finding a large number may involve correctly putting together a whole series of clues.

The mystical search for winning lottery numbers in Southeast Asia takes several basic forms. In one of these the player seeks—or accidently comes upon—a number or a clue to a number through a sign in the natural environment (such as in the bark of a special tree), the cultural environment (such as the license plate of a car that has been in an accident), or through an internal process (such as meditation, gazing, or dreaming). In a second way, the player seeks supernatural help from a spirit or deity by going to a shrine or grave and asking or using some method of divination through which the number may be revealed. In the third way an aspiring winner seeks a number through the assistance of another human being who, through spiritual powers or a divine connection, may be able to help in one way or another.[32]

Lottery Play among South Indian Plantation Workers

These several paths to supernatural help in finding a successful number are not mutually exclusive. This can be seen in several more detailed, modern accounts of lottery play by anthropologists. Studies done in the 1960s and 1970s of South Indian plantation workers in the west cost of peninsular Malaysia show that the pursuit of lottery prizes based on efforts at gaining supernatural assistance is not recent. Nor is there reason to suppose that, in general terms at least, the culture of lottery play has changed much in the more recent period.[33]

As a part of his larger detailed ethnographic study, Ravindra Jain discusses lottery play among plantation workers of a large estate he refers to as Pal Melayu.[34] Though less so than in earlier periods, such plantation workers still lived fairly circumscribed lives in socially isolated communities. Lottery play had come to form a regular expenditure in the budgets of a majority of worker households that he was tracking daily in his research. However, the particular form of lottery activity Jain found at the time he began his study was apparently recent. Previously some *kanganis* (foremen), who earned higher wages than laborers on estates, had been well known to bet on horse races, which required costly travel to the track. The usual outcome, including the expenses as well as the bets, was substantial loss, and such gambling was reputed to be a path to financial disaster. Such gambling had a certain élan because it involved a colonial sport and appealed to people who had more money than did laborers, for the latter were in no position to be involved in at-the-track betting.

The most popular form of lottery play among laborers at this time involved Forecast Three-Digit Lottery, popularly referred to as *ekor*—probably derived from the Malay phrase *tikam ekor* or "stabbing the tail" noted above. *Ekor* in this case could have a double meaning in that, as usual, the three-digit number was the end of a longer one but also could suggest the tail of a horse. This is because the Forecast Three-Digit Lottery was based on horse racing, specifically on the last three digits of the six-digit number of the winning horse in each race (with second and third prizes based on the numbers of the second- and third-place horses). *Ekor* is therefore a form of horse-race gambling but one that could be done for very small sums and modest expenses. It also required no knowledge of the chances of a particular horse winning, since the number of each horse was randomly assigned just before the beginning of each race.

Ekor has some of the usual characteristics of the three-digit lottery, including the comparatively favorable odds of eventually winning a prize, which could of course be improved by buying more tickets. However, unlike many three-digit lotteries, *ekor* was legal and backed by the authority of the government. Jain reports that the expenses and profits subtracted from the payout are relatively modest, though how important or well known this was to the players is not stated. The strongest source of motivation to play was having won previously, and the second was knowledge of someone else who had won. The number of people in Pal Melayu who had won was small, but, the plantation also being a small community, they were well known to everyone. Here also three-digit lottery play had important social values, especially for men, for whom it had become an obsession. The sequence of activity involved buying the tickets before or on race day and then gathering in the bar of the *ekor* ticket shop to wait for the results announced on the radio. Here they drank before the race to calm their nerves and then afterward to celebrate winning or, more often, to drown their sorrows. "The thought of Ekor was ever-present in the minds of most estate workers on Pal Melayu."[35]

The thoughts and efforts of men about *ekor* generally involved mystical means of finding winning numbers. The favorite appeared to be "number dreaming." Put simply, a man might awake from a night's sleep or a daytime nap and remember dreaming of a number. A man might also deliberately try to sleep in order to dream of a number before going to buy a ticket. A dream, however, might not be liable to direct interpretation. The dream might be of an animal or an object rather than a number, and if this was the case a special book would need to be consulted, one that translated animals and objects into numbers. Such books were inexpensive and sold in local Chinese provision stores. These contained tables of line drawings next to both Chinese and Arabic numerals, with relevant portions of the Chinese text translated into Malay, which the Tamil workers could read. Some knowledgeable devotees claimed the book was a publication by the devotees of a supposed mystic known as "Hong Kong Sami."

Either the direct or the indirect discovery of winning numbers could be further complicated. A dream might involve a larger or smaller number than one consisting of three numerals, it might involve animals, or it might involve objects in confusing sequence or mixture. This complexity, however, meant that failure to correctly divine a winning number (the usual outcome) was not interpreted to mean the method was incorrect, only that some mistake or bad choice had been made in its application. A common fallback strategy was to use a further form of divination that Jain describes as follows:

> Often dreaming of a number is followed by a verification ritual at the Munianti [a popular Tamil divinity] shrine. The temple, ordinarily neglected, is swept clean and a ceremonial lamp is lit. The god is prayed to, and betel leaves, water, bananas, oranges and coconuts are offered. Turmeric water is sprinkled in all corners of the temple, and lighted camphor is waved in front of the image. The ceremony is climaxed by the sacrificial offering of a white cock by the person who has dreamt of the number. The body of the cock is thrown outside the temple, while the severed head is laid before the image and turmeric water is sprinkled on it three times. If the cock opens its mouth each time water is sprinkled, the worshipper believes he has

> dreamt the true number. He breaks a coconut, lights camphor, prays to the god again, and often bathes the image with a half a bottle of beer and drinks the other half himself.[36]

In addition to number dreaming, with or without a confirming visit to the shrine, several other forms of divination were also used. One of these was to write numbers on pieces of paper, go to the shrine and perform the same ritual described above, and then draw lots in front of the image. Similar rituals may also be performed at the shrines of divinities elsewhere that have reputations for providing help with lottery numbers, though finding such shrines might require consultation with a Malay or Chinese diviner. Finally, players may consult with a Tamil bird astrologer to determine one's luck with *ekor.* As with a diviner, this will involve a small fee for service. Except for plain dreaming, the search for a winning *ekor* number therefore involves an expenditure of funds for fees and ritual materials in addition to time and effort. Playing *ekor* is hence serious business.

It is difficult to know the extent to which the passion for three-digit lottery play described by Jain for Pal Melayu is either constant or typical of estate workers elsewhere in the plantation zone of western Malaya.[37] It seems likely that enthusiasm waxes and wanes but is always present to some extent, to be revived by a local win and then perhaps eventually declining with a prolonged losing spell in the community. However, small-number lotteries generally produce enough winners to keep hope and interest alive, and the various occult practices used in the pursuit of winning numbers are not easily discredited by negative experience.

The Making of a Lottery Deity

In both Vietnam and Thailand, the rise of new deities who are venerated and who can be asked for winning lottery numbers or to provide protection or other help is an ongoing process. These are often supposed to be the ghosts of real persons, but who in reality may have never existed as such. And real or not in life, such spirits are often believed to be the ghosts of persons who have died a bad death—typically violently, by suicide, or in any case prematurely. Sooner or later a shrine is created.

The anthropologist Oscar Selamink provides an example of how this can happen in southern Vietnam.[38] The shrine in question is located along a river in an area outside of Cho Lon, the Chinese quarter of Ho Chi Minh City (formerly Saigon), and approachable only by water. It is beyond a religiously heterodox temple and near a place with a series of altars dedicated to the five incarnations of the Mother Goddess and a shrine devoted to the second president of socialist Vietnam. Here there are two graves, one made of cement and one a plain mound of earth. The story is that the graves are of two orphan children, a boy and his sister. Some years ago the boy committed suicide by hanging himself from a tree and a short while after the girl did so as well. One day a woman came to pray at the graves and then won a big lottery prize. The news quickly spread and many people began to visit the graves to seek the help of the two spirits with winning numbers. People come at night in secret because the government at first forbade the practice as superstition. However there is now an altar, one of the graves has been upgraded, and the other one will probably be as well by a thankful winner.

Some popular lottery spirits did lead real lives. One that did was Phumphuang Duangchan, the top Thai female pop star in the 1980s and early 1990s.[39] Phumphuang was beautiful, a talented singer with a kind and pleasing personality who was known throughout the country from constant personal, TV, and movie appearances. She came from a poor background with parents who had been laborers, and she had not remained in school long enough to learn to read. She became rich as an entertainment superstar who outwardly appeared to have a life of great success and glamour. She had a special appeal to young people who, like her, had moved to the city from the village.

Her private life, however, was mainly a mess, spent largely on the road and performing, with little rest and recuperation. She was married twice, and her second husband did not get along with her parents and other relatives. She suffered from two autoimmune disorders and died at the age of thirty-one. Before her death she was torn between the efforts of her husband to have her treated by modern medicine and those of her parents who believed she was suffering from malevolent occult causes that might involve her husband who was after her money. She saw both medical doctors and spirit mediums and died on the way to see a medium. The modern medical opinion was that she succumbed to kidney failure. Her parents thought it was sorcery and fought with her estranged husband over her property.

A better supernaturally laced soap opera could not be written. Her fame and the other circumstances of her life and premature death made Phumphuang a prime candidate for deification. The Thai, like some other peoples in Southeast Asia, have the notion of bad death as having the potential of spiritually favorable consequences.[40] Her transition from a tragically deceased, fondly remembered, and glamorous real human to a potent supernatural being capable of helping the living began in the years following her demise. After lying in state in Bangkok she was given a royal cremation in the Buddhist temple in her natal village, presided over by a princess and attended by fifteen thousand grieving fans. Although the country was in turmoil at the time, with clashes between the military and demonstrators in Bangkok, her death and funeral dominated the news. Copies of Phumphuang memorabilia were produced and sold in large quantities at her funeral and in markets around the country. The political and social upheavals that took place at the time of her demise and in the following months may have encouraged the notion that important mystical forces were at work.

The deification of Phumphuang was perhaps also encouraged by the holding of several annual fairs at the temple where she was cremated, which became known as her temple. However, the real beginning came with the onset of rumors linking her spirit to the lottery. Such stories began to circulate in the national newspapers and on television in the first half of 1998. The gist of such stories and urban legends was that Phumphuang was conveying winning numbers to her loyal fans. A cynical investigative newspaper timed such stories to the days before the bimonthly national lottery in an apparent effort to increase sales. One story recounted that Phumphuang's husband told reporters that he won a huge lottery prize after taking their eleven-year-old son to pay homage to the wax statues of his mother at her shrine. The son's visits to his mother's shrine were also reported to attract fortune seekers who hoped to pick up lucky numbers conveyed through the son. Other stories reported how crowded this temple became on the nights preceding lottery draws, and yet others that it had become an international occult tourist attraction. One fortune seeker was quoted in a Thai newspaper as saying that this was the hope of the poor.[41]

Buddhist Mystical Assistance: The Lottery in Burma

All over Southeast Asia people seek mystical assistance in finding winning lottery numbers, and in Buddhist areas this may involve monks. The most common involvement of monks with lotteries is probably helping members of the laity to win. One way this is done in Laos involves the blessing given by a monk at the popular string-tying or soul-calling ceremony (*baci*), several instances of which I participated in. Such blessings by monks can include phrases like "May you become rich and win the lottery." Another way that a monk may help is to suggest or hint at a winning number.[42] The detailed account of occult-oriented, small-number lottery play in Burma published recently by Rozenberg describes how this works in Myanmar.[43] He describes the Burmese (more specifically, the ethnic Burmans) as being obsessed with the lottery and inclined to go to great lengths to seek out a winning number. His account centers on a number-seeking adventure in which he participated with three Burmese friends in the climactic excitement of the final run-up to the next draw.

The lottery was the usually illegal, highly localized, three-digit version. In this case, as commonly elsewhere, the winning number is based on the final three digits of the longer winning number from an official trusted lottery draw. At first this was the twice-a-month draw of the government lottery in Thailand. Later, however, the official lottery of Myanmar, with its even more frequent draws, was added, creating more frequent opportunities for play. As elsewhere also, the illegal, small-number version is popular because the player can bet in several ways, can choose the specific number to play (even though a limited number of other players have also chosen it), and can bet any amount of money, the winning sum being based simply on some multiplier of the amount a player has wagered.[44]

Paradoxical though it might at first seem, the illegal lottery in Myanmar, as elsewhere, has to be honest. Winners are paid promptly, and cheating is rare. The organizational structure is simple and limited. At the top is the "banker" who finances the operation, stands behind the payment of all winners, and keeps everything left after the winners have been paid and other expenses met. The participation of the banker is invisible. The banker keeps no written records, which are the main form of evidence used by the police if they go after illegal lottery operations, and only those who are just below him know his identity. The latter are the vendors (frequently women) who do the retailing and keep the records of their transactions in notebooks, which include each bet made and the number of bets made for each number up to 999. The vendors visit the houses of players and spend time on the streets and in coffee and cigarette shops in return for 25 percent of each bet they take. Because, unlike the bankers, they are well known in the community, and because they keep the written records, the vendors are vulnerable to the police. The police, however, are seldom a problem unless they are pressed from above for some reason to go after the lotteries. The local police often like to play themselves and if so are seeking tips for likely winning numbers or some other favor.[45]

Lottery play as so far described would again seem to be fairly straightforward gambling. It might exist even if it did not have an occult side. But in Myanmar, as elsewhere in Southeast Asia, such a possibility is hypothetical, for what helps to motivate play is the possibility of circumventing the actual odds through mystical help in finding a winning number. The search for such occult aid has several characteristics. The first concerns the domain of Burmese religion to which the search for lottery numbers belongs. Burmese occult activities have been divided into Buddhist and non-Buddhist (an oversimplification) sectors. The non-Buddhist side, for example, includes get-rich pursuits such as alchemy, which has a prominent place in traditional Burmese magic.[46] Spirit mediums, which are also part of the non-Buddhist sector, are similarly often consulted on economic matters, but they are not sought out in the search for winning lottery numbers. Efforts to find winning numbers through occult means in Myanmar belong rather to the general domain of practical Buddhism.

A second characteristic is that the mystical search for winning lottery numbers is not a clear, straight, well-marked road. It involves the intersection of Burmese Buddhist philosophy, numerology, mystical code breaking, and guesswork. Players seeking winning numbers try to obtain them from Buddhist monks who have developed a reputation for correctly predicting them on the basis of their spiritual powers. One such famous monk had come to be known as "the Monk Who Makes the Bankers Run Away" because he was believed to have correctly predicted winning numbers several times, thereby putting fear into the hearts of the bankers at the top of the illegal lottery networks.[47] But neither this monk nor others who had gained a reputation for correct prediction would simply give out the three winning numbers, let alone in the correct sequence. There were monks who would come into town and hold up signs offering winning lottery numbers, presumably in return for donations, but this sort of behavior did not inspire confidence, the principle apparently being He Who Says Does Not Know and He Who Knows Will Not Say (directly). The information provided by a monk with real mystical knowledge would rather be expressed in an oblique form, such as one that often involved converting words into numbers according to some code that would have to be figured out. Such information might be found hidden in a public sermon the monk would give before a lottery draw, the sermon having no overt connection whatsoever to the lottery.

Buddhism is involved in ways that differ from the perspective of the lottery player and the monks who, however reluctantly, support the search for a winning number. Winning requires some amount of good karma—and in turn is probably an indication of future well-being in general. But while good karma is necessary, it is not sufficient. It is also necessary to try very hard by searching for clues to the number and then doing the calculations of words and numbers to correctly interpret them. Such clues are to be found above all in the spoken and written words of the right monk. Players who seek numbers from monks believe that forest and hermit monks have stronger occult powers than those who belong to urban monasteries, as is also true in the case of the creation and blessing of amulets.

Players and monks have different but complementary orientations to the lottery.[48] That of the player is more obvious than that of the monk. From the perspective of the monks, the lottery might at first seem entirely wrong or at least undesirable. A monk takes vows of poverty and is supposed to devote himself to making progress toward enlightenment and salvation by avoiding sinful acts and doing good works. As some players realize, many monks want nothing to do with the lottery because they prefer to spend their time in solitary meditation and wish to avoid worldly material concerns. In addition, monks are forbidden to demonstrate magical powers to the laity, for which they can be expelled from the order. Such monks may refuse to have anything to do with helping with lottery numbers or encouraging players to seek their help. They may even post signs that say they do not wish to be bothered.

Monks themselves cannot personally possess wealth—they are not even supposed to handle money. They customarily go on ritualized begging rounds for their food early in the morning, from which those members of the laity who make donations earn good karma.

At the same time, the lottery is not entirely a negative activity from the monks' perspective. One monk in Yangon had even created his own lottery, the prizes being objects of value that had been donated by the laity. But this was not the main basis of benefit. Rather, it was that lottery play tends to create a relationship of reciprocal exchange between players and those monks who are involved, from which each could benefit. For one thing, the belief that a monk had knowledge of winning numbers that he might obliquely reveal through clues in his sermons served as a way of attracting players to come and listen carefully to these, from which they might gain moral benefit even if it was not the reason they were there. This is not hard to understand. If university students believed that winning lottery numbers might be revealed in course lectures, more attention might be paid to what was being said. Also, monasteries require economic support. Monetary donations for new buildings, statues of the Buddha or of revered monks, or the construction of pagodas are also important and are considered major ways by which members of the laity can increase their positive karma. The most important goal of the monk is similarly to increase his store of karma and make progress toward enlightenment and salvation. But monks also exist in a moral and monastic hierarchy, and they seek influence that enables them to do good in the world. Monks may gain prestige and moral and political influence through the donations they attract and through other economic enterprises, such as the production of amulets, and through their reputation for learning and spiritual powers.

Though not in an entirely satisfactory manner, the lottery has been assimilated into this more traditional system of moral and economic exchange between monks and laity. Lottery players who win and believe it was because of the clues given by a monk in a sermon are apt to donate some of their winnings to the monastery. Insofar as a player has any concern that lottery winnings are ill gotten and therefore might produce bad karma, this may to some extent be offset by a generous donation.[49]

OCCULT ECONOMIC THOUGHT

Winning the lottery in Southeast Asia is, for many, never a matter of mere accident, chance, or rational probability. Nor is it necessarily assumed that winning numbers cannot be known before they are drawn. It is rather that the lucky numbers are already out there somewhere and can potentially be learned from a spirit or god at a shrine; from a living person with mystical powers; from a supernatural sign, such as the number of a license plate or one suggested by the figure in the bark of a tree; or from a dream. One principle that applies here is that bad fortune will be followed by good. This is one of the implications of bad death and has something to do with deification. It also explains the practice of playing the license number of car or motorcycle that has fatally crashed, an idea that apparently extends to airplane disasters, since Malaysian lottery firms are reported to have been forced (for whatever exact reason) to stop selling numbers involving the date and flight number of the Malaysian Airlines plane that was downed with all on board killed over Ukraine on July 17, 2014.[50]

None of these ways of finding a winning number are necessarily easy or a sure thing. They often require some knowledge, skill, and sometimes complex interpretation. This means also, however, that the general validity of mystical discovery is not readily falsified. There is always reason to hope that further effort and better calculation will have a positive result. To put this slightly differently, lottery play is not viewed as simply "gambling." It is rather an occult activity that falls within the realm of practical religion and has the same sort of possibilities for success as do other supernatural searches, such as ones aimed at passing a school exam, finding a job, getting a promotion, or causing someone to fall in love—though not necessarily with the same odds, of course. Finding a lottery number may require calculation and interpretation or verification and not merely an appeal for supernatural help or a chance discovery.

The Nature of Magical Thinking

As anthropologists have long known, magical thinking and activity are likely when outcomes of some activity are both uncertain and important, and the more of one or the other or both, the more occult thought and practices are encouraged. The uncertainty of the lottery and other efforts to gain practical help through occult efforts is obvious. The importance is more complicated. The lottery may have a particular appeal to the poor, who tend to see it as their only reasonable hope for economic improvement. The appeal, however, goes beyond the poor in that success is taken to be an indication of good karma, luck, or blessedness—something that is widely valued and sought. Lottery play combined with mystical searches for winning numbers epitomizes occult economic thought and activity, but other forms of behavior reflect such concerns as well. Many instances have been given throughout this chapter and elsewhere in the book. Success or failure in business is a different sort of example, though the basic principles are the same.[51]

8

RELIGIOUS MOVEMENTS AS POPULAR RELIGION

As we have seen earlier, the introduction of Christianity in Southeast Asia has sometimes led to the emergence of local sectarian or syncretic religious movements. Missionaries arrive (perhaps preceded by messianic rumors), seek converts, and introduce other perceived benefits. But for various reasons they are not always able to control the subsequent course of events that they had not anticipated. Local political boats get rocked or overturned, and power structures may be threatened or altered. In some instances (as with the Karen) conversion itself becomes a kind of religious movement. Once conversion occurs among indigenous peoples, a new form of popular religion comes into existence, one in which there is a set of beliefs and practices that do not simply replicate the official version of the doctrinal religion that has been brought to them or sought out. Similarly, with a religious movement that takes place among people who adhere to an existing established doctrinal religion, a new popular religion will generally be at odds with it and often with the authority of the state (if there is a controlling state) as well.

Chapter 6, which focused on conversion to Christianity, had little to say about religious movements which have been associated with other world religions or that are mainly the consequence of other developments. This chapter will take up the consideration of religious movements, both in more general terms and with regard to non-Christian instances. While Christianity is involved to some extent in several of the instances to be considered, the last three are linked to Islam. Globalization has also been involved in the more recent instances.

THE NATURE OF RELIGIOUS MOVEMENTS

Broadly put, popular religious movements can be said to be any effort to effect social, cultural, political, or economic change that has organized supernatural and ritual dimensions and departs substantially from existing beliefs and practices.[1] Such movements may involve both abandoning existing religious beliefs and practices or only adopting radical new ones. Although the underlying motives may be implicit, there will necessarily be efforts to achieve some end—that is, beyond the ordinary purposes of religious activity. All religious movements appear to arise out of change, conflict, competition, conquest, dissatisfaction, or disruption, and they often have an ethnic dimension. They appeal to people who see little or inadequate progress possible through ordinary, individual, or collective means. They usually involve a leader, central person, or visionary whose actions initiate the movement and around whom the movement revolves. The leader often is believed by followers to be of supernatural origin, or to have been supernaturally contacted, inspired, and instructed. Such individuals usually continue to demonstrate their power through what are taken to be supernatural feats or miracles. The crucial importance of such a prophet or messiah (as such persons are usually known) means that his or her death or disappearance is a crisis, often the end of the movement, or at least its fragmentation. Those movements that are carried successfully on by disciples can become new religions, sects, orders, or schools within some religious tradition.

Religious movements have often been approached in terms of their main themes or characteristics. Those aimed at preserving or returning to indigenous ways and rejecting foreign ones are commonly referred to as nativistic. Those that involve a savior or prophet are generally said to be messianic. Those that predict the end of the world or its radical transformation are labeled as millennial. One problem with such categories is that they are not mutually exclusive. Another is that the various labels may be only partially appropriate or misleading. Not all movements fit any such category. Further, those who were present at the time to provide the initial descriptions and interpretations may have been biased or misunderstood why a movement occurred or its aims, and therefore whether it was, for example, bent on eliminating foreign religious or other cultural practices and returning to the old way of life or simply preserving some of it.

Beyond such types, movements have sometimes been described as peaceful or violent. The problem here is both how much, if any, violence is involved or intended, and also who initiates the violence that occurs. Some movements involve actual attacks and killing. But in others, notions of invulnerability or the use of amulets believed to afford protection against bullets or other weapons are taken as evidence of the violent intentions of members. Movements also vary in terms of outcome or long-term developments. Here it is easy to identify examples of the extremes of success and failure. And although these terms are still used, social scientists are now less inclined to sort religious movements into messianic, millennial, and nativistic categories than to focus on what they have in common. For a long period now anthropologists have often preferred the term *revitalization* as a general label for religious movements, but as we shall see, revitalization is hardly the only, or perhaps even the usual, outcome.

In what follows I discuss six religious movements that have occurred in Southeast Asia—one in Borneo, two in northern mainland Southeast Asia, and three in peninsular Malaysia. They are not intended to be an accurate sample of all the known movements to have occurred in the recent past in Southeast Asia. They represent examples of the range of variation that occurs in movements in general. After discussing the particular instances, I shall turn to more general and comparative considerations.

Bungan in Borneo

The Bungan movement that took place in central Borneo involved several groups of people collectively referred to (in Malaysian Borneo) as Orang Ulu, or "Upriver Peoples," including Kayan, Kenyah, Berawan, Kajang, and Penan, and others. It began with what is best characterized as a reform movement, meaning one that aims at modifying rather than abandoning traditional beliefs and practices in order to create a more satisfying way of life. The movement began on the Apo Kayan Plateau in what was then Dutch Borneo (present-day East Kalimantan), but developed mainly in Sarawak, probably because Christianity was already more fully established in the former than the latter region. The movement was aimed at changing indigenous religious practices and became known simply as Bungan, after its main deity, Bungan Malan. In addition to becoming a named religion, a further effect of the movement was to create a specific identity for the old religious practices known as Adat Dipuy (the "Old Way"), a name that had not previously existed. For a time there were thus three named religions in the region: the traditional or Old Way, the new Bungan or Adat Bungan, and Christianity (of which there were several versions, depending on the village and area). As noted in the previous discussion of Christian conversion in Borneo, longhouse villages tended to be or become entirely one or another since many rituals were communal rather than individual or familial. Villages that could not agree on which religious tradition to follow tended to split up rather than remain internally divided.

An early published account of the Bungan includes an origin myth that states that the Old Way was not the first religion.[2] In the beginning there was a golden age of abundance and religious simplicity in which a single grain of rice made a meal and there were no onerous rituals and taboos. Then an incestuous marriage among the gods caused trouble, and the humans paid the price. The numerous taboos and animal auguries (above all ones involving the omen birds) at the heart of the old religion were created and imposed on the people by a new god named Dipuy. The story also tells that the Europeans, who had also been living in the region, took the magical rice and left, and that is why they became rich and the Dayaks became poor and had to struggle in order to survive. The new rituals were difficult, time consuming, and expensive, and if not performed correctly the spirits were angered and caused even more trouble. The omen birds were a constant source of worry when anything of the least consequence was to be undertaken. Many days of work were lost when the omens required people to stay home and inside their longhouses. Headhunting, which was considered necessary for the production of rice, had become a major activity.

Then sometime around 1940 a Kenyah man named Jok Apuy had a dream in which he was contacted by Bungan, a lesser goddess in the old religion. Jok Apuy had been an unsuccessful man who had lived a life of poverty and misfortune, including the loss of his children. The Dutch who had come to the Apo Kayan had told the people to become Christian and (while this is not entirely clear) Jok had done so, but this had not helped. He begged the gods to take his life, and his prayers were heard in heaven by Bungan Malam. She decided to come to earth to look into the problem. In the dream Bungan told Jok Apuy it was time for a change. When she had created the world the rituals were simple and there were no auguries, but then various new requirements were added. The solution was for humans to return to the original simple religion and get rid of all the ritual requirements that had been later added by the god Dipuy. The omens brought by the birds and other animals were to be ignored. The elaborate and costly agricultural ceremonies were to be abandoned, as were the taboos against killing and eating certain animals, most notably the *rusa* (a kind of deer that was widely hunted by some peoples in the interior but forbidden to others). Headhunting had already ended, but the cult of skulls, which had been kept, was to go as well. The skulls were to be removed from the village. All that was necessary was a simple ritual prayer to Bungan.

The reforms that Bungan told Jok Apuy to follow were not exactly new ideas. The missionaries in the interior had been saying similar things as reasons for people to become Christian. If they accepted Jesus Christ they could get rid of the bothersome taboos, omens, and headhunting ceremonies. Jok Apuy was probably familiar with such claims, but he decided to follow Bungan. The result was that he prospered, with impressive rice crops. Others in the village noticed Jok Apuy's new success and that he had also stopped attending Christian services, and some followed suit.

The news spread to other longhouses. Jok Apuy had become a prophet, and the Bungan reforms took hold, though not evenly or without change. Over the years two sorts of developments took place. The first was that Bungan achieved success beyond the Apo Kayan where it had originated. This sounds like the old story of prophets without honor in their own country, but in this instance there is probably a fairly specific historical explanation. The new Bungan religion grew and for a time prevailed, especially among the Orang Ulu peoples across the (hardly existent) border with Sarawak where large numbers of Kenyah and Kayan were also living. And while the Apo Kayan and the deep interior of northern Sarawak are not only close but also culturally and geographically similar, there were certain differences. One was that, for whatever set of reasons, Christianity was at the time more fully established in the interior of Dutch East Kalimantan than it was in the interior of British colonial Sarawak. This meant that Sarawak was open to Bungan in a way that the Apo Kayan was not. There, while some Dayaks had followed Jok Apuy and become Bungan, most stuck with Christianity.

Another difference of some possible importance was one that developed after Indonesia obtained independence from Dutch colonial rule in 1949. As noted earlier, after this time the new Indonesian government began to press all of its diverse peoples to embrace a monotheistic religion—one, moreover, "with a book"—an effort that became much more threatening with the anti-communist thrust that came with the military coup of Suharto. And while Christianity was one of the accepted religions, Bungan, let alone Adat Dipuy, was not. The government also began to press people to break up their longhouses and move into single-family dwellings. And while the conversion to Christianity and the abandonment of longhouses were different expressions of government anti-communism, they were linked. Although the government had other reasons for getting rid of longhouses as well, one being that they were regarded as fire hazards and another that they were seen as being non-hygienic, much of the ceremonial activity of the traditional religion took place in the longhouse common veranda. Therefore, people who converted for whatever reason to Christianity had less reason to want to keep longhouses. People who gave up longhouses because of government-military pressure or for whatever reason were probably also more likely to accept conversion to a government-approved religion.[3]

Religious developments took a different course in the interior of Sarawak. Both during the colonial and post-colonial periods, circumstances here were ones that made this region much more open to the spread of the Bungan movement.[4] Beginning in the late 1940s the Bungan movement began to spread into Sarawak and take hold in the upper river areas that were closest to the Apo Kayan in Indonesia. In some instances the movement simply spread from one village to another as people watched what happened in a neighboring village after they had implemented the reforms. In some other instances Bungan disciples followed the example of Christian missionaries and traveled the rivers to visit villages urging people to convert. In areas where

Christianity had not yet arrived, villages were faced with only two choices, to retain the rituals and taboos of the old religion or to accept Bungan. In either case it was mainly a village choice rather than an individual or household one since many of the rituals were communal in nature. All households were required to participate if the ritual was to work. The partial conversion of a village was therefore a bad idea. Some individual exceptions might be made in the case of older people considered to be no longer able to make the change. Elders in some families therefore remained traditionalists while younger members converted. In regions where Christianity was also spreading, people had three choices—to retain the old religion, to adopt the Bungan reforms, or to become Christian, with, however, the same tendency for villages to follow the same path or divide.

RELIGIOUS MOVEMENTS IN THE NORTHERN MAINLAND

The two movements to be discussed here concern the Hmong, though the Khmu were also involved in the later one. Like other groups the Hmong had stories about once having writing in China and of supernatural beings that would restore their lost scripts. They had words for both paper and writing and were familiar with written amulets.[5] Over the course of the twentieth century the mystical power of writing and scripts became associated with the power of military technology and warfare. The French anthropologist Jack Lemoine studied the development of writing and scripts among the Hmong.[6] He noted that the long civil (and American) war that engulfed Laos after the end of colonial rule brought military goods from all over the world that were stockpiled, moved around, and abandoned as front lines shifted. The writings on the cases of munitions and the instructions for the use of weapons included Chinese, Vietnamese, French, English, Russian, Czechoslovakian, and other languages. The Hmong, who generally could not read, not unreasonably assumed that the writing was related to the awesome destructive power of the weapons.

The Pa Chai Rebellion

As the link between writing and warfare and military power might further suggest, the religious movements that took place among the Hmong in northern Laos did so in the context of political dissatisfaction, competition, rebellion, and armed conflict. In brief, the first such movement began in 1919 and involved a rebellion against French colonial rule and the domination of the lowland Lao. The French referred to the rebellion as *les guerre des fous*, or "the war of the insane," because the Hmong rebels held magical beliefs including notions of invulnerability. They believed it was instigated and led by a Hmong man named Pa Chai. It involved a minority of the Hmong in the area and lasted for only several years. The general story of what took place seems similar to other rebellions against colonial government authority in which an insurrection is sparked by rumors of the appearance of a divine messenger.

As the story goes, Pa Chai lived as an ordinary villager until one day he was summoned to heaven by the Lord of the Sky and the Earth, who dwelt in a palace made of golden bricks. The Lord of the Sky and the Earth told Pa Chai that he was a special person who had been sent to live with the Hmong to teach them how to have a better life, but he failed to do so. Pa Chai was then told to return and try again to convince the Hmong to change their ways so that their lives would improve.

Word spread of Pa Chai's miraculous visit to heaven and return to earth where he displayed his newly acquired magical powers. The Hmong urged him to use his power to exterminate the Lao (lowlanders), who had been oppressing them. Pa Chai resisted this suggestion saying he had not been told to do this by the Lord of Heaven and Earth. He then made a further trip to heaven to explain how miserable the Hmong had become. Other Hmong, however, then took matters into their own hands and began to urge an insurrection against the government. But a Hmong headman who had become aware of what was going on informed the French, who sent Vietnamese soldiers to put down the rebellion. Pa Chai, however, had empowered a gunsmith to make a magical gun that enabled the Hmong rebels to hold off the government forces for two years. The Hmong rebels then attacked a government stronghold and poisoned its water supply. They also began to attack people living in the area. The French organized a counter-attack, and Pa Chai performed special rituals to seek divine help. But the Lord of Heaven and Earth was displeased with how the rebels had behaved and withdrew his protection. Pa Chai and his followers then gave up their arms to the French and fled into the jungle to hide. But a Hmong traitor led four Lao assassins to the hiding place where they killed Pa Chai and took his head away in a bag in order to collect the bounty they had been promised by the French.

This was not quite the end of the story, however. Some of Pa Chai's powers remained, and his spirit had final revenge. When the assassins arrived at the French headquarters and opened the bag to take Pa Chai's head out, it was missing, and in its place was the head of the Hmong traitor.[7]

The Pahawh Movement

The Pa Chai movement does not seem to have involved scripts or books, but a sequel to it in the same area did. The story in this case is that of another also apparently ordinary Hmong village farmer whose name was Shong Lue. Writing was central to the movement he inspired. Although he himself was illiterate, Shong Lue created an alphabetic script (a complete set of written symbols that represents the elementary sound units of the spoken language) that could be used for both Hmong and Khmu, each of which belonged to different language families. The story of Shong Lue includes the scripts he created, apparently entirely on his own; the turbulent circumstances in which he grew up and worked; and—like Pa Chai—a violent death at a young age. This story is told at book length by the missionary and anthropological linguist William Smalley and two Hmong co-authors, including one that had been a disciple of Shong Lue.[8]

Shong Lue was born in 1929 just across the border from northern Laos in Vietnam. He was the son of a Hmong father and Khmu mother but was raised as Hmong by his paternal grandparents after he became an orphan at an early age. According to believers, the miraculous events that shaped his life began in childhood. One day while guarding a field of corn from monkeys he fell asleep and had a dream in which two young men came and spoke to him. They asked if he had taught the alphabet yet. Shong Lue replied that since he could not read or write, how could he? The men then said they had already given the alphabet to him. When he denied this, they said look at your hands, and when he did he saw he was holding a book. Shong Lue protested further that he could not teach, but the men replied that if they told him to teach he could teach.

Shong Lue then awoke in a state of fright and returned home. Nothing more out of the ordinary happened for many years. He married and had children, and then in 1959 he began to have visions in which he received the Pahawh Hmong and the Pahawh Khmu, the alphabet for the two languages. Shong Lue and his now scattered disciples and followers believe that the alphabets he created were given to him directly by the god Vaj. In this view Shong Lue was a messiah who held the key to all knowledge and through whom God intended to help the Hmong to renew their lives. By the time that Shong Lue began to produce the alphabet and his followers to carry out the other instructions he had received, the civil war in Laos between royalists (supported by the Americans) and communists (supported by the North Vietnamese and the Chinese) was in full swing. The Pahawh "was a part of a grassroots nativist and messianic movement in which God, the spirit Vaj gave writing and knowledge to an unlettered people through the prophet Shong Lue Yang."[9]

The sequence of mystical experiences that led to the creation of the Pahawh also involved Shong Lue's wife Pang Xiong. As she was one day bringing him breakfast in the field where he was working, Pang Xiong was knocked unconscious by a whirlwind and remained so throughout the morning. When she revived and reached Shong Lue and told him what had happened, he decided to return to the village to seek a powerful shaman who could find out what had occurred. But as they were preparing for the ceremony, Shong Lue heard a voice from the air. The voice said that a shaman was not needed because his two brothers were being sent to help. The voice also instructed Shong Lue that he must not sleep with his wife or leave the house to work in the fields until his two brothers were born. He was further told to acquire an opium pipe and opium, and to build a round house as a temple for worship (Hmong houses and other buildings are rectangular and temples of any sort are lacking) and to furnish it with candles and flowers as offerings. Last, he was told to make ink from indigo and paper from bamboo, after which he would receive the alphabet.

Shong Lue wondered if he was going insane. But he was then slapped hard three times and heard the voice in the air say, "I am God, your father, who sent you to be born on earth as a human being. You are not crazy but you must do what I tell you." Shong Lue wondered in his mind how he, a poor man, could do all of this. Again the voice responded to his thoughts and said not to worry because he would send three kings to help him.

Much more happened in the sequence of miraculous events that led to the revelation of the Pahawh alphabet to Shong Lue and his effort to teach it to the Hmong. In brief, his two brothers were born as twin sons, but they soon died. Then three kings appeared as men dressed in black uniforms of officials with gold medals. On the 15th of the month, Shong Lue smoked opium and the two brothers appeared as grown men and began to teach him the Pahawh. The three kings then brought him the things he would need and showed him where to find buried treasure in the form of silver bars that he could use to pay for his activities. Then they disappeared. After seven months he was allowed to return to his rice field and discovered that it had been mysteriously cared for and was doing well. After nine months his wife gave birth to twin sons. They only lived a short while, but when they died Shong Lue was consoled by finding a message with one of the departed twins' footprint on it. The message explained more to Shong Lue about who he was and what he had been sent to do. The Pahawh script was to be made available for only a limited time. The message explained that the Hmong had had writing in the past but that their enemies had destroyed it each time. This time those nations that destroy the Pahawh would themselves be destroyed, while God would bless those who helped the Hmong. If the Pahawh were not established this time, it would not be available again for nine generations of eighty-five years each (or seven hundred and sixty-five years). The message concluded by saying that now Shong Lue would remember everything, because he was the Son of God sent to earth to be born as a human being with the power to save people.

After reading the message, Shong Lue remembered that God the Father had twelve sons, including himself and his two brothers, whom God had chosen to teach the Pahawh on earth. He was now in a state of total recall and knew everything in the universe from the beginning to the end. He remembered his earlier full name and that his title was "Savior of the Common People." He now assumed his full name and title and began to teach the Pahawh script to the Hmong and the Khmu. The message was preserved by Shong Lue and shown to others including his disciple Chia Koua Vang, one of the authors of the book. When he was later arrested, he left the message with his wife, but she was subsequently murdered.[10]

Both the message and Shong Lue's ensuing recall of his messianic nature and purpose raise the issue of outside influences and the larger context. Left out of Smalley's account is much discussion of the role that Christianity would seem to have played as a background influence for the movement.[11] It probably cannot be assumed that none of the Hmong known by Smalley and his co-authors had been directly exposed to missionary activities or Christian doctrine. It seems even less likely that the Hmong involved in the movement at that time in that region were unaware of Christianity or the central Christian story of Christ the Messiah, the Son of God, sent to earth to save mankind. There are structural elements in the story of Shong Lue that seem strikingly Christian. Shong Lue was one of *twelve* brothers (the number of Christ's disciples) in heaven. The importance of the number three, which is fundamental to Christian doctrine (crucifixions; Father, Son, and Holy Ghost; Mary, Joseph, and Jesus; the wise men in the Christian story), also recurs in the story of Shong Lue. Here there are three brothers who were sent to earth by God as well as three kings. As a Christian missionary linguist himself, it seems unlikely that Smalley was not aware of such apparent links, though he does not place much emphasis on them.[12]

As word spread of Shong Lue and the movement he led, he became involved in the ongoing civil war between royalists and communists in Laos. Whatever Shong Lue's own political views (he seems to have been more closely tied to the anti-communist supporters of the Royal Lao government than to the communists), he came to be mistrusted by both sides, each of which suspected that he was aiding the other. The communists told people that the Pahawh was created by the CIA, which by that time was recruiting Hmong to fight against them. By 1963 the communists were seeking to capture Shong Lue, which he was able to avoid by hiding in the forest when he was warned of danger by his supporters.

Over the next several years Shong Lue's movement continued to grow as it was also drawn into the civil war in Laos. New followers sought out Shong Lue and attended worship services in the round temple, but over time the movement had to shift periodically to a new location. Shong Lue gained a reputation for being able to predict the location of communist attacks in the region, for which he was at first rewarded by the Royalist–CIA led forces. But eventually these also came to distrust him and denounce him as a communist.[13] In 1967 he was arrested by the Royal Lao government and imprisoned for three years. The anti-communist Hmong leaders in the Lao government were alarmed at the size of his following and the widespread belief in his supernatural powers as well as his alleged communist ties. At the end of this time Shong Lue let his supporters know that he and his two divine brothers were going to return to heaven because he expected to be killed, which turned out to be correct. His supporters then arranged a successful rescue after which Shong Lue was kept in hiding, where he continued his work on the Pahawh script. Eventually found by Royal Lao spies, Shong Lue and his wife Pang were assassinated in 1971 by members of General Vang Pao's royalist army.

After Shong Lue's death, one of his disciples attempted to keep the movement going by continuing to teach the Pahawh script, though only to the Hmong—the Khmu had been frightened off. Later that year, however, this disciple was also assassinated along with several other Hmong followers. The Royal Lao government soldiers were again responsible, though this time dressed in communist uniforms and using bazookas furnished by the CIA.[14] This brought an end to the further spread of the movement before the collapse of the Royal Lao government in 1975.

The publication of *Mother of Writing* came at a time (1990) when anthropologists and other social scientists had become sensitive about issues of representation and polyethnic perspectives. Thus Smalley, the lead author and voice of the book, intends to show the differences between his own views and that of his two Hmong co-authors, one of whom was the main disciple of Shong Lue, the other the research assistant of the latter. The first chapter presents an account of the creation of the alphabet, including Shong Lue's early life and his visions and supernatural experiences. Smalley ends this chapter by pointing out that Hmong co-authors, as inside participants in the movement, believe the information about the extraordinary events and powers, including the revelations, to be all literally true and that contrary evidence has been fabricated by outsiders seeking to discredit the movement. He also notes that they think that most Westerners don't really believe in the supernatural and practice their religion only for social or political reasons.[15]

THREE RECENT MOVEMENTS IN MALAYSIA

We turn now to three recent movements in west or peninsular Malaysia, all mainly involving Malays. One of these involved highly publicized events that took place in 2000, another gained considerable attention in 2005, and the most recent involved developments that became news in late 2012 and early 2013. The first is known as Al-Ma'unah (Brotherhood of Inner Power), a radical Islamist movement that sought to replace the Malaysian government with a religious state. The second was Kerajaan Langit (Sky Kingdom), a syncretic, ecumenical, communal movement that had existed for several decades before it was attacked and destroyed in 2005 by the government as Islamically deviant. The third is the Panji Langit (Sky Pendant), a movement that formed around popular rumors of the end of the world based on the supposed ancient Mayan calendrical prediction that at that time was receiving wide attention in the world.

Al-Ma'unah

Al-Ma'unah was the first of the three movements to gain public attention.[16] Al-Ma'unah is the shortened name of Persaudaraan Ilmu Dalam Al-Ma'unah, which translates as Brotherhood of Al-Ma'unah Inner Power. Leaders of the movement claimed at the time to be a part of a broader, international movement with a thousand members, including ones in Brunei, Egypt, and Saudi Arabia as well as throughout Southeast Asia, though such assertions were never verified. The movement may have begun (in Indonesia?) as a not unusual effort to develop inner mystical powers to be used in martial arts (*silat* in Malay) and in "Islamic" curing. In Malaysia the effort became focused on the establishment of an Islamic state in Malaysia, by violence if necessary. The total number of members or supporters appears to remain unknown. And while it may be assumed that most followers supported the establishment of a religious state based on sharia law, the portion of followers that favored violent means of doing so also remains unknown. Government action against Al-Ma'unah, which appears to have focused much of the popular attention the events received, concentrated on the thirty-odd individuals actually involved in the attacks and siege rather than whatever sort of broader membership, following, or support there was.

The overt efforts by Al-Ma'unah to force the creation of an Islamic state took place early in July 2000 in the northern state of Perak. Led by an ex-Malay soldier named Mohamed Amin, a group of members undertook raids on two military armories from which they obtained large numbers of small-arms munitions, including assault rifles, machine guns, grenade launchers, and ammunition. The attackers also had Malay *parang* (heavy chopping knives) incised with inscriptions from the Koran that gave them magical power. Following the raid, the group made their way to a jungle camp. Other Al-Ma'unah members also attempted to attack the Anchor and Carlsberg breweries (beer being forbidden to Muslims but not other Malaysians) outside Kuala Lumpur using grenade launchers, though with little damage. Shots were also fired at the temple at Batu Caves in Kuala Lumpur, the most important Hindu shrine and pilgrimage site in the country, though again without damage.

The rebellion was brief. The entire operation as carried out by the rebels was sufficiently inept as to suggest they were counting on divine assistance in order to succeed. Within several days the police and army had surrounded the insurrectionists' camp in the forest. Al-Ma'unah spokesmen then broadcast a threat to surround the city of Kuala Lumpur if Prime Minister Mahathir Mohamad did not resign within twenty-four hours. Fighting then took place at the jungle camp, resulting in several deaths, including those of two of the hostages taken by Al-Ma'unah who were executed. Some of the rebels then agreed to give up, though after first refusing to give up their magical chopping knives. Eventually the entire Al-Ma'unah force surrendered, to be put on trial several years later. The Malaysian government charged those involved in the attacks with treason and acts of war against the country and succeeded in having them convicted and sentenced to prison or execution for their crimes—four were executed. It is notable, however, that neither the government nor its controlling political party (UMNO—the

United Malay National Organization) chose to label the participants as "terrorists" or to refer to Al-Ma'unah as a terrorist organization.

Beyond the trials and executions, the political and religious aftermath was significant. The political exchanges between UMNO and PAS (the two Malay parties) following the incidents were strident. The Malaysian prime minister and UMNO leader Mahathir stated that members of Al-Ma'unah were mainly PAS supporters, thus implying that the party was involved. For its part, PAS counter-attacked by stating that the Al-Ma'unah military attacks had in actuality been staged by the government in order to discredit the Islamist opposition. This claim was supported by the argument that it was too much to believe that a military arsenal could be tricked into turning over a large quantity of weapons, ammunition, and explosives to a group that showed up pretending to be real military. This was followed by an angry demand by UMNO for an apology for making an outrageously false claim, followed in turn by a denial by PAS of any need for an apology.

Aside from the party political fallout, the government decided that religious deviation was a continuing potential problem in the country, one that would have to be dealt with more forcibly. A list of deviant Muslim organizations was drawn up, and groups charged with violating religious fatwas declaring them to be Islamically incorrect were also liable to be found to be threats to national security. These all appear to have been consequences of the Al-Ma'unah incident, as was probably also the arrest and imprisonment in 2001 of Ayah Pin, the leader of the eclectic Kerajaan Langit movement, to which we now turn.

Kerajaan Langit

Though it had begun long before this time, the Sky Kingdom (Kerajaan Langit) movement in Malaysia gained wide popular attention in August 2005 after the commune established by its members was raided and then destroyed by the police and many of its members arrested.[17] The attention was due in part to the actions of the government and in part to the icons created and displayed by the group and then attacked and obliterated by the police. As shown in published photos, these monuments, including a two-story-high bright yellow teapot and a slightly smaller bright blue vase, were widely published in newspapers and online. One photo includes Ayah Pin, the leader of the movement, wearing a baseball cap and standing in front of the teapot and vase. The teapot inspired a popular reference to the movement as the "teapot cult," and the site was likened in descriptions to a Disneyesque theme park. The photos had been taken before the government demolished all of the monuments as well as the other buildings on the site. The photos did not include several other important symbolic objects, including a yellow umbrella (a traditional emblem of Malay royalty) and an ornamental Malay fishing boat that stood for Noah's Ark.

The matter attracted strong public interest as another matter of controversy (mainly dividing Muslims and non-Muslims) involving the violation of the constitutional guarantee of freedom of religion in Malaysia and its apparent qualifications. The facts as reported here are that, as usual, the Malay-dominated government had acted on the assumption that religious law—to which all Muslim Malaysians are subject—trumped constitutional provisions for religious liberty, an interpretation that non-Muslim Malaysians tend to both fear and resent. In this case the leader and followers were charged with either apostasy, a serious violation of sharia law, or with failing to obey a fatwa banning the movement as deviant. To add secular weight to the charges, the movement was also found to be a "threat to national security," though no actual or threatened acts of violence were attributed to the leader or members, and no weapons were reported as being found in the compound.

The movement was led by a Malay named Araffin Mohamed but popularly known as Ayah Pin (in English, Father Pin—Ayah meaning "father" and Pin being the local pronunciation of the last syllable of "Araffin"). Ayah Pin was born in 1943 in a village in Bachok, Kelantan. His initial supernatural experience is not untypical of those who become prophets. At the age of ten he became seriously ill and reported being visited by an angel. The angel returned after another twenty years, in 1973, which launched him on his spiritual quest. Two years later he became associated with a religious group in Penang, on the other side of the peninsula, perhaps as a follower of Hassan Tuhan (Hassan God, also known as Anak Rimau, that is, Child of the Tiger) who also claimed divinity. By the mid-1980s Ayah Pin had returned to the northeast coast and upriver of Besut, Trengganu, not far from his natal village in Kelantan, and formed the Sky Kingdom commune on its permanent site. Some reports note that when the Office of Islamic

Affairs learned of the Sky Kingdom they declared it to be deviant, and therefore off limits to Muslims. But if so, no further action was taken at the time, and the movement and its commune continued to grow. By 1995 the group had begun to build the monuments for which it became known. At about this time, however, the state of Trengganu's Religious Affairs Council issued a fatwa against the group and had four members arrested for apostasy. Those arrested, however, gained their release by arguing that since they were no longer Muslims, the sharia court had no jurisdiction over them. This was a strategy that continued to be used, though with little success. The government declared that the renunciation of Islam is itself subject to the approval of the religious courts—a sort of a legal catch-22—not simply the right of the individual charged, the constitutional guarantee of freedom of religion for all Malaysians notwithstanding.

Several years later, in 2001, the government took direct action against Ayah Pin, who had renounced Islam, though unsuccessfully in the official view. This may have been in part the result of the government decision to take religious deviation more seriously after the Al-Ma'unah incident. Ayah Pin was accused of committing a violation of "Section 25," specifically that his teachings and beliefs were "false, deviant, corrupting," and "a threat to public peace." He pleaded guilty to the somewhat less serious charge of "belittling Islam," though he apparently did not repent his renunciation. The sharia court sent him to prison for eleven months and fined him 2,900 ringgit (about $900 in current U.S. dollars). The Religious Affairs Department expected that this action against Ayah Pin would serve to diminish the further growth of the movement, but this does not seem to have occurred. The Sky Kingdom continued to attract new members and the commune developed accordingly.[18] The group supported itself (and the photos of the compound suggest it was doing well) in ways that required the goodwill of the members of the local public and visitors who dealt with it, though just before the first raid the compound had been attacked by a local vigilante mob wearing masks. The members of the commune do not appear to have been accused of living in violation of Islamic sexual or marital laws, though perhaps only because such additional charges were deemed unnecessary.

The police raid and the destruction of the central icons and the buildings of the compound did not end the movement or the commune, though it certainly changed it. Of the members of the movement that had been arrested, some forty initially charged had been released as of 2005 after renouncing the group. Twenty-six were still facing criminal charges in the sharia court in Trengganu. Of those arrested, two women received special attention. One was from New Zealand and had been married to a man from northern Sumatra for seven years and had presumably converted to Islam. She was charged for violating the fatwa that had declared the Sky Kingdom to be deviant and illegal.[19] The other was a Malay woman who had appealed to civil courts to renounce Islam as her religion under the freedom-of-religion provision of the Malaysian constitution. She had also been charged with failing to obey the fatwa after refusing to repudiate the Sky Kingdom. Her request, which had been made in order to avoid imprisonment, was refused on the grounds that permission to abandon Islam as her religion was a matter for the religious courts—the same ones that had convicted her of violating the fatwa in the first place. This was announced in 2011, six years after the arrest of the Sky Kingdom members.[20]

Although the police arrested three of Ayah Pin's wives, they failed to capture him. According to a report published in 2006, he had escaped to Thailand and was living in refuge just across the border in the province of Narathiwat. Whether or not the Malaysian authorities had sought to have him extradited is not reported, but they may have been satisfied to have him simply gone so long as he was not causing trouble. There is no mention of members following Ayah Pin to Thailand and reestablishing the commune there. But by this time twenty-five members of the commune were back living at the site, though neither their legal status nor their activities are reported.

By 2007 the membership of the commune was said to be down to twenty-four and to have chosen a new leader, a former police chief, though the significance of the "former" (he was in his thirties) is not noted. What the members were doing in terms of religious activities or otherwise is again not reported. Nor is it reported whether or not the teapot or other of the main icons had been rebuilt, though this seems unlikely. The commune had changed in another way as well. Before the raids it had welcomed religious tourists and other visitors. By this time, as a result of previous developments and publicity, the members had become reclusive and suspicious of outsiders. On the other hand, if the government still considered the existing members of the reorganized commune to be apostates or violators of the fatwa, it would not seem to have been concerned strongly enough to take further action.

As for Ayah Pin himself, according to a much more recent account (published in March 2012) he was back living at the commune site in Hulu Besut, Trengganu. Here he is described as a "fugitive cult leader," but apparently no longer actively sought by the police. According to his brother, who was interviewed for the article, Ayah Pin was then seventy-one years old and seriously ill, semi-paralyzed by a stroke, and being treated by a village curer. His brother reported pleading with him to repent but without success.[21]

Of what may have initially attracted the members and motivated some of them to remain even after the government raid and the complete destruction of the compound little has been said in published sources. Throughout the world there are doubtless innumerable free spirits or disillusioned seekers on the lookout for something and someone new and interesting to believe in and follow. That some of them found their way to an obscure corner of peninsular Malaysia and a commune led by a Malay guru espousing eclectic and ecumenical doctrines, and with a wonderful giant teapot and vase symbolizing everflowing and bountiful water, does not seem very surprising.[22]

The Malay Muslims, who are reported to have formed the bulk of the Sky Kingdom following, are a different matter. Unlike the non-Muslims who joined the movement without danger of being arrested for violating a fatwa, the Muslims were taking risks since such violations take precedence over constitutional guarantees of religious rights. The previous arrest, fining, and imprisonment of Ayah Pin for nearly a year was certainly probably well known to most Malays. Ayah Pin's fine of 2,900 ringgit is a large sum in rural Malay society. The motives or goals of the Malays who were willing to take the risk and become followers of Ayah Pin are not discussed in the newspaper accounts.

Panji Langit

The final Malaysian movement is a further example of the globalization of the supernatural and the use of the Internet for occult purposes. Known as Panji Langit or the "Sky Banner" in English, the group was labeled as another deviant sect in a fatwa and compared by one government official to the earlier Panji Kerajaan.[23] The Sky Banner group became public knowledge early in January 2013, following a police raid on a rural Malay house in Kampung Chabau in Malacca state, where the leader lived with his family. According to the initial statement by the chief of the state police, the Sky Banner appeared to have been in existence for about a year. The leader was a forty-six-year-old Malay man named Mohammad Jaffar Robani (known as "the Imam"), who was originally from the neighboring state of Johor. The group reportedly had a membership of about forty persons and met in his house. The neighboring villagers claimed that they had nothing to do with the group, and that those who did were all strangers from elsewhere who were at the house on weekends. The group for the most part kept to itself. One villager reported that he had attended a religious meeting in the house at which, however, the Imam had little to say. The villagers also claimed to have been suspicious about what was going on in the house and that they had informed the local mosque committee, which in turn contacted the state religious authorities. Published pictures of the house show an ordinary but prosperous-looking Malaysian rural bungalow that lacked statues or distinctive architectural features or other indications of the identity of the group of the sort used by the Sky Kingdom. The group was said to have recruited members through its website and through its door-to-door sales of traditional medicine.

There were two main topics in the initial news reports.[24] The first was that the group had formed to prepare for the end of the world on December 22, as supposedly specified by Mayan prophecy and disseminated widely in the world through the Internet and other mass media. Even before failure of the Mayan prophecy had become known, the National Fatwa Council of Malaysia had issued a proclamation stating that the Panji Langit's teachings were deviant according to the Sunnah. But according to the police report, while the group not surprisingly appeared to have lost some of its following after the world failed to end on schedule, it did not disband.

This led to the police raid of January 7, which in turn revealed another matter of concern. This was a large store of weapons, including bows and arrows, Malay chopping knives, swords, and imitation pistols and rifles. These were being kept in preparation for the end of the world, though there was uncertainty about how the weapons were to be deployed in such an event. The police were satisfied that the weapons were not intended to be used in attacking other persons and that the group was not a threat. The Imam, however, was arrested and charged in court with two counts of possession of dangerous weapons.

It is again notable that the charges against the Imam involved violations of ordinary criminal law rather than of sharia statutes. A fatwa had been issued against the Imam's teachings, which he appears to have violated. He was not, however, prosecuted under religious law. The state Islamic Religious Department (JAIM) also said that the Sky Banner was similar to the Sky Kingdom cult. However, beyond the partial overlap in the names of the two groups and the likelihood that those involved in the former likely knew of the latter, no specific connections were noted, and the similarities seem limited. Ayah Pin and some of the members of the Sky Kingdom appear to have set themselves much more seriously against Malaysian Muslim doctrine than did anyone in the Sky Banner. The police were said to be looking for the members of the Sky Banner because they were seeking information.

THE DEVELOPMENT OF POPULAR RELIGIOUS MOVEMENTS

Since the nineteenth century the anthropological interpretation of religious movements has been that they begin as efforts by people who have become demoralized or even desperate, often as a result of conquest and the destruction or great alteration of their traditional way of life. They seek salvation through a miraculous transformation. The classic example here is the Ghost Dance of the Native Americans of the western plains of North America circa 1889–1890, but there are a great many others. Later the psychological anthropologist Anthony Wallace developed the theory of revitalization, a functionalist approach to religious movements.[25] This theory holds that these are efforts by a group of people to create a more satisfying and effective culture. It was important in that it went beyond the usual effort of putting religious movements into various categories and discussing their particular histories, characteristics, and causes. Instead, it attempted to show that the notion of revitalization in some form or other is probably applicable to most movements in the sense that they at least implicitly involve efforts to produce positive social, cultural, and religious change.

So conceived, revitalization involves a series of stages. A society begins in a "steady state," that is, one of satisfactory psychological integration and adaptation. Then it enters a state of stress, conflict, and disintegration, often as a result of intrusion, conquest, and exploitation. The traditional culture, including religion, appears to be failing. Then a prophet appears, often an ordinary person who has visions and receives messages and instructions from a commanding spirit or divinity. The message explains why the society is suffering and what it must do to correct its mistakes. The instructions include both practical and more distinctly ritual matters. The people are at first skeptical, but eventually some listen and follow the instructions. Their lives improve, and others follow. The new religion then undergoes a period of development, further expansion, and consolidation. In psychological terms the society undergoes a complete cognitive reorganization. The eventual outcome is a new steady state. The movement has become an established religion or even a world religion.

But while certain religious movements seem to bring at least some revitalization, others do not. "Revitalization" or success really only occurs as the final outcome of the sequence of developments that usually fail for some reason along the way. Of the movements considered here, only Bungan in Borneo provides an example of what could be called revitalization in the sense of having gone through the relevant stages. Traditional life among the upriver peoples was based on hunting and gathering, cultivation, trade, great mortuary ceremonies, social stratification, headhunting, and residence in communal longhouses. It was also linked to spectacular artistry in painting and carving. It was not a Garden of Eden, but it was all anyone knew. Then the world began to change. Colonial rule was established, trade increased, and missionaries arrived and urged religious conversion as a way to a better spiritual and material life. Some people converted while others did not, and of those who did, some were satisfied while others were not. Some villages divided over religious differences. This opened the way to an effort at revitalization brought by a local prophet. The message spread, bringing changes in beliefs, ritual practices, and in other lifeways. Bungan became the new traditional religion among many upriver peoples who had not yet committed fully or at all to Christianity, and a new if not unchanging steady state of sorts was reached. But this generally does not last more than a few decades because the broader sequence of change cannot be stopped. In the long run, Bungan cannot compete with the spiritual hope and the promise of modernization, political respect, and economic progress associated with conversion to Christianity.

The Pa Chi and Pahawh movements in Laos fit the classic model of religious movements, though both were aborted before going very far along the path of revitalization. The leaders of these movements were assassinated, though in the case of the Pahawh some effort was made to continue and achieve the goals set out through the visions and efforts of the prophet. But because of the outcome of the war in Laos and the movement of many of the Hmong into refugee camps and then into a wider diaspora, the achievement of a successful transformation probably could not have been attained. Among those who remained in Laos and those who left for Thailand and the United States were former followers and disciples of Shong Lue. Some of these attempted to keep the movement going, because they believed Shong Lue was a messiah sent to save the Hmong, and because they believed that the Pahawh script would help keep Hmong culture alive and provide protection against complete assimilation in a new and very different society.[26]

Hmong refugees carried the Pahawh script to the United States, which formed the largest part of the Hmong diaspora by far. Some of these refugees had learned the Pahawh and did believe in its divine origin or saw it as a way to keep Hmong culture alive and preserve their ethnic identity. But there were many more who had only a vague idea of the Pahawh or who had never heard of it at all. And of those who were familiar with the Pahawh, not all saw much value in it. For some, the supernatural powers attributed to Shong Lue and to the shamans, magical writers, and other traditional religious specialists were backward superstition that was out of place in the United States. Although the authors made inquiries, they found no evidence that the round houses of worship associated with the Pahawh had been built in any of the American communities where the Hmong had settled.[27] This would seem to have been the end.

The Malay Movements

Of the three Malay (or mainly Malay) movements, none proceeded far through the stages of revitalization. There is little about Al-Ma'unah that suggests revitalization. Including both those who were killed during the siege and those subsequently executed by the government, nearly a dozen people appear to have died and many more were sent to prison for long periods. And aside from this, the accounts indicate little in the way of positive development. In the case of the Sky Kingdom, how the movement fits the model of revitalization remains unclear, though insofar as any took place it was probably at the individual level rather than a wider one. What seems notable is how long the commune lasted before it was destroyed, given its location. The Sky Banner could probably not have lasted either once it was reported to the authorities. Here there is also the question of how a date-specific end-of-the-world movement could bring revitalization.

All three of these movements of course involved religion and fall within the general Malaysian governmental and news media category of "cults" or "sects." Kerajaan Langit and Panji Langit were both declared to be Islamically incorrect by official and legally binding fatwas. However, in the case of the latter the fatwa was not the basis of the prosecution of the movement, whereas in the case of Kerajaan Langit it was. Apparently no fatwa was issued regarding Al-Ma'unah, perhaps simply because one was not necessary.

All three of the movements reflect in part global or external connections. And different as they were, all suggest something about the changing nature and circumstances of Malay popular religion and its context. All formed in a period of increasing turbulent and highly politicized Islamization in Malaysia. This involved the adoption and imposition of a more restrictive or standardized version of Islam, though one favored by some Malays more than others. The ability (and inclination) of the government, religious authorities, and the Malay political parties to impose a religiously and politically correct version of Islam varies considerably from one region of the country to another. It has been weaker in the more developed, urbanized, and Westernized west coast than in the east coast. Increasing Islamism has been a national trend in peninsular Malaysia for many decades. It was begun especially by the PAS political party and government in their stronghold in Trengganu and Kelantan. However, it was soon taken up by the originally secularist and nationalist UMNO, which (under Mahathir) was unwilling to be outdone by PAS and made Islamism a central plank in its platform as well.

The rise of Ayah Pin and the Sky Kingdom, the sudden and brief appearance of Al-Ma'unah, and the recent emergence of the Sky Banner end-of-the-world movement overlap with the latest phase in growth of Islamism in Malaysia. This includes the return of PAS to power in Kelantan in 1990, its passage of the *huded* enactments in 1993 (passed also ten years later in Trengganu, though also without being put into effect), and its other ongoing efforts to establish or enhance political Islamism wherever it could. Different as they are, Al-Ma'unah, the Sky Kingdom, and the Sky Banner all seem to be a consequence of some dissatisfaction with contemporary official, orthodox Islam as defined, interpreted, and determined by committees of ulamas, official fatwas, sharia courts, state religious councils, religious police, and the main Malay political parties. While these developments are not exactly new, they have been carried to greater extremes in recent decades.

The Sky Kingdom movement developed in the northwest corner of the country, generally known to be the main stronghold of Islam and PAS. This suggests that Islam or Malay religion in this region is a more complex matter than simply embracing Muslim orthodoxy or Islamism.

The leader of the movement, Ayah Pin, advocated ecumenicalism, and the commune welcomed groups from other religions and discussions with them. Aside from the particular meaning of the teapot and other symbols, the reported religious beliefs of the group were syncretic. Though having renounced Islam, Ayah Pin was held by followers to be the incarnation of Mohammad—as well as Jesus, Buddha, and Shiva (covering all the bases of the major world religions)—who will return one day as the Imam Mahdi, the future savior in Islam. But this does not mean progress toward revitalization. The photos of the compound of the commune suggest that it was doing fairly well as an enterprise supporting itself through donations, religious tourism, and the manufacture and sale of confections. But this tells us only a little. Many rural and small-town Malays earn a living by making and selling snacks, especially in the poor areas of the country such as Kelantan and Trengganu.

Though this cannot be proved, both the Sky Kingdom and the Sky Banner suggest that popular Malay religious interests, concerns, inclinations, beliefs, and activities are not entirely contained within the framework of authoritarian orthodox Islam. To return briefly to a point made earlier about religion in Kelantan as I first came to know it in the late 1960s, Islam then was still in some ways a folk religion, one passed on mainly by oral tradition and example (though radio broadcasts were also involved). The Malays in Kelantan at that time were devoutly committed to Islam, but their popular religious interests, beliefs, and practices went considerably further. These were not limited to or contained by orthodox or textual Islam as it has more recently come to be defined and insisted upon. The movements suggest that such more complex and eclectic interests and orientations still exist for some, though they are no longer officially tolerated as they once were.

THE SUCCESS OF RELIGIOUS MOVEMENTS

The Pahawh movement and most of the others we have considered in this chapter can be seen as (in quite different ways) efforts at revitalization. However with historical hindsight we can also see that the circumstances that led to and shaped the movements were also ones that prevented most of them from achieving revitalization in a new steady state, or in some instances from even coming close to it. The Bungan movement in the interior of Borneo is the only real exception. And the Bungan movement also had the most limited goals—reforms (doing away with onerous taboos and ritual burdens) rather than a larger transformation of the religion and way of life, not to mention political rebellion or resistance. It did, however, in most places eventually give way to conversion to Christianity. As forms or expressions of popular religion, religious movements are often transient, though there have of course been great exceptions, including the development of several of the world religions.

9

POPULAR RELIGION IN SOUTHEAST ASIA

To revisit the question with which I opened this book, what is popular religion in Southeast Asia? Popular religion refers to beliefs and activities that have a supernatural dimension and that are widely characteristic of ordinary people in contrast to only elite or orthodox adherents as informed by textual scripture. Popular religion is sometimes referred to as folk religion, but this phrase is inadequate insofar as it implies oral transmission that, while important, overlooks the influence of modern mass media and technology. The notion of popular religion applies mainly to religious traditions that are complex and exist at different levels or are developing in this way. Some popular beliefs and practices may be denigrated by scripturally oriented religious elites as backward or improper animism or superstition, or accepted as harmless or even valuable folklore. The differentiation between popular and orthodox religion I have discussed throughout this book may be greater in some parts of the world than others. It is probably more significant in Southeast Asia and other developing areas than in the Western world, for example, but I have made only occasional reference to these.

In Southeast Asia itself there are also differences. The notion of popular religion has little applicability to indigenous religions where everyone (except perhaps for a few specialists and differences of age and gender) knows, believes, and does much the same things. As indigenous people convert to one or another world religion, or seek to have their own religious traditions accepted as such (as some have done in Indonesia), the notion of popular religion becomes applicable to them as well. Religious movements of revitalization form a particular sort of popular religion. They tend to express a radical dissatisfaction with things as they are and seek a miraculous transformation. Such movements develop among both the adherents of existing complex religions and among those on the margins of these.

In Southeast Asia popular and elite religion tend to be differentiated in a number of ways, although such differences are matters of degree. As set out in the introduction the differences include contrasting social and physical spaces, forms of hierarchy, doctrinal elaboration, reliance on writing and literacy, different sorts of moral and legal codes, purposes, and concerns. In conclusion, it should be emphasized that the differences between popular and elite religion are themselves subject to variation among different named religions, countries, and periods of time. As to religions, at the current time it would seem that Islam has the narrowest gap between popular and elite levels of religion. Buddhism is probably at the opposite extreme from Islam in terms of having the greatest difference between popular religious beliefs and those of elite or textually inspired perspectives and practices. But here there are several problems with making comparisons. Far more has been studied and written regarding Thailand in recent decades than the other Theravada Buddhist countries of Burma/Myanmar, Laos, and Cambodia.

Christianity and Hinduism fall somewhere between Islam and Buddhism in terms of the gap between popular and elite or orthodox forms of religion. But both are probably closer to Buddhism than to Islam in terms of openness to officially deviant or disreputable or at least nonsanctioned sorts of popular religious activities. The problem here is again the difficulty in making comparisons. Christianity is the national religion of identity only in the Philippines. Here the population is predominantly Roman Catholic, but the ability of the Catholic Church to get people to do and not do as Catholics are supposed to has waned, as it has elsewhere in the world. Outside of the Philippines, Christianity is mainly the religion of the ethnic and geographical margins, of indigenous minorities and fragmented areas. Except for suppressing religion in general, the governments of these countries almost certainly know or care little about any differences between popular religions and those of the official church involved, unless they were causing trouble.

The problem with understanding the differences in Hinduism between popular and elite versions is that, except in terms of identity,

Hinduism is not a single religion in Southeast Asia—even in comparison to Buddhism, Islam, and Christianity. Here, rather, there are several separate and distinct versions. These include Balinese traditional and modern Hinduism, and the very different South Indian popular Hinduism brought by immigrant plantation laborers during the colonial period. There is also the government-mandated neo-Hinduism adopted and developed by various indigenous groups in Indonesia as a means of holding on to their indigenous religious traditions. As popular religions, these different versions have tended to develop and change in varying ways.

Popular religion in Southeast Asia also varies in other ways. In terms of differences among countries, the most important variation has been between the socialist and non-socialist ones (though even within these groupings, there have been variations). The socialist countries in the beginning were generally hostile to religion and saw it as something that needed to be eliminated, reduced, or at least altered to better conform with state goals and political priorities. Though the anti-religious efforts varied, all failed or were scaled back. In Cambodia the communist efforts to annihilate Buddhism at both the popular and elite levels did not so much fail as they were prevented from being completed by the downfall of the Khmer Rouge—and their replacement by a much more moderate socialist government that permitted the beginning of the restoration of Buddhism. Of the two remaining socialist (or now neo-socialist) countries, Laos has probably made the lesser effort to diminish or alter popular religion. It fairly quickly developed efforts to moderately socialize Buddhism while using it also to legitimize and popularize the Communist Party and state. In Vietnam the change came especially with the abandonment of a socialist economy and the introduction of market-based reforms—the question being whether the related surge in popular religious activity was a return to traditional, pre-socialist practices or to a higher level of occult involvement than had formerly existed.

In contrast, most if not all of the non-socialist countries have been officially pledged to religious liberty and pluralism. That said, in probably all instances the official model of religious tolerance leans toward the various world religions rather than the popular mixture of these with various and localized occult beliefs and practices. The differences between the two predominant religions of Buddhism and Islam and within these the differences among various countries have been noted. The two larger non-socialist countries with the most authoritarian attitudes and policies toward popular religion in recent times have been Malaysia and Indonesia. But these have been different—Malaysia being restrictive and authoritarian regarding Islam and Indonesia being so in terms of requiring citizens to have an officially approved religion. Between Indonesia and Malaysia there is Singapore, which has different attitudes and policies regarding religion. While Singapore has a reputation for authoritarian and punitive attitudes and policies (as with chewing gum, caning, and the suppression of political dissent), its approach to religion is pluralistic. Here the ethnic composition and religious diversity of the country may be important. Singapore is somewhat similar to Malaysia in terms of ethnic and religious composition, but the proportions are very different. The Chinese form the vast majority of the population, but their religious composition is mixed and includes (to keep it simple) Buddhism, Christianity, Confucianism, and traditional Chinese "folk religion," including various combinations of some of these and probable differences within families. Under such conditions religious pluralism is likely to be generally favored.

There have also been changes over time in both the socialist and non-socialist countries, although those taking place in the non-socialist countries have been less abrupt. In Thailand or Siam/Thailand, the state has gone from its nineteenth-century (or earlier) patterns of seeking increased control over both Buddhism and some aspects of popular religion (for example, spirit medium practices) to today's lack of concern or control over either except in the case of secular crime. In Indonesia the policy of encouraging or coercing all citizens to belong or convert to an officially approved religion extends back to the early post-colonial period and the adoption of the national principles in the constitution. But it was further developed over time in various ways, reaching an authoritarian peak during the Suharto regime. In Malaysia religion has also changed over time, especially with elections and shifts in political power. When I first came to know something about Islam and other dimensions of popular religion in the Malay state of Kelantan in the late 1960s, many popular religious and cultural activities that were later banned were still flourishing. Though perhaps in an oblique or beneath-the-surface way the various religious movements that have taken place in recent years in Malaysia suggest popular dissatisfaction with the course of change in religion and culture.

Finally, the beliefs and activities of popular religion tend to fall into two categories. There are first those beliefs and activities that are linked to one or another specific world religion. Here we therefore have popular Hinduism, popular Buddhism, popular Islam, and popular Christianity, though it is usually necessary to be more specific, usually by adding an ethnic, national, or sub-religious designation.

The other category includes those beliefs and practices that are not specific to any named religion of identity. They include spirit beliefs and notions of bad death and such activities as spirit medium practices, supernaturally oriented healing, searches for winning lottery numbers, sorcery and counter-sorcery, the creation and use of charms or amulets, and shrines, of which uses and practices cross most boundaries of religious identity. These vary from place to place but also show cross-cultural (or cross-religious) regularities. The notion that how people die (violently and suddenly or peacefully and naturally), where, and at what age will determine what sort of spirit their soul becomes is widespread and foundational in popular religion in Southeast Asia—as evidence from eastern Indonesia, Borneo, Vietnam, Thailand, and Burma shows.[1] Basic ethnological logic suggests that such notions about good and bad death are probably older than the development of any of the world religions. Some of the popular religious practices that such beliefs underlie are recent. The belief that the license number of a car involved in a fatal crash (or the flight number or date of a fatal plane crash) can have mystical significance in the search for a winning lottery number is of course modern in the sense that automobiles, license plates, airplanes, and lotteries are all recent developments, but the underlying belief in supernatural causality is ancient. The belief in diverse forms of spirits, including those of ancestors and other persons, saints, places, and divinities, is also pervasive and foundational in popular religion and associated with the belief that some persons have or can acquire the ability to interact with, interpret, or control spirits in ways that ordinary persons cannot. The notion that a person or an agent can supernaturally influence, harm, or counteract such practices is also probably pervasive in popular religion. Further examples could be cited as well, but those noted above serve to make the point.

NOTES

1. INTRODUCTION

1. Discussed more fully in Winzeler 2011, chaps. 8 and 9.
2. Aslan 2014.
3. Chan 2012, 19. It is true that popular religion cannot always be as easily separated from elite, institutionalized, or orthodox religion as this quote suggests regarding China.
4. De La Paz 2012, 185.
5. Ibid., 185.
6. Yeoh 2012, 79–94.
7. Ibid., 89–90.
8. For a fuller discussion, see Winzeler 2012, 27–31.
9. Mandelbaum 1964.
10. Chan 2012, 204.
11. Reader and Tanabe 1998.
12. Yeoh 2014, 165.
13. Yeoh 2012, 83–84.
14. Ibid., 82.
15. Redfield 1957.
16. Goody 1968.
17. As will be discussed in detail later, in northern continental Southeast Asia the minority hill peoples sometimes link the political domination of the lowland majorities to their possession of mystically powerful books and writing. Here also religious movements prophesize the return of lost magical books or the creation of miraculous forms of writing (see Keyes 1977, 55–56).
18. Kitiarsa 2012, 19.

19. Kitiarsa 2012, 7.
20. Fischer 2012, 27.

2. THE DEVELOPMENT OF RELIGION IN SOUTHEAST ASIA

1. Bautista and Reid 2012, 3.
2. Ibid., 3; Evans 1998, 27–31; Hefner 1994.
3. Hefner 1994, 75–76.
4. Yang 1961, 122–23.
5. Chan 2012, 206.
6. Howe 2001, 1–2.
7. Hanks 1972, 90.
8. Keyes 1977, 74–75.
9. Ibid., 74–75.
10. For developments in North Sumatra, see Kipp 1990, 223–30; Pedersen 1970, 47–79; and Steedly 1993, 52–60, 65–69.
11. Bigalke 2005, 76–104; Volkman 1985, 35–37.
12. Chapter 12 in my book on the anthropology of religion (Winzeler 2012, 249–80) contains a general comparative discussion of religion under capitalism and communism.
13. From Marx's 1843 *Contribution to Hegel's Philosophy of Right*.
14. Malarney 2002, 52–76, 80–83.
15. Taylor 2004, 40.
16. Malarney 2002, 102–5.
17. According to Shaun Malarney, in the village of Thinh Liet, a bust of Ho was placed in the central position on a refurbished altar devoted to memorializing the souls of the dead. The older men with party backgrounds who supported the placement claimed that it was strictly a matter of memorialization and that no superstition was involved. But by 1991, their position changed to advocating that Ho be recognized as the guardian spirit of the village and treated accordingly. The existing guardian spirit had not been doing a very good job and should be replaced, and no spirit was more deserving of the position than Ho. Some villagers went even further and took the position that Ho had actually been a living god in his lifetime, sent to free the Vietnamese from French colonial and American oppression (Malarney 2002, 201).
18. Quoted from a Vietnamese newspaper article by Evans (1998, 27–28).
19. "Many communal houses [village temples] once regarded as tools of the elite or forms of superstitious activity were embraced as fine examples of the nation's arts, traditions and culture" (Taylor 2004, 43). After being closed for

more than a decade, temples and shrines were reopened and used for their traditional purposes.

20. Wells-Dang 2007, 401.

21. Salemink 2008, 147.

22. Jellema 2007, 69–72.

23. According to an account by the Vietnamese anthropologist Do Thien, a three-year study of several villages in northern and southern Vietnam showed a very large expenditure (from 30 to 60 percent of all household spending!) for life-crisis rituals, including those of birth, marriage, death, and death anniversaries (Thien 2007, 173). These are presumably the kinds of expenditures the Communist Party and government had previously sought to discourage but apparently gave up trying to enforce.

24. See Evans 1998, 57; Harris 2008, 170–79; 2013; Stuart-Fox 1996, 65.

25. Stewart-Fox 1996, 73.

26. Evans 1998, 24–25, 72. Not all monks supported the socialist regime or aided the resistance that continued after 1975. Some such monks were assassinated (Evans 1998, 71). Most of those who survived are now living in the United States or Canada (Baird 2012). See also the recent general collection on Buddhism and violence in modern Asia (Tikhonov and Torkel Brekke 2012).

27. Evans 1998, 71.

28. Ibid., 72.

29. See Harris's (2013) comprehensive treatment in *Buddhism in a Dark Age*.

30. Harris (2013, 131–35) thinks that as bad as it was, later reports overstated the number of deliberate killings. He suggests that, in all, perhaps some twelve thousand died violently, of which only a portion were executed—but what portion?

31. A considerable number of monks had died before the Khmer Rouge came to power, especially as "collateral damage" when the United States carpet-bombed eastern Cambodian settlements as an extension of the war in Vietnam (Harris 2013, 129).

32. Harris 2013, 128.

33. Ibid., 124.

34. Ibid., 156.

35. Ibid., 156.

36. Ibid., 168–69.

37. Available statistics on adherents of the various religious *identities* of Indonesia are 88 percent Muslim (including 99 percent Sunni), 9 percent Christian (including 7 percent Protestant and 3 percent Catholic), 2 percent Hindu, .84 percent Buddhist, and .3 percent Confucian. Such figures are not

broken down by ethnic affiliation. See also Suryadinata, Nurvidya Arifin, and Ananta 2003, chapter 5.

3. THREE VERSIONS OF POPULAR HINDUISM

1. Prakash 2003, 44.
2. Coedès 1967.
3. Terwiel 1994, 5–6, 12–13.
4. Beatty 1999, 218–19.
5. Sandhu 1969, 167.
6. Wiebe and Mariappen 1979, 135–36.
7. Jain 1970.
8. Willford 2006.
9. Ibid., 27–59.
10. Ibid., 84–116.
11. Most Westerners, however, probably also think of "religion" as meaning the various world religions as opposed to the broader anthropological notion of supernatural beliefs and practices in general.
12. Abalahin 2005, 121. The religious beliefs and practices of Indonesian peoples that did not qualify as official *agamas* were also put under the authority of a different ministry, that of education and culture rather than religion.
13. Ibid., 120.
14. Why Protestantism and Catholicism are listed as separate religions rather than together as "Christianity" is not clear, although the importance of the distinction had ancient roots in the colonial history of Indonesia: Catholicism was introduced by the Portuguese in the mid-sixteenth century and Protestantism in the early seventeenth by the Dutch, who were very hostile to the former.
15. The question of whether the religious beliefs and practices of the Indonesian Chinese were actually "Confucian" was also an old one, as was whether Confucianism was a religion in the first place. In any case, Confucianism was given *agama* status under the administration of Sukarno, the first president of Indonesia. Then, however, it was "de-*agama*-ized" after the military takeover in 1965 by the dictator General Suharto, who ruled until 1998. During this period, public displays of any Chinese religious activities, including festivals, were forbidden. This, however, had to do with anti-Chinese ethnic hostility as well as with the criteria of *agama*.
16. Howe 2001, 7.
17. Roughly speaking—see later.

18. Howe 2001, 4; Picard 2004.
19. Howe 2001, 18–19.
20. Ibid., 18.
21. Ibid., 59.
22. This included some highland communities in eastern Java that had never become Muslims. Such groups looked to the Balinese as a model of how to develop Hinduism among themselves. See Hefner 1985.
23. Volkman 1985, 33.
24. Schiller 1997, 9.
25. Steedly 1993, 68–69.
26. Volkman 1985; Bigalke 2005.
27. Bigalke 2005, 76–78.
28. Ibid., 104–6.
29. Volkman 1985, 37.
30. Ibid., 167.
31. Ibid., 165–71.
32. Ibid., 169.
33. Bigalke 2005, 292–93.
34. Schiller 1997, 9.
35. Ibid., 3–6.
36. As explained long ago by the French anthropologist Robert Hertz (1960), the basic idea is that the soul of the deceased cannot leave the body for the afterworld or for reincarnation into another person until the body itself has disappeared except for the bones and the final ceremony has been completed. It is the spectacular ritual activities of the final ceremony that, while not having become a tourist attraction as in Tanah Toraja, were a focal celebration for families, communities, and the wider society. And here their attraction and importance crossed religious lines. By the late twentieth century, while neither Christian nor Muslim Ngaju viewed the ritual and beliefs that formed *tiwah* with approval, family members and kin belonging to both groups tended to participate along with Kaharingan adherents.
37. Schiller 1997, 23, 124.
38. Ibid., 126.
39. bin Mohamad 1970, 2.

4. BUDDHISM AND POPULAR RELIGION

1. There are various cultural differences between the Burmese and the Thai peoples and between the histories of the two countries. The Burmese and Thai languages belong to different major linguistic families. And Burma and

Thailand have had very different experiences with colonialism. Over the course of the nineteenth century, the British conquered Burma, abolished its monarchy, and ruled it as a colony joined to India. Post-colonial Burma/Myanmar has mainly been ruled as a military dictatorship. Thailand (or Siam/Thailand) by contrast was never conquered, at least by a Western colonial power, and still retains its monarchy, which is closely linked to Buddhism. In terms of popular religion, the most prominent non-Buddhist supernatural cult in Burma is that of the Thirty-Seven Nats (spirits), of which there is no real equivalent in Thailand. These and other possibly significant differences—the greater importance of religiously based rebellion in Burma and the greater development, and greater prosperity and modernization, in Thailand—should give pause to efforts to make easy comparisons of Buddhism and other dimensions of popular religion in the two countries.

2. Condominas 1998.

3. De Young 1955, 110.

4. This is an observation made also by the anthropologist May Ebihara (1966, 190) in her account of Buddhism in rural Cambodia.

5. Spiro 1967, 251.

6. Ibid., 253–63.

7. Ibid., 220.

8. One that does, however, is Stanley Tambiah's 1970 study *Buddhism and the Spirit Cults in Northeast Thailand*. Tambiah was highly critical of Spiro's interpretation. Although he does note that some categorical distinction is made between Buddhism and animism in Thailand, he asserts that Spiro overstates it for Burma. He also objects to Spiro's psychological reductionism. Tambiah contributes much specific information on Buddhist forest monks, the importance of magic and amulets, and Thai animism. But his overall interpretation of Thai religion is far from clear, for it is hard to see the forest for the trees. He also seems to underestimate the possible differences between religion in Burma and Thailand that might mean that the Burmese see a more emphatic distinction between Buddhism and animism than do the Thai. While the Thai have an abundant and diverse range of animistic beliefs and practices, they appear to lack recognition of a category of spirits comparable to the Thirty-Seven Nats, with their well-known royal mythological associations. Nor do the Thai have spirit festivals, at least not on the scale of the major ones held on Mount Popa and Taungbyung in Burma. Nor, finally, do Messianic Buddhism and the magical practices associated with it appear to exist in Thailand, at least not on the same scale as in Burma.

9. Terwiel 1994.

10. Ibid., 1–18.

11. Ibid., 3–5.

12. Ibid., 17.
13. Ibid., 98.
14. Ibid., 112–13.
15. Ibid., 111.
16. McDaniel 2011.
17. Terwiel is an anthropologist who bases his account on traditional participation, especially as a monk in a rural monastery. McDaniel's discipline is religious studies with a focus on Buddhist religious texts, but he is familiar with anthropology and tends to write like an anthropologist who frequently bases his analysis on participant observation.
18. McDaniel 2011, 1.
19. Fuller 2013.
20. McDaniel 2011, 5–6.
21. There are many websites, including one on Wikipedia, devoted to the Erawan Shrine.
22. Fuller 2013.
23. McDaniel 2011, 6–7.
24. Ibid., 123.
25. Ibid., 156; see also the more detailed discussion of the new downtown shrines on page 155.
26. Ibid., 188.
27. Ibid., 15.
28. Ibid., 17. He writes, "We will see in chapters 3 and 4 especially that liturgical handbooks and monastic altars are sites of *accretion* [italics added], where texts and objects from disparate religious origins are welcome." And later we learn that Valentine's Day, like Christmas, is now widely celebrated in Thailand—at the Trimurti Shrine in Bangkok with offerings of long-stemmed red roses, red candles, and red incense sticks—despite its Christian origins, about which people probably do not care, to the extent they know.
29. Avonius 2004, 50–53.
30. Brown 1987; Avonius 2004, 52.
31. Avonius 2004.
32. Ibid., 20–21.
33. Cederroth 1996, 23.
34. Avonius 2004, 54.
35. Brown 1987; Avonius 2004, 53–54.

5. POPULAR ISLAM IN MALAYSIA AND INDONESIA

1. This may also be part of the explanation for why the Chinese, who (in my experience in Sarawak at least) are happy to eat and drink and intermarry with the Dayaks (and vice versa), were able, for example, to displace the Malays from trade in the interior of the Balui (the upper Rajang River) after the colonial establishment of a fort and market at Belaga, as recently reported by Alexander and Alexander (2002).

2. Skeat 1900.

3. Wilkinson 1957, 1.

4. Winstedt 1961.

5. There were also more modernized versions of *pondok* schools that were known by the Arabic term *madrasah*.

6. There are also reports of occult interaction between Malay spirit mediums and the shamans of aboriginal communities, including ones in Kelantan. These, however, had little if any significance among Malays of the Kelantan plain.

7. The anthropologist Louis Golomb (1978) studied the interaction of Muslim Malays and Buddhist Thais in the 1970s. He found that Malays did rely heavily on monks and other Thais for occult services, including love magic, sorcery, and in particular the more acceptable practice of counter-sorcery as in the case of Mat's mother. He interpreted this as another example of interethnic ecological specialization and exchange in areas of ethnic complexity—part of the Thai adaptation to living near large non-Thai populations. He then pursued the question in Thailand. Here he found a more general occurrence in both southern Thailand and in the Bangkok area of central Thailand. In the latter region there were small Malay communities that had been established in the nineteenth century when Malay political prisoners were brought from the south by the Siamese government. Here there was also a pattern of ritual exchange, but it was the opposite of the one in Kelantan. It was the Malays who had developed a reputation as occult practitioners and were sought out by Thais for love magic and counter-sorcery. He also went to a region of southern Thailand where the proportions of Thais and Malays were more equal, and here, while Malays tended to think that the Thai had particular occult skills, the Thai held the same view of the Malays. The Malays therefore sought out Thai ritual specialists while the Thai preferred Malay ones.Golomb (1985, 2–3) points out that "out-group" curing and magic is an ancient occurrence that can be found in antiquity (among the Greeks and the Romans) and Western history (among Jews, Muslims, and Christians). He also suggests, as have others, that notions of out-group occult powers probably played a role in the processes of

religious conversion and change that have occurred throughout Southeast Asian history. Southeast Asians became "Hinduized" because Hindu traders and adventurers brought superior forms of magic, as did Buddhists and then Muslims. Even Christian missionaries seem to have benefitted in some instances from such notions. Rumors spread in northern continental Southeast Asia and southwestern China among the hill-dwelling minorities that white men were bringing magical books that would restore their lost power and wealth.

Sorcery accusations therefore form a pattern. Golomb (1985, 194–229) found that in both Thailand and Malaysia they are more common in regions where there are ethnic-religious minorities around that can be blamed for sorcery than where such groups are lacking. In the latter sorts of places, such as northeastern Thailand, misfortune was more apt to be attributed to attack by malevolent spirits than sorcery. This suggests that people are more comfortable with making accusations and gossiping about sorcery when some of the blame can be placed on nearby members of an ethnic and religious out-group. They are more reluctant to attribute sorcery, which is regarded as immoral or forbidden entirely, to others who are adherents of their own religion and members of their own ethnic community. This is, of course, classic scapegoating, though this does not mean that it does not in some instances take place. Golomb is convinced that some Thai in Kelantan do provide sorcery (at least or especially love magic) and counter-sorcery to Malays. And similarly in Thailand, some Malays provide occult services to Thai clients.

8. Sweeney 1972, 36.
9. Ibid., 36–37.
10. Ibid., 35.
11. Goody 1968.
12. Hoffstaedter 2011.
13. Ibid., 120–21.
14. Ibid., 119–28.
15. Ibid., 123–24.
16. Avonius 2004; Cederroth 1981; 1996.
17. Cederroth 1996, 9. See also Avonius 2004 and Hitchcock 1996 on Islam in eastern Indonesia.
18. Cederroth 1996, 17–31.
19. Geertz 1960.
20. Ibid., 5.
21. Ibid., 5–6.
22. Ibid., 6–7.
23. See Hitchcock 1996 and Hefner 2011 for discussions of the criticisms made of Geertz's treatment of Javanese religion.

24. See Beatty 1999, 28–29; Hefner 2011.
25. Hefner 2011.
26. Cederroth 1981; 1996. See also Avonius 2004.
27. Pelras 1996, 137–38, 187–97.
28. Beatty 1999, especially 247–48.
29. Hefner 2011.
30. Avonius 2004, 11.
31. Siegel 2005.

6. CONVERSION AND POPULAR CHRISTIANITY

1. On the Orang Asli, see Edo 2012 and Arabestani and Edo 2011.
2. Winzeler 2011, 203–19.
3. Winzeler 2011.
4. Connolly 2003; Cooper 1984; Kammerer 1990; Metcalf 1989, 214–15; Tapp 1989b.
5. Hayami 2004, 247.
6. Kammerer 1990.
7. Cooper 1984, 79, 82, 169, 189. Nicholas Tapp reports that the Hmong converts he knew were primarily motivated by the desire to achieve some economic advantage.
8. Tapp 1989b, 101.
9. According to the American anthropologist Lorraine V. Aragon (2000, 113), who did a lengthy study of Christians in central Sulawesi, eastern Indonesia, these villagers had become Salvation Army Protestants because of such a decision. After the Dutch had succeeded in pacifying the region they invited missionaries in as a way of promoting colonial development. They divided the people and territory up and awarded the western area to the Salvation Army. Their first choice had been the Dutch Reformed Church, but its missionaries were already fully engaged elsewhere.
10. See Freeman 1979 on Iban beliefs about headhunting and rice fertility.
11. Winzeler 1999.
12. Whittier 1973, 40–42.
13. Rousseau 1998, 21–26.
14. Whittier 1973, 57.
15. Ibid., 146.
16. Ibid., 53.
17. I found the same thing in an old mountaintop Bidayuh village in West Kalimantan where I spent several days in 1996. Here the village was composed

of Baptists and Catholics, each clustered in a different hamlet, between which there was some rivalry—one of the villagers told me, for example, that he had made the right decision in becoming a Baptist rather than a Catholic because the Baptists were getting better rice crops.

18. Whittier 1973, 149.

19. Tapp 1989a.

20. Hayami 2004, 203.

21. Ibid., 209.

22. Ibid., 257–58.

23. Ibid., 33–44; Stern 1968.

24. Keyes 1977, 52.

25. Hayami 2004, 40–41.

26. Stern 1968, 304.

27. Hayami (2004, 29), who has provided the fullest account to date, reports that the Karen are creative storytellers who will readily incorporate new information into their existing tales as they retell them.

28. The Kachin of far northern Burma have a missing-book myth in which they had consumed the book. The Lahu of Thailand and Yunnan Province in Southwestern China had a missing-book story and a prophecy that it would be returned by a brother. Such stories were sometimes linked to political movements against authorities. The Hmong also have a missing-book story. The nineteenth-century Hmong in South China who had been involved in numerous rebellions against the Chinese were aroused by rumors that missionaries were bringing a book that would enable them to regain the writing they had lost, and with it their former wealth and territory.

29. Stern 1968, 306–8.

30. Ibid., 305.

31. Ibid., 313.

32. At which time we were able to spend four days at Mae Ra Ma, a camp near Mae Hong Son. Here the most striking thing to be seen was the religious diversity shown by the religious buildings (all of which had to be constructed, like the houses and other buildings, of "impermanent" materials including lumber and thatch). In addition to a Buddhist temple, there were Baptist, Methodist, and Catholic churches, all supported by various mission organizations.

33. On the Hmong of Germany and Texas, see Nibbs 2014; on the Hmong of California and in general, see Fadiman 1997; on the Lao, see Van Esterik 1993; on the Khmer in the Boston area, see Smith-Hefner 1999; on the Khmer with special reference to the San Francisco Bay Area, see Aihwa Ong 2003; on the Khmer of Canada, see Van Esterik 1993 and McLellan 2009.

34. Van Esterik 1993, 20–26.

35. Smith-Hefner 1999, 23–24; McLellan 2009, 125–26.
36. Harris 2013.
37. McLellan 2009, 126–27.
38. Ibid., 141.
39. Ong 2003, 197, 205; McLellan 2009, 141–42.

7. THE MAGIC OF THE MARKET

1. Comaroff and Comaroff 1999; 2000.
2. Foster 1967, 151.
3. Nash 1972.
4. Taussig 1980, 13.
5. Lomnitz-Adler 2005, 57.
6. Comaroff and Comaroff 2000, 310.
7. Salemink 2008, 147.
8. Buckley 2013; see also Levin 2013.
9. Yeoh 2012.
10. Taylor 2004, 41.
11. Salemink 2008, 147.
12. Taylor 2004, 41–42.
13. Ibid., 111–14.
14. Ibid., 191–203.
15. Many scholars have written about various facets of the occult economy in Thailand over the past several decades. Here I draw heavily on the recent account of the Thai scholar Pattana Kitiarsa. His *Mediums, Monks and Amulets* (2012) is the most recent, comprehensive, and explicit treatment of the nature and development of the occult economy in Thailand. As both a locally born and raised Thai from a poor area (the northeast) of Thailand, and a trained anthropologist with a PhD from the University of Washington, Kitiarsa writes confidently and critically and with great personal knowledge about popular religion in Thailand. Like Barend Terwiel and Justin McDaniel, Kitiarsa became a Buddhist monk. He explains, however, that because his motives for doing so were religious and personal—to fulfill an obligation he felt to make merit for his deceased mother—he remained a monk for only a few weeks and chose to do so mainly in isolation rather than with other monks. Perhaps because of this limited experience, he does not (unlike McDaniel and especially Terwiel) draw upon his personal experience as a monk to illustrate his interpretation of popular Thai Buddhism or other religious matters.
16. Kitiarsa 2012, 35–36.
17. Ibid., 36–44.

18. Ibid., 48.

19. However, Kitiarsa (2012, 31) cites a study done by the Thai Farmers' Bank in 1995 that estimated that clients spent more than twenty billion baht (then $800 million) a year on the services of mediums. It also reported that mediums exist in every type of community, though especially in urban areas.

20. Kitiarsa 2012; McDaniel 2011; Tambiah 1984.

21. Kitiarsa 2012, 12–13.

22. Ibid., 113.

23. White 2005; Kitiarsa 2012, 57–79.

24. Kitiarsa 2012, 4.

25. White 2005.

26. Ibid., 69–70.

27. Ibid., 74.

28. Ibid., 75.

29. Ibid., 78–82.

30. Ibid., 84.

31. Rozenberg 2005. See also Shway Yoe 1963, 528–30. According to Kitiarsa (2012, 70–71) the lottery was introduced into Thailand by Chinese immigrants in the early nineteenth century.

32. This third way may be subject to some religious variation. Several accounts indicate that certain Buddhist monks may be willing to help with numbers whereas, in my own experience, Muslim holy men are not, even though they may be able to do so. The folklore of *tikam ekor* in Kelantan included the popular notion that a *tok wali* (a holy recluse believed to have magical powers) would know a winning number but because gambling was sinful would not reveal it—but that the number might be found through stealth by reading behavioral clues of the sort a skillful poker player might look for in an opponent during a game, such as a blink or twitch when a correct number was said.

33. Jain 1970; Wiebe and Mariappen 1979.

34. Jain 1970, 115–19.

35. Ibid., 115.

36. Ibid., 116.

37. See also Wiebe and Mariappen 1979, 144.

38. Salemink 2008, 158.

39. Whose life and afterlife are described and analyzed by Kitiarsa (2012, 57–79).

40. One such example already discussed is the very popular spirit of Mae Nak, whose shrine in Bangkok is visited by people seeking favors from all over Thailand, and who may be a folk and mass media creation. Another is Ya Mo, a guardian spirit of the town of Korat whose legend is inscribed on a monument erected in her honor at the town center and who makes regular appearances in

séances of many local spirit mediums. In life Ya Mo is supposed to have been a heroic woman who in the early nineteenth century led a successful revolt against the Lao army then occupying the town—but who, according to a book written by a modern Thai historian (that caused a scandal and outraged the town), never had an earthly existence. Keyes 2002; Kitiarsa 2012, 30.

41. Kitiarsa 2012, 67.

42. Kitiarsa 2012, 38–39; Rozenberg 2005.

43. Kitiarsa (2012, 39–40) reports that helping with lottery numbers is one of the routine services provided by magic monks.

44. Rozenberg 2005.

45. Ibid., 20.

46. Nash 1965, 190–92.

47. Rozenberg 2005, 21.

48. Ibid., 33–36.

49. Ibid., 37–39.

50. See "Lottery firms stop sales of tickets," *Asia Gaming Brief*, July 24, 2014, http://agbrief.com/news/lottery-firms-stop-sales-tickets-linked-downed-malaysian-airliner.

51. The Chinese in Southeast Asia are a famous instance of being at once highly successful in business and strongly oriented to notions of luck and other occult beliefs and practice. The Protestant ethic is clearly not the only spirit of capitalism.

8. RELIGIOUS MOVEMENTS AS POPULAR RELIGION

1. My *Anthropology and Religion* (Winzeler 2012) has a fuller discussion of religious movements.

2. Baling Avun 1961, as later summarized by Jérôme Rousseau (1998, 21–25) in his ethnographic account of Kayan religion. See also Metcalf 1989, 216–17.

3. How seriously the peoples of the remote interior of Kalimantan (Indonesian Borneo) at first took the wishes of the government (or how many were even aware of them) about having a proper monotheistic religion is open to question. However, by the late 1960s after the Suharto military regime took power, the issue became more serious. The Suharto dictatorship was virulently anti-communist and had killed (or had encouraged or permitted to be killed) large numbers of people accused of being communists. Most of the massacres took place in Java and Bali, but rumors about them were widespread elsewhere in Indonesia as well. Since atheism or "not having a religion" was taken as a

marker of communism, and since people in Indonesia who were not recognized as adherents of a government-certified religion were defined as not having a religion at all (only "beliefs"), they were open to the charge of being communists—even if they had never heard of Karl Marx nor had the faintest idea of what revolutionary socialism was about. In some areas of Kalimantan, Dayak peoples were able to successfully recreate their traditional religion as a form of "Hinduism," one of the government-approved religions. This does not seem to have occurred in the Apo Kayan region, however. Here no apparent effort was made to turn Bungan into politically acceptable Hinduism.

4. To begin with, Christianity had not yet spread into many of the more remote areas of Sarawak in the upper branches of the Baram, Rajang, and other rivers of northern Sarawak before the arrival the Bungan. For its part the colonial government of the Brooke regime, which lasted until 1941, tended to follow policies of benevolent paternalism and indirect rule. Beyond requiring loyalty to the Brooke government and efforts to suppress indigenous warfare and headhunting, the government did little to change native life—and there were few if any Europeans or other non-natives around to provide examples of other ways of life. The stratified Orang Ulu peoples continued to be stratified and continued to live in longhouses. The colonial government remained fairly neutral in matters of religion, as in most other things. Nor were there changes of the sort that brought destabilization to some other interior or highland areas of Borneo and other islands of Southeast Asia. Plantations or other European colonial enterprises did not develop. Following the occupation of the Japanese during World War II, the British returned to impose a more orthodox form of colonial government on Sarawak, but it remained a form of indirect rule involving minimal interference in native culture, little in the way of economic change, and religious neutrality. See Rousseau 1998, 26–27.

5. Smalley et al. 1990, 87–88.

6. Lemoine 1972.

7. Smalley et al. 1990, 8–9.

8. Smalley et al. 1990.

9. Ibid., 17; the events that occurred, or are believed to have occurred, are recounted on pages 21–39.

10. Ibid., 24.

11. Neither "Christian" nor "Christianity" (or for that matter "missionary") are included in the index to the book.

12. Smalley et al. 1990, 181; such influences are noted also by Tapp (1989a; 1989b, 95–104).

13. Smalley et al. 1990, 31–32.

14. Ibid., 37–39.

15. Ibid., 25. Smalley presents his own ambivalent views of Shong Lue in the last section of the final chapter. As a linguistic anthropologist he was well aware of the nature of religious movements and their historical and cultural context, and how they are explained by social science. As an expert on alphabets and scripts and on other writing systems developed for the Hmong (one of which he himself was involved in creating), he is completely convinced that the Pahawh script created by Shong Lue is genuine, original, and a brilliant accomplishment. In his view Shong Lue was either a natural genius who had accomplished something done only rarely in human history, or what he did was a true miracle. The Western rationalist will choose the former explanation—that the creation of the Pahawh script and the religious movement that developed around it were natural human events in which a gifted and well-meaning but otherwise ordinary, illiterate village man responded to the tumultuous circumstances in which he grew up. These circumstances included war, turmoil, danger, poverty, exploitation, and the cultural belief that writing is a form of magical power, as well as Christian missionary activity and previous messianic occurrences. The achievement was extraordinary but within the range of natural possibility. As a trained Western social scientist, Smalley cannot reject this explanation. But as a committed Christian missionary whose faith includes the acceptance that miracles or supernatural causation has a role in human affairs, he is also not prepared to dismiss the literal religious interpretation held by his Hmong co-authors. He ends by saying he will never understand Shong Lue.

16. See Mustapha 2004.

17. See "Teapot cult under attack," "Ayah Pin followers wary of more raids," and further articles referenced in Wikipedia under "Sky Kingdom." The complete stories of all of the movements remain untold. Beyond news reports, there are fuller accounts in Wikipedia articles that seem reliable for the first two, while for the very recent end-of-the-world Panji Langit movement, no such account has yet appeared.

18. The lengthy and substantial account published in Wikipedia reports university students and Orang Asli (Malayan aborigines) in particular as being attracted to the movement at this time, though neither is further mentioned. More generally at the time of the government raid on the compound, the Sky Kingdom membership was reported to be mainly Malay but to also include Africans, Indians, British, and a New Zealander. Outside those in Malaysia, some followers lived in Singapore and Bali. Estimates of the number of members are probably unreliable. The Wikipedia account states that most estimates put the number at several thousand but notes that any number will depend on the criteria used for inclusion. This account also reports that the Sky Kingdom is one of twenty-two heretical Islamic organizations in the country listed as deviant "cults" or "sects" said to have a total membership of twenty-two thou-

sand. Even if such a total is correct, it tells nothing about the portion to be assigned to the Sky Kingdom. The number of buildings in the compound at the time of its destruction is given as thirty-three, but this includes both non-residential as well as residential ones, the nature of which (single or multiple residence), moreover, is not mentioned. Unless there were high-density living quarters, such a number of buildings suggests a resident population ranging in the low to mid-hundreds.

19. See Gregory 2005.

20. See "Malaysian 'teapot cult' woman not allowed to leave Islam," *Religion News Blog*, July 21, 2011, http://www.religionnewsblog.com/26083/malaysian-teapot-cult-woman-not-allowed-to-leave-islam.

21. "Ayah Pin very ill," *New Straits Times*, March 28, 2012.

22. Compared, for example, to beliefs in UFOs that sometimes spy, land, crash, or kidnap earthlings; protection against zombies being included in the 2011 edition of the Army Training Manual; or, for that matter, magical underwear.

23. Murali 2013.

24. Maketab 2013.

25. Wallace 1956.

26. Smalley et al. 1990, 124.

27. Ibid., 126.

9. POPULAR RELIGION IN SOUTHEAST ASIA

1. Discussed in my *Peoples of Southeast Asia Today*, 153–60.

BIBLIOGRAPHY

Abalahin, Andrew J. 2005. "A sixth religion? Confucianism and the negotiation of Indonesian-Chinese identity under the Pancasila State." In *Spirited politics: Religion and public life in contemporary Southeast Asia*, ed. Andrew C. Willford and Kenneth M. George, 119–42. Southeast Asia Program Series No. 38. Ithaca, NY: Cornell University Southeast Asia Program Publications.

Ackerman, Susan, and Raymond L. M. Lee. 1988. *Heaven in transition: Non-Muslim religious innovation and ethnic identity in Malaysia.* Honolulu: University of Hawai'i Press.

Al-Attas, Syed M. al-Naquib. 1978. *Islam and secularism.* Kuala Lumpur: ABIM.

Alexander, Jennifer, and Paul Alexander. 2002. "Gender and ethnic identity among the Lahanans of Sarawak." In *Tribal communities in the Malay world: Historical, social and cultural perspectives*, ed. Geoffrey Benjamin and Cynthia Chou, 457–73. Leiden, Holland: International Institute for Asian Studies.

Ang, Chouléan. 1986. "The place of animism within popular Buddhism in Cambodia: The example of the monastery." *Asian Folklore Studies* 47:5–41.

Arabestani, M., and J. Edo. 2011. "The Semai's response to missionary work: From resistance to compliance." *Anthropological notebooks, Slovene anthropological society*, 5–28.

Aragon, Lorraine V. 2000. *Fields of the lord: Animism, Christian minorities and state development in Indonesia.* Honolulu: University of Hawai'i Press.

Arasaratnam, Sinnappah. 1979. *Indians in Malaya and Singapore.* Rev. ed. Kuala Lumpur, Malaysia: Oxford University Press.

Asad, Talal. 1993. *Genealogies of religion: Disciplines and reasons of power in Christianity and Islam.* Baltimore, MD: Johns Hopkins University Press.

Askew, Mark. 2008. "Materializing Merit." In *Religious commodifications in Asia: Marketing gods*, ed. Pattana Kitiarsa, 89–119. London: Routledge.

Aslan, Reza. 2014. "Bill Maher isn't the only one who misunderstands religion." *New York Times*, October 8.

Atkinson, Jane Monnig. 1987. "Religions in dialogue: The construction of an Indonesian minority religion." In *Indonesian religions in transition*, ed. Rita Smith Kipp and Susan Rodgers, 171–86. Tucson: University of Arizona Press.

———. 1989. *The art and politics of Wana shamanism.* Berkeley: University of California Press.

Attagara, Kingkeo. 1968. *The folk religion of Ban Nai: A hamlet in central Thailand.* Bangkok, Thailand: Kurusapha Press.

Avonius, Leena. 2004. *Reforming Wetu Telu Adat: Islam, adat, and the promises of regionalism in Post-New Order Lombok.* PhD diss., Leiden University.

Baird, Ian. 2012. "Lao Buddhist monks and their involvement in political and military resistance to the Lao People's Democratic Government since 1975." *Journal of Asian Studies* 71 (3): 655–77.

Baling Avun. 1961. *Adat Adat Bangsa Kayan*. Unpublished manuscript in Kayan, 61 pages, cited and excerpted in Rousseau, 1998, 21–25.

Barker, John, ed. 1990. *Christianity in Oceania: Ethnographic perspectives*. Lanham, MD: University Press of America.

Bautista, Julius. 2010. *Figuring Catholicism: An ethnography of the Santo Niño de Sibu*. Quezon City: Alteneo de Manila University Press.

Bautista, Julius, and Anthony Reid. 2012. "Introduction: Materiality in a problematically plural Southeast Asia." In *The spirit of things: Materiality and religious diversity in Southeast Asia*, ed. Julius Bautista, 1–10. Ithaca, NY: Cornell University Southeast Asia Program Publications.

Beatty, Andrew. 1999. *Varieties of Javanese religion: An anthropological account*. Cambridge: Cambridge University Press.

Benjamin, Geoffrey. 2002. "On being tribal in the Malay world." In *Tribal communities in the Malay world: Historical, social and cultural perspectives*, ed. Geoffrey Benjamin and Cynthia Chou, 7–76. Leiden, Holland: International Institute for Asian Studies.

Benjamin, Geoffrey, and Cynthia Chou, eds. 2002. *Tribal communities in the Malay world: Historical, social and cultural perspectives*. Leiden, Holland: International Institute for Asian Studies.

Bigalke, Terance W. 2005. *A social history of an Indonesian People*. Singapore: Singapore University Press.

bin Mohamad, Mahathir. 1970. *The Malay dilemma*. Kuala Lumpur: Federal Publications.

Bird-David, H. Benjamin. 1999. "'Animism' revisited: Personhood, environment, and relational epistemology." *Current Anthropology* 40 (February supp.): S67–S91.

Boland, B. J. 1971. *The struggle of Islam in modern Indonesia*. The Hague: Nijhof.

Boon, James A. 1977. *The anthropological romance of Bali 1597–1972: Dynamic perspectives in marriage, caste, politics and religion*. Cambridge: Cambridge University Press.

Bosquet, G. H. 1939. "Researches de la deux sects Musulmanes (Waktou Telous et Waktou Lima) de Lombok." *Revue des studies Islamiques* 13:149–77.

Bowen, John. 1993. *Muslims through discourse: Religion and ritual in Gayo society*. Princeton, NJ: Princeton University Press, 1993.

Brac de la Perrière, Bénédicte. 1989. *Les Rituals de Possession en Bermane, du Cult d'aus Ceremonies Privées*. Paris: ERC.

———. 2005. "The Taungbyon Festival: Locality and nation-confronting in the cult of the 37 lords." In *Burma at the turn of the 21st century*, ed. Monica Skidmore, 65–89. Honolulu: University of Hawai'i Press.

———. 2009. "An overview of the field of religion in Burmese studies." *Asian Ethnology* 68 (2): 185–210.

Brown, Iem. 1987. "Contemporary Indonesian Buddhism and monotheism." *Journal of Southeast Asian Studies* 18 (1): 108–17.

Bown, Patricia Leigh. 2009. "A doctor for disease, a shaman for the soul." *New York Times*, September 19.

Buckley, Chris. 2013. "Success brings scrutiny to Chinese mystic." *New York Times*, July 30.

Budiwanti, Erni. 2014. "The purification movement in Bayan, north Lombok: Orthodox Islam versus syncretism." In *Between harmony and discrimination: Negotiating religious identities within majority-minority relationships in Bali and Lombok*, ed. Brigitta Hauser-Schäblin and David D. Harnish. Leiden: Brill.

Bunnag, Jane. *Buddhist monk, Buddhist layman: A study of monastic organization in central Thailand*. Cambridge: Cambridge University Press.

Cannell, Fenella. 1998. *Power and intimacy in the Christian Philippines*. Princeton, NJ: Princeton University Press.

———. 2006. *The anthropology of Christianity*. Durham, NC: Duke University Press.

Cassaniti, Julia. 2012. "Agency and the other: The role of agency for the importance of belief in Buddhist and Christian traditions." *Ethos* 40 (3): 297–316.

Cederroth, Sven. 1981. *The spell of the ancestors and the power of Mekkah: A Sasak community on Lombok.* Goteberg: Universitatis Gothobergensis.

———. 1996. "From ancestor worship to monotheism: Politics and religion in Lombok." *Temenos* 32:7–36.

Chambert-Loir, Henri, and Anthony Reid, eds. 2002. *The potent dead: Ancestors, saints and heroes in contemporary Indonesia.* Honolulu: University of Hawai'i Press.

Chan, Margaret. 2012. "Bodies for the gods: Image worship in Chinese popular religion." In *The spirit of things: Materiality and religious diversity in Southeast Asia*, ed. Julius Bautista, 197–216. Ithaca, NY: Cornell University Southeast Asia Program Publications.

Chandra Muzaffar. 1987. *Islamic resurgence in Malaysia.* Kuala Lumpur: Penerbit Fajar Bacti Syn Bhd.

Chatterjee, Partha. 1996. *The nation and its fragments: Colonial and postcolonial histories.* Princeton, NJ: Princeton University Press.

Chinyong, Joseph Liow, and Nadirsyah Hosen, eds. 2010. *Islam in Southeast Asia.* 4 vols. London: Routledge.

Coedés, G. 1967. *The making of Southeast Asia.* Berkeley: University of California Press.

Comaroff, Jean, and John L. Comaroff. 1999. "Occult economies and the violence of abstraction: Notes from the South African postcolony." *American Ethnologist* 26 (2): 279–303.

———. 2000. "Millennial capitalism: First thoughts on a second coming." *Public Culture* 12 (2): 291–343.

Condominas, Georges. 1998. *La buddhismi au village.* Vientiane: Editions des Cahiers de France.

Connolly, Jennifer. 2003. *Becoming Christian and Dayak: A study of Christian conversion among Dayaks in East Kalimantan, Indonesia.* PhD diss., New School University, Ann Arbor, Michigan.

Cooper, Robert. 1984. *Resource scarcity and the Hmong response.* Singapore: Singapore University Press.

Darlington, Susan M. 2012. *The ordination of a tree: The Thai Buddhist environmental movement.* Albany, NY: SUNY Press.

DeBernardi, Jean. 2006. *Chinese popular religion and spirit mediums in Penang, Malaysia.* Stanford, CA: Stanford University Press.

De La Paz, Cecelia. 2012. "The potency of poon: Religious sculpture, performativity, and the *Mahal na Senyor* of Lucban." In *The spirit of things: Materiality and religious diversity in Southeast Asia*, ed. Julius Bautista, 183–96. Ithaca, NY: Cornell University Southeast Asia Program Publications.

De Young, John E. 1955. *Village life in modern Thailand.* Berkeley: University of California Press.

Doré, Amphay. 1979. "Profiles médiumniques Lao." *Cahiers de l'Asie duSud Est.*, no. 5, 7–25.

Ebihara, May. 1966. "Interrelations between Buddhism and social systems in Cambodian peasant culture." In *Anthropological Studies in Theravada Buddhism*, by Manning Nash et al., 175–96. Southeast Asian Studies, Cultural Report Series No. 13. New Haven, CT: Yale University Press.

Edo, Juli. 2012. "Folk beliefs vs world religions." Unpublished MS.

Endicott, Kirk. 1970. *An analysis of Malay magic.* Oxford, UK: Clarendon Press.

———. 1979. *Batek Negrito religion: The world-view and rituals of a hunting and gathering people of peninsular Malaysia.* Oxford, UK: Clarendon Press.

Endres, Kirsten W. 2011. *Performing the divine: Mediums, markets and modernity in urban Vietnam.* NIAS Monographs No. 118.

———. 2011. "'Trading in spirits': Transnational flows, entrepreneurship, and commodification in Vietnamese spirit mediumship." In *Traveling spirits: Migrants, markets and mobilities*, ed. Gertrude Hülwelmier and Kristine Krause, 118–32. London: Routledge.

Evans, Grant. 1990. *Lao peasants under socialism.* New Haven, CT: Yale University Press.

———. 1993. "Buddhism and economic action in socialist Laos." In *Socialism: Ideals, ideologies and local practice*, ed. C. M. Hann, 130–47. ASA Monographs No. 31. London: Routledge.

———. 1998. *The politics of ritual remembrance: Laos since 1975*. Honolulu: University of Hawai'i Press.

Fadiman, Anne. 1997. *The spirit catches you and you fall down: A Hmong child, her American doctors, and the collision of two cultures*. New York: Farrar, Strauss and Giroux.

Fealy, G., and S. White, eds. 2008. *Expressing Islam: Religious life and politics in Indonesia*. Singapore: Institute of Southeast Asian Studies.

Felstad, Karen. 2011. "Spirited migrations: The travels of Len Dong spirits and their mediums." In *Traveling spirits: Migrants, markets and mobilities*, ed. Gertrude Hülwelmier and Kristine Krause, 52–66. London: Routledge.

Felstad, Karen, and Nguyen Thi Hien, eds. 2006. *Possessed by the spirits: Mediumship in contemporary Vietnamese communities*. Southeast Asia Program Series No. 23. Ithaca, NY: Cornell University Southeast Asia Program Publications.

Fischer, Johan. 2012. "Of Proton, Mercedes, MPVs: Car culture among middle-class Malays in suburban Malaysia." In *The spirit of things: Materiality and religious diversity in Southeast Asia*, ed. Julius Bautista, 27–42. Ithaca, NY: Cornell University Southeast Asia Program Publications.

Forest, Alain. 1980. *Le cult des genies au Cambodge: Analyyse et tradition d'un corpus de texts sur les "neak ta."* Paris: L'Harmattan.

Forth, Gregory L. 1998. *Beneath the volcano: Religion, cosmology and spirit classification among the Nage of Eastern Indonesia*. Leiden, Holland: KITLV Press.

Foster, George M. 1967. *Tzintzuntzan: Mexican peasants in a changing world*. Boston: Little, Brown.

Fox, James J. 1973. "On bad death and the left hand." In *Right and left: Essays on dual symbolic classification*, ed. Rodney Needham, 342–68. Chicago: University of Chicago Press.

Fox, Margarlit. 2012. "Life went on around her, redefining care." *New York Times*, September 13.

Freeman, Derek. 1979. "Severed heads that germinate." In *Fantasy and symbol: Studies in anthropological interpretation*, ed. R. H. Hook and George Devereux, 233–46. London: Academic.

Fried, Morton H. 1987. "Reflections on Christianity in China." *American Ethnologist* 14, no. 1 (special issue).

Fuller, Thomas. 2012. "Monks lose relevance as Thailand grows richer." *New York Times*, December 18.

———. 2013. "Plane crash? murders? time to play Thai lottery." *New York Times*, January 2.

Geertz, Clifford. 1960. *The religion of Java*. Glencoe, IL: Free Press.

———. 1964. "Internal conversion in contemporary Bali." In *Malayan and Indonesian studies presented to Sir Richard Winstedt*, ed. J. Bastin and R. Roolvink, 282–302. Oxford, UK: Clarendon Press.

Geertz, Hildred. 1963. *Indonesian cultures and communities*. New Haven, CT: Human Relations Area Files Press.

Goh, Robbie B. H. 2005. *Christianity in Southeast Asia*. Singapore: Institute of Southeast Asian Studies.

Golomb, Louis. 1978. *Brokers of morality: Thai ethnic adaptation in a rural Malaysian setting*. Asian Studies at Hawaii no. 23. Honolulu: University of Hawai'i Press.

———. 1985. *An anthropology of curing in multiethnic Thailand*. Illinois Studies in Anthropology 15. Urbana: University of Illinois Press.

Goody, Jack, ed. 1968. *Literacy in traditional societies*. Cambridge: Cambridge University Press.

Gregory, Angela. 2005. "Storm over teapot cult." *New Zealand Herald*, July 22. Accessed July 29, 2013.

Hanks, Lucien M. 1972. *Rice and man: Agricultural ecology in Southeast Asia*. Chicago: Aldine-Atherton.

Harris, Ian. 2008. *Cambodian Buddhism: History and practice*. Honolulu: University of Hawai'i Press.

———. 2013. *Buddhism in a dark age: Cambodian monks under Pol Pat.* Honolulu: University of Hawai'i Press.

Hauser-Schäblin, Brigitta, and David D. Harnish. 2014. *Between harmony and discrimination: Negotiating religious identities within majority-minority relationships in Bali and Lombok.* Leiden: Brill.

Hayami, Yoko. 1996. "Karen tradition according to Christ or Buddha: The implications of multiple reinterpretations for a minority ethnic group in Thailand." *Journal of Southeast Asian Studies* 27 (2): 342–449.

———. 2004. *Between hills and plains: Power and practice in socio-religious dynamics among Karen.* Kyoto, Japan: Kyoto University Press.

Hefner, Robert. 1985. *Hindu Javanese: Tenggir tradition and Islam.* Princeton, NJ: Princeton University Press.

———. 1993. *Conversion to Christianity: Historical and anthropological perspectives on a great transformation.* Berkeley: University of California Press.

———, ed. 1993. "Of faith and commitment: Christian conversion in Muslim Java." In *Conversion to Christianity: Historical and anthropological perspectives on a great transformation,* ed. Robert Hefner, 99–125. Berkeley: University of California Press.

———. 1994. "Reimagined community: A social history of Muslim education in Pasuran, East Java." In *Asian visions of authority: Religion and the modern states of East and Southeast Asia*, ed. Charles F. Keyes, Laurel Kendall, and Helen Hardacre, 75–95. Honolulu: University of Hawai'i Press.

———. 1997. "Introduction." In *Islam in an era of nation states: Politics and religious revival in Muslim Southeast Asia*, ed. R. W. Hefner and P. Horvatitch, 231–72. Honolulu: University of Hawai'i Press.

———. 2011. "Where have all the *abangan* gone? Religionization and the decline of non-standard Islam in contemporary Indonesia." In *The politics of religion in Indonesia: Syncretism, orthodoxy and religious contention in Java and Bali*, ed. Michel Picard and Rémy Madinier, 71–91. New York: Routledge.

Hertz, Robert. (1907) 1960. *Death and the right hand.* Glencoe, IL: Free Press.

Hitchcock, Michael. 1996. *Islam and identity in Eastern Indonesia.* Hull: University of Hull Press.

Hoffstaedter, Gerhard. 2011. *Modern Muslim identities: Negotiating religion and ethnicity in Malaysia.* Copenhagen: NIAS Press.

Holt, John Clifford. 2009. *Spirits of the place: Buddhism and Lao religious culture.* Honolulu: University of Hawai'i Press.

Hoskins, Janet. 1987. "Entering the bitter house: Spirit worship and conversion in west Sumba." In *Indonesian religions in transition*, ed. Rita Smith Kipp and Susan Rodgers, 136–60. Tucson: University of Arizona Press.

———, ed. 1996. *Headhunting and the social imagination in Southeast Asia.* Stanford, CA: Stanford University Press.

Howe, Leo. 2001. *Hinduism and hierarchy in Bali.* Oxford, UK: James Currey.

———. 2005. *The changing world of Bali: Religion, society and tourism.* London: Routledge.

Howell, Brian M. 2008. *Christianity in the local context: Southern Baptists in the Philippines.* New York: Palgrave Macmillan.

Hülwelmier, Gertrude, and Kristine Krause, eds. 2010. *Traveling spirits: Migrants, markets and mobilities.* London: Routledge.

Jackson, Peter. 1999a. "The enchanting spirit of Thai capitalism: The cult of Luang Phor Khoon and the post-modernization of Thai Buddhism." *Southeast Asia Research* 7 (1): 5–60.

———. 1999b. "Royal spirits, Chinese gods and magic monks: Thailand's boom-time religions of prosperity; The cult of Luang Phor Khoon and the post-modernization of Thai Buddhism." *Southeast Asia Research* 7 (3): 245–320.

Jain, Ravindra K. 1970. *South Indians on the plantation frontier in Malaya.* New Haven, CT: Yale University Press.

Jay, Robert R. 1963. *Religion and politics in rural central Java.* Cultural Report Series 12. New Haven, CT: Yale University, Southeast Asian Studies.

Jellema, Kate. 2007. "Returning home: Ancestor worship and the nationalism of Doi Moi Vietnam." In *Modernity and re-enchantment: Religion in post-revolutionary Vietnam*, ed. Philip Taylor, 57–89. Singapore: ISEAS.

Kabilsingh, Chatsumarn. 1991. *Thai women in Buddhism.* Berkeley, CA: Paralax Press.

Kammerer, Cornelia Ann. 1990. "Customs and Christian conversion among Akha highlanders of Burma and Thailand." *American Ethnologist* 17 (2): 277–91.

Karim, Wazir Jahan. 1992. *Women and culture: Between Malay adat and Islam.* Boulder, CO: Westview Press.

Kartodirdjo, Sartono. 1973. *Protest movements in rural Java: A study of agrarian unrest in the 19th and early twentieth centuries.* Kuala Lumpur: Oxford University Press.

Keane, Webb. 1996. "Materialism, missionaries and modern subjects in colonial Indonesia." In *Conversion to modernities: The globalization of Christianity*, ed. Peter van der Veer, 137–70. London: Routledge.

———. 2007. *Christian moderns: Freedom and fetish in the mission encounter.* Berkeley: University of California Press.

Kent, Alexandra. 2004. *Divinity and diversity: A Hindu revitalization movement in Malaysia.* NIAS monographs, 98. Singapore: ISEAS Press.

Kessler, Christi, and Jürgen Rüland. 2008. *Give Jesus a hand: Popular religion and politics in the Philippines.* Manila: Ateneo Manila University Press.

Keyes, Charles F. 1977. *The golden peninsula: Culture and adaptation in mainland Southeast Asia.* New York: Macmillan.

———. 1987. *Thailand: Buddhist kingdom as modern state.* Boulder, CO: Westview Press.

———. 1993. "Why the Thai are not Christian: Buddhist and Christian conversion in Thailand." In *Conversion to Christianity: Historical and anthropological perspectives on a great transformation*, ed. Robert Hefner, 259–83. Berkeley: University of California Press.

———. 2002. "National heroine or local spirit? The struggle over memory in the case of Thao Suranari of Nakhon Ratchasima." In *Cultural crisis and social memory: Modernity and identity in Thailand and Laos*, ed. Shigaharu Tanabe and Charles Keyes, 113–36. Honolulu: University of Hawai'i Press.

Kipp, Rita Smith. 1990. *The early years of a Dutch colonial mission: The Karo field.* Ann Arbor: University of Michigan Press.

Kipp, Rita Smith, and Susan Rodgers, eds. 1987a. *Indonesian religions in transition.* Tucson: University of Arizona Press.

———. 1987b. "Introduction: Indonesian religions in society." In *Indonesian religions in transition*, ed. Rita Smith Kipp and Susan Rodgers, 1–31. Tucson: University of Arizona Press.

Kitiarsa, Pattana. 2008a. "Buddha Phanit: Thailand's prosperity religion and its commodifying tactics." In *Religious commodifications in Asia: Marketing gods*, ed. Pattana Kitiarsa, 120–44. London: Routledge.

———, ed. 2008b. *Religious commodifications in Asia: Marketing gods.* London: Routledge.

———. 2012. *Mediums, monks and amulets: Thai popular Buddhism today.* Chiang Mai: Silkworm Books.

Kuipers, Joel C. 1998. *Language, identity, and marginality in Indonesia: The changing nature of ritual speech on the island of Sumba.* Cambridge: Cambridge University Press.

Kwon, Heonik. 2006. *After the massacre: Commemoration and consolation in Ha My and My Lai.* Berkeley: University of California Press.

Laderman, Carol. 1991. *Taming the wind of desire: Psychology, medicine, and aesthetics in Malay shamanistic performance.* Berkeley: University of California Press.

Landa, Jocano F. 1969. *Growing up in a Philippine barrio.* New York: Holt, Rinehart and Winston.

Landon, Kenneth P. 1949. *Southeast Asia: Crossroad of religions.* Chicago: University of Chicago Press.

Lee, Raymond. 1988. "Patterns of religious tension in Malaysia." *Asian Survey* 28 (4): 400–18.

Lemoine, Jacques. 1972. "Les Ecritures du Hmong." *Bulletin des Amis du Royaume Lao* 7–8:123–65.

Levin, Dan. 2013. "Beijing Journal: Festival's resurgence has Chinese sending manna to heavens." *New York Times*, April 4.

Lieban, Richard. 1967. *Cebuano sorcery: Malign magic in the Philippines*. Berkeley: University of California Press.

Liow, Joseph, and Nadirsyah Hosen, eds. 2009. *Islam in Southeast Asia*. 4 vols. London: Routledge.

Lomnitz-Adler, Claudio. 2005. *Death and the idea of Mexico*. New York: Zone Books.

Love, Robert. 2004. *The Samahan of Papa God: Tradition and conversion in a Tagalog peasant religious movement*. Manila: Anvil.

Maketab, Hanis. 2013. "Sect believed world will end on December 21." *New Straits Times*, January 11. Accessed June 29, 2013. news@nst.com.my.

Malarney, Shaun Kingsley. 2002. *Culture, ritual and revolution in Vietnam*. Honolulu: University of Hawai'i Press.

Malaysian woman not allowed to leave Islam. ReligiousNewsBlog.com, July 21, 2011. Accessed June 30, 2013.

Mandelbaum, David. 1964. "Introduction: Process and structure in South Asian religion." In *Religion in South Asia*, ed. E. B. Harpur, 5–20. Seattle: University of Washington Press.

Marston, John, and Elizabeth Guthrie, eds. 2004. *History, Buddhism, and new religious movements in Cambodia*. Honolulu: University of Hawai'i Press.

McDaniel, Justin Thomas. 2011. *The lovelorn ghost and the magical monk: Practicing Buddhism in modern Thailand*. New York: Columbia University Press.

McLellan, Janet. 2009. *Cambodian refugees in Ontario: Resettlement, religion, and identity*. Toronto: University of Toronto Press.

Mearns, David. 1995. *Siva's other children: Religion and social identity amongst overseas Indians*. Delhi: Sage.

Mendelson, E. M. 1963. "The uses of religious skepticism in modern Burma." *Diogenes* 41:94–116.

Metcalf, Peter. 1982. *A Borneo journey into death: Berawan eschatology from its rituals*. Philadelphia: University of Pennsylvania Press.

———. 1989. *Where are you spirits: Style and theme in Berawan prayer*. Washington, DC: Smithsonian Institution Press.

Miller, R. F., and T. H. Rigby. 1986. *Religion and politics in communist states*. Research School of Social Sciences and Pacific Studies. The Australian National University.

Mills, Mary Beth, 1995. "Attack of the widow ghosts: Gender, death and modernity in Northeast Thailand." In *Bewitching women, pious men: Gender and body politics in Southeast Asia*, ed. Aiwa Ong and Michael G. Peletz. Berkeley: University of California Press.

Morris, Rosalind. 2000. *In the place of origin: Modernity and its mediums in northern Thailand*. Durham, NC: Duke University Press.

Mulder, Niels. 1996. *Inside Southeast Asia: Religion, everyday life, cultural change*. Amsterdam, Netherlands: Pepin Press.

Murali, R. S. N. 2013. "Deviant sect leader believed doomsday was on Dec 21, 2012." *The Star*, January 10.

Mustapha, Kasmiah. 2004. "Book gives insight into Al-Ma'unah." *New Straits Times*, April 18. Accessed July 9, 2013. http://www.emedia.com.my.

Mydans, Seth. 2011. "Vietnam persecutes Christian minority, report says." *New York Times*, March 31.

Nash, June. 1972. "The devil in Bolivia's nationalized tin mines." *Science and Society* 36 (2): 221–33.

Nash, Manning. 1965. *The golden road to modernity: Village life in contemporary Burma*. New York: Wiley.

Nash, Manning, et al. 1966. *Anthropological studies in Theravada Buddhism*. Cultural Report Series No. 13. New Haven, CT: Yale University, Southeast Asian Studies.

Nguen Van Hue and Laurel Kendall, eds. 2003. *Vietnam: Journeys of body, mind, and spirit.* New York and Hanoi: American Museum of Natural History Press and the National Museum of Ethnology.

Nguen Van Ku and Luu Hung. 1902. *Funeral houses in the central highlands of Vietnam.* Hanoi: Gioi Publishers.

Nibbs, Faith N. 2014. *Belonging: The social dynamics of fitting in as experienced by Hmong immigrants in Germany and Texas.* Durham, NC: Carolina Academic Press.

Nobuta Toshihiro. 2008. *Living on the periphery: Development and Islamization among the Orang Asli.* Kyoto: Kyoto University Press.

Norton, Barley. 2006. "'Hot tempered' women and 'effeminate' men: The performance of music and gender in Vietnamese mediumship." In *Possessed by the spirits: Mediumship in contemporary Vietnamese communities*, ed. Karen Felstad and Nguyen Thi Hien, 55–76. Southeast Asia Program Series No. 23. Ithaca, NY: Cornell University Southeast Asia Program Publications.

Ong, Aihwa. 2003. *Buddha is hiding: Refugees, citizenship, the new America.* Berkeley: University of California Press.

Pedersen, Paul B. 1970. *Batak blood and Protestant soul: The development of national Batak churches in North Sumatra.* Grand Rapids, MI: Eerdmans.

Peletz, Michael. 1997. "'Ordinary Muslims' and Muslim resurgents in contemporary Malaysia: Notes on an ambivalent relationship." In *Islam in an era of nation states: Politics and religious revival in Muslim Southeast Asia*, ed. R. W. Hefner and P. Horvatitch, 231–72. Honolulu: University of Hawai'i Press.

Pelras, Christian. 1996. *The Bugis.* Oxford: Blackwell.

Pham Quyuh Phuong. 2007. "Empowerment and innovation among Saint Tran's female mediums." In *Modernity and re-enchantment: Religion in post-revolutionary Vietnam*, ed. Philip Taylor. Singapore: ISEAS.

Picard, Michel. 2004. "What's in a name? Agama Hindu Bali in the making." In *Hinduism in modern Indonesia: A minority religion between local, national and global interests*, ed. M. Ramstedt, 56–75. London: Routledge.

Picard, Michel, and Rémy Madinier, eds. 2011.*The politics of religion in Indonesia: Syncretism, orthodoxy and religious contention in Java and Bali.* New York: Routledge.

Pieterse, J. P. Nederveen. 1992. *Christianity and hegemony: Religion and politics on the frontiers of social change.* New York: Berg.

Prakash, Gyan. 2003. "Between science and superstition: Religion and the modern subject of the nation in colonial India." In *Magic and modernity: Interfaces of revelation and concealment*, ed. Birgit Meyer and Peter Pels, 39–59. Stanford, CA: Stanford University Press.

Rafael, Vincente L. 1988. *Contracting colonialism: Translation and Christian conversion in Tagalog society under early Spanish rule.* Ithaca, NY: Cornell University Press.

Rajadhan, Anuman. 1986. *Popular Buddhism in Siam and other essays on Thai studies.* Bangkok: Sathirakoses Nagapradipa Foundation.

Ramstedt, Martin, ed. 2004a. *Hinduism in modern Indonesia: A minority religion between local, national and global interests.* London: Routledge.

———. 2004b. "Introduction: Negotiating identities—Indonesian 'Hindus' between local, national and global interests." In *Hinduism in modern Indonesia: A minority religion between local, national and global interests*, ed. Martin Ramstedt, 1–34. London: RoutledgeCurzon.

Reader, Ian, and George Tanabe Jr. 1998. *Practically religious: Worldly benefits and common religion in Japan.* Honolulu: University of Hawai'i Press.

Redfield, Robert. 1957. *The primitive world and its transformations.* Ithaca, NY: Cornell University Press.

Roff, William R., ed. 1974a. *Kelantan: Religion, society and politics in a Malay state.* Kuala Lumpur: Oxford University Press.

———. 1974b. "The origins and early years of the *Majlis Ugama.*" In *Kelantan: Religion, society and politics in a Malay state*, ed. William Roff, 101–52. Kuala Lumpur: Oxford University Press.

———. 1984. "Islam obscured? Some reflections on studies of Islam and society in Southeast Asia." *Archipel* 29:7–34.

———. 1990. *Islam and the political economy of meaning.* London: Croon Helm.

Rousseau, Jérôme. 1998. *Kayan religion: Ritual life and religious reform in central Borneo.* Leiden, Holland: KITLV Press.

Rozenberg, Guillaume. 2005. "The cheaters: Journey to the land of the lottery." In *Burma at the turn of the 21st. century*, ed. Monica Skidmore, 19–40. Honolulu: University of Hawai'i Press.

Russell, Susan D., and Clark Cunningham, eds. 1989. *Changing lives, changing rites: Ritual and social dynamics in Philippine and Indonesian uplands.* Ann Arbor: Center for South and Southeast Asia.

Ruth, Richard A. 2012. "Dressing for war in old-fashioned magic: Traditional protective charms of Thailand's forces in the Vietnam War." In *The spirit of things: Materiality and religious diversity in Southeast Asia*, ed. Julius Bautista, 129–46. Ithaca, NY: Cornell University Southeast Asia Program Publications.

Rutherford, Danilyn. 2002. "After syncretism: The anthropology of Islam and Christianity in Southeast Asia." *Comparative Studies in Society and History* 44 (1): 196–205.

Salemink, Oscar. 2008. "Spirits of consumption and the capitalist ethic in Vietnam." In *Religious commodifications in Asia: Marketing gods*, ed. Pattana Kitiarsa, 147–68. London: Routledge.

Sandhu, Kernial Singh. 1969. *Indians in Malaya: Migration and settlement, 1786–1957.* Cambridge: Cambridge University Press.

Schiller, Anne. 1997. *Small sacrifices: Religious change and cultural identity among the Ngaju of Indonesia.* New York: Oxford University Press.

Schneider, Jane, and Shirley Lindenbaum, eds. 1987. "Frontiers of Christian evangelism." *American Ethnologist* 14 (special issue).

Schober, Julianne. 1995. "The Theravada Buddhist engagement with modernity." *Journal of Southeast Asian Studies* 26 (2): 307–25.

———. 2005. "Buddhist visions of moral authority and civil society: The search for the postcolonial state in Burma." In *Burma at the turn of the 21st. century*, ed. Monica Skidmore, 113–33. Honolulu: University of Hawai'i Press.

———. 2008. "Communities of interpretation in the study of religion in Burma." *Journal of Southeast Asian Studies* 39 (2): 255–67.

Scott, James George. 2009. *The art of not being governed: An anarchist history of upland Southeast Asia.* New Haven, CT: Yale University Press.

Sell, Hans Joachim. 1955. *Der Schlimme Tod bei den Völkern Indonesiens* [Bad death among Indonesian peoples]. 's-Gravenhage: Mouton.

Shamsul Amri Baharuddin. 1983. "A revival in the study of Islam in Malaysia." *Man* 18:399–404.

Shaw, Rosalind, and Charles Stewart, eds. 1994. *Syncretism/anti-syncretism: The politics of religious synthesis.* London: Routledge.

Shway Yoe (James George Scott). 1963. *The Burman: His life and notions.* New York: The Norton Library.

Siegel, James. 2005. *Naming the witch: Cultural memory in the present.* Stanford, CA: Stanford University Press.

Sinha, Veneeta. 2008. "'Merchandizing' Hinduism: Commodities, markets and possibilities for enchantment." In *Religious commodifications in Asia: Marketing gods*, ed. Pattana Kitiarsa, 169–85. London: Routledge.

Skeat, Walter William. 1900. *Malay magic: An introduction to the folklore and popular religion of the Malay Peninsula.* New York: Barnes and Noble.

Smalley, William A., Chia Koua Vang, and Gnia Yee Yang. 1990. *Mother of writing: The origin and development of a Hmong messianic script.* Chicago: University of Chicago Press.

Smith-Hefner, Nancy. 1999. *Khmer American: Identity and moral education in a diasporic community.* Berkeley: University of California Press.

Spiro, Melford E. 1967. *Burmese supernaturalism: A study in the explanation and reduction of suffering*. Englewood Cliffs, NJ: Prentice Hall.

Stauth, Georg. 2002. *Politics and cultures of Islamization in Southeast Asia: Indonesia and Malaysia in the 1990s*. Bielefeld: Transcript Verlag.

Steedly, Mary Margaret. 1993. *Hanging without a rope: Native experience in colonial and postcolonial Karoland*. Princeton, NJ: Princeton University Press.

Stern, Theodore. 1968. "Ariya and the golden book: A millenarian sect among the Karen." *Journal of Asian Studies* 27 (2): 297–328.

Strong, John. 2003. *Relics of the Buddha*. Princeton, NJ: Princeton University Press.

Stuart-Fox, Martin. 1996. *Buddhist kingdom, Marxist state: The making of modern Laos*. Bangkok, Thailand: White Lotus Press.

———. 2003. "The Hmong problem in Laos." *Irawaddy Magazine* 11 (7): 1–2.

Suryadinata, Leo, Evi Nuridya Arifin, and Aris Ananta. 2003. *Indonesia's population: ethnicity and religion in a changing political landscape*. Singapore: ISEAS.

Swearer, Donald K. 1995. *The Buddhist world of Southeast Asia*. Albany, NY: State University of New York Press.

Sweeney, Amin. 1972. *The Ramayana and the Malay shadow play*. Kuala Lumpur: National University of Malaysia Press.

Tambiah, Stanley. 1970. *Buddhism and the spirit cults in northeast Thailand*. Cambridge: Cambridge University Press.

———. 1976. *World conqueror and world renouncer: A study of Buddhism and polity in Thailand against a historical background*. Cambridge: Cambridge University Press.

———. 1984. *The Buddhist saints of the forest and the cult of amulets: A study in charisma, hagiography, sectarianism, and millennial Buddhism*. Cambridge: Cambridge University Press.

Tanabe, Shigaharu, and Charles Keyes, eds. 2002. *Cultural crisis and social memory: Modernity and identity in Thailand and Laos*. Honolulu: University of Hawai'i Press.

Tannenbaum, Nacola, and Cornelia Kammerer, eds. 1996. *Blessing and merit in mainland Southeast Asia*. New Haven, CT: Yale University Southeast Asia Monograph Series.

Tapp, Nicholas. 1982. "The relevance of telephone directories to a lineage-based society: A consideration of some messianic myths among the Hmong." *Journal of the Siam Society* 70:114–27.

———. 1989a. "The impact of missionary Christianity upon marginalized ethnic minorities: The case of the Hmong." *Journal of Southeast Asian Studies* 20 (1): 70–95.

———. 1989b. *Sovereignty and rebellion: The white Hmong of northern Thailand*. Singapore: Singapore University Press.

Tapp, Nicholas, Jean Michaud, Christian Culas, and Gary Yia Lee, eds. 2004. *Hmong/Mia in Asia*. Chiang Mai, Thailand: Silkworm Books.

Taussig, Michael T. 1980. *The devil and commodity fetishism in South America*. Chapel Hill: University of North Carolina Press.

Taylor, Jim. 1999. "(Post-) modernity, remaking tradition and the hybridization of Thai Buddhism." *Anthropological Forum* 9 (2): 163–88.

———. 2008. *Buddhism and postmodern imaginings in Thailand*. Burlington, VT: Ashgate Press.

Taylor, Philip. 2004. *Goddess on the rise: Pilgrimage and popular religion in Vietnam*. Honolulu: University of Hawai'i Press.

———. 2005. "Modernity and re-enchantment in post-revolutionary Vietnam." In *Modernity and re-enchantment: Religion in post-revolutionary Vietnam*, ed. Philip Taylor, 1–56. Singapore: ISEAS.

Terwiel, B. J. 1976. "A model for the study of Thai Buddhism." *Journal of Asian Studies* 35 (3): 391–403.

———. (1975) 1994. *Monks and magic: An analysis of religious ceremonies in central Thailand*. Bangkok: White Lotus Press.

Thien, Do. 2003. *Vietnamese supernaturalism: Views from the southern region*. London: RoutledgeCurzon.

———. 2007. "Unjust-death deification and burnt offering: Towards an integrative view of popular religion in contemporary southern Vietnam." In *Modernity and re-enchantment: Religion in post-revolutionary Vietnam*, ed. Philip Taylor, 161–93. Singapore: ISEAS.

Tikhonov, Vladimir, and Torkel Brekke, eds. 2012. *Buddhism and violence: Militarism and Buddhism in modern Asia.* London: Routledge.

Trier, Jesper. 1986. "The Mlabri people of northern Thailand: Social organization and supernatural beliefs." *Contributions to Southeast Asian Ethnography* 5:3–41.

U. Chit Hiang. 2008. "Anthropological communities of interpretation for Burma: An overview." *Journal of Southeast Asian Studies* 39 (2): 239–54.

Van Esterik, Penny. 1993. *Taking refuge: Lao Buddhists in North America.* Tempe: Program for Southeast Asian Studies, Arizona State University.

Volkman, Toby Alice. 1985. *Feasts of honor: Ritual and change in the Toraja highlands.* Urbana and Chicago: University of Illinois Press.

Wallace, Anthony. 1956. "Revitalization movements: Some theoretical considerations for their comparative study." *American Anthropologist* 58:264–81.

Wallace, Julia. 2014. "Workers of the World Faint." *New York Times*, January 19.

Watson, C. W., and Roy Ellen, eds. 1993. *Understanding witchcraft and sorcery in Southeast Asia.* Honolulu: University of Hawai'i Press.

Weber, Max. (1922) 1963. *The sociology of religion.* Boston: Beacon Press.

Weinstock, Joseph A. 1987. "Kaharingan: Life and death in southern Borneo." In *Indonesian religions in transition*, ed. Rita Smith Kipp and Susan Rodgers, 71–97. Tucson: University of Arizona Press.

Weller, Robert P. 1994. "Capitalism, community, and the rise of amoral cults in Taiwan." In *Asian visions of authority: Religion and the modern states of East and Southeast Asia*, ed. Charles F. Keyes, Laurel Kendall, and Helen Hardacre, 141–64. Honolulu: University of Hawai'i Press.

Wells-Dang, Andrew. 2007. "Strangers on the road: Foreign religious organizations and development in Vietnam." In *Modernity and re-enchantment: Religion in post-revolutionary Vietnam*, ed. Philip Taylor, 399–444. Singapore: ISEAS.

White, Erick. 2005. "Fraudulent and dangerous popular religiosity in the public sphere: Moral campaigns to reform, prohibit and demystify Thai spirit mediums." In *Spirited politics: Religion and public life in contemporary Southeast Asia*, ed. Andrew C. Willford and Kenneth M. George, 69–92. Southeast Asia Program Series No. 38. Ithaca, NY: Cornell University Southeast Asia Program Publications.

Whittier, Herbert L. 1973. *Social organization and symbols of social differentiation: An ethnographic study of the Kenyah Dayak of East Kalimantan.* PhD diss., Michigan State University.

———. 1978. "Concepts of adat and cosmology among the Kenyah Dayak of Borneo: Coping with the changing socio-cultural milieu." *Sarawak Museum Journal* 26 (47): 103–13.

Wiebe, Paul D., and S. Mariappen. 1979. *Indian Malaysians: The view from the plantation.* Durham, NC: Carolina Academic Press.

Wiegele, Katherine L. 2005. *Investing in miracles: El Shaddai and the transformation of popular Catholicism in the Philippines.* Honolulu: University of Hawai'i Press.

Wilkinson, R. J. (1906) 1957. "Malay customs and beliefs. Papers on Malay subjects." *Journal of the Malayan Branch of the Royal Asiatic Society* 30 (4): 1–87.

Willford, Andrew C. 2006. *Cage of freedom: Tamil identity and the ethnic fetish in Malaysia.* Ann Arbor: University of Michigan Press.

Willford, Andrew C., and Kenneth M. George, eds. 2005. *Spirited politics: Religion and public life in contemporary Southeast Asia.* Southeast Asia Program Series No. 38. Ithaca, NY: Cornell University Southeast Asia Program Publications.

Winstedt, Richard. (1925) 1961. *The Malay magician: Being shaman, Saiva, and Sufi.* London: Routledge and Kegan Paul.

Winzeler, Robert L. 1974. "The social organization of Islam in Kelantan." In *Religion, society and politics in a Malay state*, ed. William Roff, 259–71. Kuala Lumpur: Oxford University Press.

———. 1985. *Ethnic relations in Kelantan: A study of the Chinese and Thai as ethnic minorities in a Malay state*. Singapore: Oxford University Press.

———. 1999. "Notes on two engraved half-skulls in Kampong Grogu, Bau." *The Sarawak Museum Journal* 54 (75 [New Series]): 201–205.

———. 2004a. *The architecture of life and death in Borneo*. Honolulu: University of Hawai'i Press.

———. 2004b. "Southeast Asian shamanism." In *Shamanism: An encyclopedia of world beliefs, practices, and culture*, ed. Mariko Namba Walter and Eva Jane Neumann Fridman, 834–42. Santa Barbara, CA: ABC-CLIO.

———. 2008. "Religious conversion on the ethnic margins of Southeast Asia." In *Living on the margins: Minorities and borderlines in Cambodia and Southeast Asia; Siem Reap, Cambodia, March 14–15, 2008*, ed. Peter J. Hammer, 45–64. Phnom Penh, Cambodia: Center for Khmer Studies.

———. 2011. *The peoples of Southeast Asia today: Ethnography and change in a complex region*. Lanham, MD: AltaMira.

———. 2012. *Anthropology and religion: What we know, think, and question*. 2nd ed. Lanham, MD: AltaMira.

Woodward, Mark R. 1989. *Islam in Java: Normative piety and mysticism in the sultanate of Yogyakarta*. Tucson: University of Arizona Press.

Yang, C. K. 1961. *Religion in Chinese society: A study of contemporary social functions or religion and some of their historical factors*. Prospect Heights, IL: Waveland Press.

Yeoh, Winnie. 2012. "*Empat ekor* number a pressing need at God of Wealth Temple." *The Star*, September 13.

Yeoh Seng Guan. 2012. "Holy water and material religion in a pilgrimage shrine in Malaysia." In *The spirit of things: Materiality and religious diversity in Southeast Asia*, ed. Julius Bautista, 79–94. Ithaca, NY: Cornell University Southeast Asia Program Publications.

———. 2014. "Actually existing religious pluralism in Kuala Lumpur." In *Religious pluralism, state and society in Asia*, ed. Chiara Formichi, 153–71. London: Routledge.

INDEX

ABOUT THE AUTHOR

Robert L. Winzeler is professor emeritus of anthropology at the University of Nevada, Reno. He received his AM and PhD from the University of Chicago and has done extensive long-term fieldwork in both insular and mainland Southeast Asia. His numerous books include *The Peoples of Southeast Asia Today* (2011) and *Anthropology and Religion, Second Edition* (2012).